"*Alone* is a compelling journey of personal discovery, religious questioning and spiritual awakening. At times deep, at times sad, at times funny, Heron invites the reader to ride along each day of this remarkable adventure. When it's over, you'll feel each of the 4,000 miles in your own soul."

- IAN DOESCHER, Presbyterian Pastor and *New York Times* bestselling author of the *William Shakespeare's Star Wars* series

---

"In *Alone*, Brian Heron takes us on a tour de force through the landscape of grief, both personally and professionally, as he faithfully bears witness to the erosion of traditional religious institutions. With honesty, humor, and emotional and physical determination, his pilgrimage to rediscover his place in a rapidly changing world, inspires us all to surrender and trust in the journey of being fully alive."

- AMY LIVINGSTONE, M.A., Sacred Art Studio. Visionary Artist and Spiritual Activist

ALONE

A 4,000 Mile Search For Belonging

ALONE

A 4,000 Mile Search For Belonging

BRIAN HERON

Wild
ginger
Press

Alone: A 4,000 Mile Search for Belonging
© 2016 Brian Heron
www.pedalpilgrim.com

I have tried to recreate events, locales and conversations from my memories of them. In order to maintain their anonymity in some instances I have changed the names of individuals and places. I may have also changed some identifying characteristics and details such as physical properties, occupations and places of residence.

All photography by Brian Heron.

Printed in the USA
ISBN: 978-1-943190-05-8

Ordering Information:
If you are interested in quantity sales for your organization, please contact Brian Heron at brian@pedalpilgrim.com.

Wild Ginger Press
www.wildgingerpress.com

This book is dedicated to the faithful and courageous people of Eastminster Church in Portland, Oregon. You have left a remarkable legacy and hold a place in my heart.

CONTENTS

PART ONE

Answering The Call

July 10 – July 19

Heading into the Cascade Range.

DAY 1
Portland to Silverton, OR
57 miles

IN LESS THAN THREE YEARS, I lost the three most important women in my life.

My wife of 25 years left our marriage suddenly one night. My mother-in-law, to whom I was especially close, died just over a year later after a long struggle with dementia. Eleven months later my stepmother (my father's third wife of 25 years) died during a routine, though risky, open heart surgery.

After such gut-wrenching loss, I had hoped I could build a successful life in Portland, Oregon, as a church minister after a nine-year detour into hospice, probation and foster care work. I took the position as minister of Eastminster Church knowing it was facing possible closure and that I could lose my job. Four years on, it was clear the end was in the not-too-distant future—Mother Church was about to abandon me as well, it seemed. My personal and professional life was crumbling at an alarming rate.

I was determined not to let these losses define me. I would win this war against the world by sheer grit and determination. Trading Forrest Gump's running shoes for cycling shoes, I resolved to ride my bike. "Walter," I told a pillar of Eastminster Church, "I need to take a pilgrimage. It's not a matter of 'if'. The only question is for how long and whether you'll let me come back."

The planning took eight months. First, the long process of convincing the church leaders to give me time off and to plan for other church leadership and pastoral care in my absence. I had numerous logistical issues to handle, such as the care of my sixteen-year-old cat, who would tend and water my tomato plants and flowers, and how to handle numerous bills while I was on the road.

I planned to visit every place I had lived, and get back in touch with the people who shaped me. My itinerary included the College of Idaho, my alma mater in Caldwell, Idaho; Bozeman, Montana, where I was born and where my life was permanently altered when my mother left our family after divorce; and Thermopolis, Wyoming, where my sister and I lived for a time while my dad put the pieces of his life back together. I would spend time in Loveland, Colorado, location of some of my most formative and painful experiences while growing up, and where my first stepmother still lived. Then on to the West Coast, where marriage and ministry had collided, and my beloved children Phil and Julie were born. The route would take me across five mountain ranges, over the highest paved highway in the world, and across the Nevada desert in the heat of August.

Of course, there was the rather significant issue of physical preparation as well. I had raced bicycles in my twenties and been pretty good at it, qualifying twice for the National Championships in short one-day races of 25–60 miles. But now I was three decades older, carried twenty-five more pounds of body weight, and would be adding fifty pounds of gear to my bike.

Riding 4,000 miles over several Western mountain ranges and a couple of desert landscapes—I dared not start such a grand adventure without any conditioning. That scared me. I spent much of the winter before the trip swimming three or four days a week and walking on the other days. As the cold winter Portland rain turned to warmer April showers, I planned to ride 1,000 miles in the six weeks before departure, but unfortunately, time pressures kept me to just under 700 miles. At least it was something.

Most of all I had to prepare the people in my life for my departure and absence. I met with family and friends, often describing my excitement, fears and anxieties. I shared a growing sense that something was coming to an end in my life. In each of my last six weeks in the pulpit, I preached from the closing benediction that I gave nearly every Sunday; should I not return, I wanted to leave them with that benediction we had shared weekly. I fully intended to come back, but none of us knew whether this was "goodbye, see you again soon" or "goodbye, thanks for everything."

Finally the day of departure arrived. Since I was leaving on a Sunday, I rode to church on my bike loaded down with gear, and for the first time in my life preached in cycling clothes hidden by my long, bleached white robe.

I walked my way through the service feeling neither more nor less emotional than on a typical Sunday. It was important to leave the congregation with something hopeful so they didn't feel I was abandoning them—ten weeks is a long time for a pastor to be absent.

I concluded the service with my usual benediction, "Now go out into the world in peace. Have courage..." As our pianist played the postlude, I walked down the middle of the aisle toward the back as I had done hundreds of times in the five years I had been there. Taking my position at the rear of the church, I shook hands, greeted my parishioners, and invited visitors to join us in the fellowship hall. But as people came by, shook my hand and hugged me, the emotion finally caught up to me. With each successive person, the tears became more impossible to hold back.

Strangely, the tears didn't seem rooted in the sadness of saying goodbye. I felt gratitude more than anything else. It finally hit me how much trust this bunch of people I called "Eastminster" had in me. They were letting me go with full pay for an estimated ten weeks on a cycling trip. Not only might I choose not to come back, but they also had to be worried that I might be seriously injured or even killed by some careless driver, a stray rock on a steep downhill, or simple foolishness and overconfidence on my part. They were supporting me and also taking the risk that I might never return.

Their farewell took me by surprise. I made my way into the fellowship hall to find it filled with members of the congregation as well as a handful of community partners. The choir had composed new words to one of our familiar hymns and serenaded me delightfully. It was corny, but I loved it. I took off my robe, exposing my tight touring shorts, cycling shoes and fluorescent yellow jersey. Finally, I checked my bike one more time to make sure everything was secure. Over the back wheel hung two panniers loaded with fifty pounds of gear, including my tent, sleeping bag and pad, and a backpacker's pillow was bungeed to my back rack.

I rolled the bike out of the fellowship hall, through the narthex, and into the breezeway outside. Small groups of white-haired ladies gathered around me while pictures were taken. The young, attractive pianist with whom I had an old man infatuation gave me a big hug and started to tear up. People patted me on the back and said, "Good luck" and "God bless you." I strode with my bike a few feet into the parking lot, turned, and snapped one final picture of them all.

I waved goodbye and pedaled through the potholed parking lot onto Halsey Street, the busy four-lane city thoroughfare running past the church. I looked back one more time: the crowd of sixty people were waving one last goodbye. I waved back. After all the preparation I'd expected this to be an adrenaline-pumping moment, like the send-off soldiers receive as they board a ship for some foreign land. Instead, the whole thing felt almost surreal and routine. I had cycled in Portland for the nine years I had lived there, and was familiar with the first half of this day's ride, so it didn't feel like embarking on some grand adventure—it felt like I was out for one of my four-times-a-week rides. The only difference was my bike was loaded down like a pack mule.

I hadn't gone a full mile before I realized that my bicycle computer was registering kilometers rather than miles. I wasn't about to spend the entire trip multiplying everything by 1.61 in order to report my distance and confirm my speed. And with an ego like mine, it was really important that I report my mileage every night to readers of my blog. I was used to doing these distances, but I was aware of how impressive they looked to armchair athletes. Luckily, Performance Bicycles was situated between the church and the city-maintained MUP (multi-use path). I was hoping for a quick in-and-out as it was already about noon, but the bike mechanics were as stumped as I was. Finally, they tracked down a code on the internet, pushed a couple of buttons, and completed the conversion. I rolled my bike out of the shop anxious to make some progress toward Silverton, over fifty miles away.

But I had to stop again. Just before entering the small town of Gladstone I stopped at a convenience store, grabbed a Gatorade and sat down on a ledge. My heart was aching for a friend of mine. Pam and I had dated for over a year before a breakup the previous March. We remained very close. She had thrown a going-away party for me the week before, but couldn't bring herself to see me off at the church that morning. To make matters more sensitive, her younger sister had died of ovarian cancer the same night as the party. This followed the accidental death in February of her high school nephew, her ailing younger sister's son—one of the cruelest twists of fate I have ever witnessed. I knew Pam was in a world of emotional pain.

In the past I might have postponed my trip a week to be present at the memorial service. But I had come to know in the months leading up to the pilgrimage that this was something I had to do; even Pam's need for support could not deter me from embarking on this journey. It tore at me terribly, but I knew I was making the right decision by following through on my plan. Nonetheless, I could not depart without leaving her one final voicemail reminder of my concern and my care.

I might have promised her, "Please feel free to call me at any time on the trip if you just need to cry on my shoulder." I didn't. I called and said, "Hi Pam. I just couldn't roll out without letting you know how much I care for you and love you. I know that this is a really hard time for you. I would be there for you if I could. I think you know that. Bye, dear Pam." I closed the phone and sat there shaking. This was hard.

Back on the bike, it felt good to experience the transition from city to countryside. Gladstone marks the dividing line between the busier energy of the city and the quieter forests and farmland of the Willamette Valley. Of all the places I have lived as an adult, Portland has felt most like home. I enjoy the culture: any night of the week I can find a variety of mainstream, foreign, documentary and art films somewhere close to my home. The quality and variety of dining establishments rivals even places like New York—or so Portlanders like to think! The climate is temperate; it is green year round and the "Keep Portland Weird" bumper stickers make me feel like I am part of a big extended family of nerds and artists. Plus, my adult children live in Portland and I have gained many friends since my arrival.

Still, for the purposes of the pilgrimage I needed this day where the terrain, the scenery, and the environment changed. I needed some visual reminder that I was leaving my life behind, even if for a brief time. I made my way along the MUP trail, following the Sunday interstate traffic just 40 feet away over a grassy embankment. As I inched my way through Gladstone and then Oregon City, I transitioned from the protected MUP to the overcrowded county highways leading to rural Oregon.

I have been cycling for over thirty years so I am quite comfortable riding in traffic, yet I was anxious to get beyond the heavy traffic and busy roads, as if the pilgrimage couldn't really start until I was in the clear. The trip was intended to create space to encounter myself, and to face both recent and impending losses in my life. But I was nervous. Large trucks lumbered by, spewing diesel smoke. Vehicles flowed around me like a line of ants headed for an uneaten sandwich. At one intersection a car made a right turn, clear enough to miss me but close enough to make me shake my head and mutter, "What the hell?!"

I wanted to get into the clear, beyond the city traffic and onto long, safe stretches of road that would allow me to be free of distractions and dangers. Eventually I would cross the plains of eastern Oregon, the high prairies of Wyoming, and the Nevada desert. There would be long periods, weeks even, of complete solitude. Wouldn't it just be ironic if I got clipped on the first day of riding, erasing everything I had planned for, prayed for, and prepared for over the past eight months? I rode anxiously forward.

Before long the traffic thinned, as more and more vehicles turned off on side streets and into driveways. Twenty minutes beyond Gladstone I was riding in the countryside, where my lungs expanded, my jaw loosened, and I finally relaxed.

My legs felt sluggish—the result of not enough training in the month prior and the sudden addition of fifty pounds of gear to my bike. Still, I found myself enjoying the bucolic farmland of Oregon's Willamette Valley. When I passed two men driving tractors, clearly a father and son team, I asked for directions, thinking I would attempt a short cut. We were the epitome of opposites: they, with dark, unshaven beards and missing teeth, working on a piece of property strewn with old cars and broken-down washing machines; me, in aerodynamic helmet, on my expensive two-wheeled machine loaded down with gear stuffed into brand new black and yellow Ortlieb panniers. Despite our lifestyle differences, they were courteous and curious and were glad to point me in the right direction.

I had arranged a week ahead of time to stay with fellow cyclists who are part of the Warmshowers network (an internet-based social networking site where cyclists host other cyclists). I arrived at my hosts' home early in the evening in the quaint and attractive town of Silverton, where cute shops teeter just above the riverbank and Victorian homes line the main streets. Rod, a thin, muscular cyclist, greeted me a few blocks from his home and we threaded our way along paths and dirt roads until we reached his retreat-like property and home. He and his wife Laura, a short, fit woman with shoulder-length brown hair, had planned a wonderful barbecue chicken dinner and we enjoyed the meal, along with beer, on their darkly stained deck overlooking a well-groomed lawn cut among the thicker vegetation of the forest. Rod and Laura shared stories of their many travels around the world by bike. With the exception of a handful of one-week tours I had taken, their stories introduced me to a whole new world of adventure and possibility. Listening to them, I felt I was getting glimpses of my own future. Was this pilgrimage the first of many cycling adventures? I was entering a new world that had been off-limits to me before, given the responsibilities of raising a family.

I left the dinner table filled and satisfied by the food, the conversation and the images of future travel. Making my way to a nice soft flat spot on their manicured lawn, I set up my tent for the first night of the pilgrimage. I rolled out the tent, pushed the stakes into the ground and threaded the poles into place. As I bent the poles the 150 degrees required to create a cozy little home—snap! One pole gave way. I couldn't believe it. The pilgrimage had barely begun and I had already needed to re-calibrate my bike computer, and now my tent was severely compromised.

It reminded me of the coming-of-age vision quest I took my son on when he was fifteen. We had planned to ride over the 11,000-foot volcanic Mt. Lassen in California in recognition of his transition from childhood to adulthood. I had bought a set of panniers for Phil at a garage sale, proud of the couple hundred dollars I had saved. Of course, I didn't test them out until the first day of the trip; when we attempted to attach them to his bike, they were useless. We finally decided they were packs designed for large dogs, as they had straps, but not the type of attachments needed for a bike. Although the trip was ultimately successful, I clearly had not planned well. I wondered if this narrative was about to play out again.

DAY 2
Silverton to Detroit Lake, OR
58 miles

MY WORLD WAS FALLING APART, but I was determined to build something new from the ashes. My intention was to blog every day so that the church and the wider community could take the journey with me and benefit from my experiences. Although Eastminster was facing likely closure, I felt that this pilgrimage might just save the church—or my job.

The Eastminster story had enjoyed great media coverage in Portland: could this pilgrimage be the catalyst for a new kind of church? If Eastminster closed, I wanted its passing to contribute to the larger conversation about the decline of the Church. I wanted other churches to hear its story and recognize themselves. I wanted to show the church world how to bridge the gap between religious adherents and those who think of themselves as spiritual.

More than fifty miles from Portland, I was still very much in the world of church. I was to meet with two people who, I felt, would have something to contribute to the story of the decline of Eastminster and the broader church. I first had a date with Christine. She'd grown up in Eastminster Church and her father Walter was the pillar of the church who had first heard my crazy idea to take a pilgrimage. I made my way over the thickly forested hill of Rod and Laura's property and descended into Silverton to meet Christine for breakfast. Her parents,

Walter and Florence, had kept her informed of my pilgrimage plans.

Christine, like most of her contemporaries, had left the church when she reached adulthood. She was one of millions of people in the Northwest who consider themselves spiritual but not religious. I knew the future of the church—and probably the future of my ministry and job security—would depend on an ability to create a meaningful spiritual community for those who fit this profile.

I wanted Christine to tell her story to my blog followers, but I had a deeper reason for getting her story. I had shared similar sentiments as a young pastor. In Lake County, California, I had written publicly in the early 90's about the compelling virgin birth and resurrection myths of the Bible. I angered many in the community, including some in the church where I was a pastor, who understood the term "myth" to imply a fictional tale rather than a story that informs our cultural values and identity. Letters to the editor flowed for weeks, accusing me of being a heretic, the anti-Christ and a wolf in sheep's clothing. A petition was circulated in the church asking that my ordination be removed. It didn't gain enough traction to be successful, but I paid a deep price for my intellectual and theological honesty. I wanted people to hear the story from someone else—especially someone who had family in the church still, but who wouldn't pay as heavy a cost as myself.

Christine was the perfect candidate. She shared my script: months before, she had been interviewed and quoted in a *Portland Tribune* article about why she no longer attended church. She didn't mince her words and some at Eastminster were stung by her comments. She said they had lost their way and no longer focused on Christ's mission, but had become concerned only about themselves and their own fellowship. It was not easy for many Eastminster members to hear this, especially from one they had raised and was the daughter of current members.

I met with Christine over a casual breakfast in one of the cute restaurants situated right on Abiqua Creek in downtown Silverton.

It's the type of place where one expects a few regulars to show up every morning, mixed with a handful of travelers passing through the area.

"Thanks for taking the time to meet with me," I said.

She grinned. "I am glad to."

The grin let me know that she knew exactly what was going on: I was using her and she was glad to assist in my covert mission.

"I'm hoping to capture some of this story of the shift toward spirituality," I began. "Eastminster may not make it, but they hope they can at least tell the story of what is happening as part of their legacy to other churches."

"I am not opposed to what they do," Christine said, "but it just holds no interest for me anymore. They're good at taking care of each other, but have forgotten about reaching out to the community."

"Is there anything the church can do to attract you back?"

"I think Eastminster is beginning to change," she conceded, "but it's too late. My husband and I have our own spiritual beliefs and practices. We believe in a divine being of sorts still, but we blend elements of Wicca and Buddhism. I don't think Eastminster could change enough to make us feel welcome. I think our beliefs would scare them all away." She smiled again, and I imagined we were both picturing her talking about witches from the pulpit and hearing gasps from the pews.

"The same thing is happening for me," I said. "Even though I pastor a church, my own religious stew is a blend of Christianity, Buddhism, and Native American spirituality. I feel like I have spiritual schizophrenia—straddling two different worlds of religion and spirituality."

"Yeah," she said. "Quite honestly, I don't know how you do it. You are a very patient man."

I knew what she meant, but inside I didn't feel patient at all. I want things to be different. I want to be able to speak freely about my beliefs and spiritual practices.

I changed the topic. "How do feel about your parents taking your two children to church when they visit?" I asked, wondering if this was a sensitive topic.

"We're okay with that now. I don't like the subtle pressure I feel from my parents about going to church or having our children in church. But as long as they don't press it too much we don't put up much of a fight. And the kids seem to like it," she said, with a hint of resignation.

We begged the waitress to take a picture of us together. Looking at the shot, I felt I was with one of my own. It was refreshing to be with someone who understood me, who shared a common language. I had grown tired of having to explain or censure myself in the church. I was hoping to have many more conversations like this in the weeks ahead, exposing the church world to my spiritual world through the stories of those I met on the road.

I didn't have to wait long. Just fifteen miles down the road I was to visit the daughter of long-time members of Eastminster who had since left. But by the time I reached Michelle's home I was getting worried. I had ridden only eighteen miles, yet my legs were showing signs of cramping. I had reserved a campsite at the base of Mt. Jefferson on Detroit Lake, still forty miles away and one-third of the way up the pass that crosses from Salem to Sisters over the volcanic Cascade Range.

I had a physically uncomfortable conversation with Michelle as she told her family's story. I sat, constantly massaging my legs. Under usual circumstances, I am sure this would have been considered rude, but I was truly concerned that at any moment one or both of my legs was going to go into a massive spasm, which is not only terribly painful, but leaves those present feeling helpless and maybe embarrassed for me. I would have loved to have her massage my legs like an athletic trainer on a football field, but that was a line I didn't dare cross! I kept massaging and she kept talking, clearly worried about me.

Unlike Christine, Michelle and her husband were one of the rare couples in their fifties who continued to attend a church similar to the

Presbyterian Church in which they grew up. Statistics bear out that the Baby Boom generation largely split between detouring to more evangelical conservative churches, or abandoning church altogether; very few stayed in the mainline Protestant churches of their childhood.

"What about your children?" I asked.

Michelle let out a sigh. "Neither of my children has any interest in church at all. I've asked them if they are angry about church or feel rejected by it, but they say, 'No, the church is just irrelevant to our lives. We don't even think about it.'"

Of course, I already knew this. While the Baby Boomers grew up in the church and later left it, the Millennials (the next generation) by and large haven't even been exposed to it. They know churches exist, but churches simply aren't on their radar or in their life.

I left the Willamette Valley feeling I was getting the story that I wanted Eastminster and the larger church to hear. At some level I knew I was manipulating the story that was emerging. In some ways this was less a pilgrimage and more of a marketing ploy.

It was time to face the reality of my already sluggish legs. The next four hours of riding were painful and left me worried. Just the year before, I had pushed myself too far on the first day of a week-long cycling trip through Yosemite National Park. Toward the end of the day, a four mile, 2,000-foot vertical climb hit me like a Mack truck. Before I reached the top, I was forced to lie in a crumpled mass on the side of the road when four or five muscle groups all went into torturous lock-down at the same time. I had become dangerously dehydrated without knowing it. Somehow I clawed my way to the top on foot where I spent the next eight hours fighting off deliriums as I tried to slowly rehydrate my body between hallucinations. It was the scariest moment I had ever had on a bike.

Given my Yosemite experience and similar signs of exhaustion, I rode slowly, working out each little cramp one at a time before they had a chance to knot up and force me into resignation. As I ascended to Detroit Lake, I made mental note of the few motels I rode by, aware that the cramps might force me to stop suddenly. If that happened, I wanted to be able to turn around and let gravity and the descending road take me back to the closest motel.

This was not a day when I broke any speed records. I simply listened to the messages my legs were giving me. Every time a twinge or hint of a cramp appeared, I stood up on my bike and stretched the twitching muscle. For forty miles and five hours I did this. I thought repeatedly of an elderly church member who had suffered a stroke ten years prior, and who bravely climbed physical and emotional hills every day: his courage pulled me forward. I reached the final little push up to Detroit Lake and suddenly felt a surge of energy. I couldn't believe I had ridden that many miles on legs that were begging to stop way down in the valley. Clearly the training I had put in before this pilgrimage was not enough. It was also clear that if I could learn the lesson of pacing and listen to my physical limits, I had more endurance in this 51-year-old body than I had given myself credit for.

I knew I still had two-thirds of the pass to climb the next day. But I went to sleep saying—in a moment of manic overconfidence—"Okay, Santiam Pass…let's see what you can throw at me tomorrow!"

DAY 3
Detroit Lake to Sisters, OR
60 miles

OKAY, SANTIAM PASS… That's how I ended my post yesterday. I had felt a strange confidence after surviving the day-long battle with dead tired legs and cramps threatening for 40 miles. I must have caught the mountain's attention, because she rewound the clock about three months and treated me to a wintry/spring day in Oregon, more typical of March than July.

I had left the rain fly off the tent during the night so I could enjoy the stars and the night breeze coming off Detroit Lake. I awoke as morning light was filtering through the trees. Allowing my senses to adjust to the new day, I began to hear a pitter-patter on my tent. I sprang up and flung the rain fly loosely over the top of the tent to keep my gear from getting wet. Inside, I continued to prepare for the day's ride while listening to the soft drizzle. It wasn't much of a rain, really; Oregon, I swear, has twenty different ways of categorizing rain and this was more in the heavy mist category.

I dressed lightly, as a little mist would serve to keep me cool until the clouds burned off (or so I assumed). Only one problem: the further I traveled up the mountain, the heavier the rain and the colder the air. The rain had moved up one category from heavy mist to light rain. It still was not a full rainstorm, so I kept putting off changing into heavier gear, thinking the clouds would melt away anytime.

The highlight of the day was encountering other cyclists who had heard the same call to strike out on the road in search of something unknown, or simply for the raw pleasure of cycling through America's landscape. I first met a newlywed couple who were riding many miles ahead of their sag wagon, leaving the bride's father busy trying to repair the broken-down vehicle and meet them at their next destination. After a short conversation, they passed me and continued on up the pass. Thirty years before, my competitive nature wouldn't have allowed that—but given their youth and the luxury of a sag wagon to carry their gear, I simply enjoyed the memory of an earlier age and let them go.

It wasn't too many more miles before I was the one doing the passing. As I made my way around a wide sweeping left turn toward the top of the pass, a couple riding separate bikes and barely moving came into view.

I quickly pedaled up on their rear wheel. "Wow, you two are really loaded down," I said. "Where are you going?"

"We've decided to go camping for a week," the man said. "We're riding to Malheur Lake."

"Malheur Lake? Isn't that in southern Oregon? Are you really riding all the way there?"

"Yep," he said proudly. "We don't own a car and we do everything by bike, including going camping. I have 114 pounds of gear on this trailer," he bragged.

I let out an I-can't-believe-it laugh. "I thought my 4,000-mile trip was impressive, but this looks almost crazy!"

"Well, we aren't as young as we used to be. We're in our fifties now and we like to camp in luxury. We each have a ten-pound cot loaded onto our trailer."

I laughed again. Their commitment to camping in luxury required a physical feat that was anything but luxurious—more like torturous. But I loved meeting this couple as they ground their way up the pass at three miles per hour.

By the time I reached the top of Santiam Pass at 4,817 feet in elevation, I was completely drenched and cold. Even my computer started complaining by shorting out: I had to continually disconnect it from its housing and wipe off the metal connections to keep it giving me the data I wanted. I finally dug out my rain gear buried deep in my panniers, but it was too late—I was already as wet as I could be and the rain gear would only serve to keep the moisture from escaping from my body. I would be slightly warmer, but no drier for the rest of the day.

I arrived at my destination—Sisters, Oregon—and immediately checked in to a motel where I could concentrate on unpacking my gear, letting it dry, and repacking it in a way that would allow me greater flexibility and ease for unseen circumstances—like rain in July! While doing laundry I met another cyclist, a strong-looking young man with two weeks of whiskers who was on the last leg of a three-month trip across America. He had dipped his rear wheel in the Atlantic Ocean off the coast of Florida as he left on May 2. In one week he expected to dip his front wheel in the Pacific Ocean in Astoria, Oregon. I could only think that I was with my kind of people—pedaling pilgrims. I had waited a lifetime for an adventure like this where I felt completely in my element and where my soul felt alive.

I went to sleep that night wrung out from the wet, cold day. Yet I was also feeling optimistic. After an especially fragile ride the day before, fighting off leg cramps, my body had recovered quickly. How I went from cramping one day to feeling strong at the end of a mountain pass climb, I don't know. But it was encouraging. I knew there were at least twenty major passes to cross on this trip and felt good that I had conquered this one with little more than annoyance at the surprise July rainfall. My confidence rose at least two notches from the previous day.

DAY 4
Sisters to Ochoca State Park, OR
47 miles

I TOOK FULL ADVANTAGE of the 11:00 a.m. checkout time in the motel. After the logistical challenges of the first three days (bike computer, broken tent pole, and a soggy ride for which I was unprepared), I needed to get back on the road feeling a little more organized and refreshed. I still had to address the broken tent pole. Bend boasted an REI, but it was twenty miles out of my way, adding nearly a full day to my schedule. Boise was less than a week away and I decided I could survive in my tent for a few more days and address the issue there.

My clothes, sleeping bag and gear were once again dry. The rainstorm over the Cascades motivated me to be more intentional about my packing. Part of the reason I hadn't fetched my rain gear the day before was because I wasn't sure where it was, and I didn't want to stand out in the rain digging for it. I know—that doesn't make much sense since I was already riding in the rain getting wet! Anyway, that morning I reorganized my panniers, putting items I would need while riding toward the top of my panniers, and items for camping near the bottom.

I had a pretty leisurely ride planned of only 47 miles from Sisters to Ochoco State Park. On the way, I stopped in Redmond to share lunch with the mother of Pam, my close companion who had lost her sister the week before I left. I knocked on her door and her dog immediately went into a barking frenzy, just as she had every time Pam and I showed up. Her mother came to the door as thin as I had ever seen her, with the bones of her arms showing through her skin.

"Hi Mary," I said. "It's so good to see you."

"I'm so glad you stopped by to see me on your way through."

"I felt it was the least I could do. I am so sorry about Carley's passing and missing her memorial service."

"You can't just put your life on hold," she said, erasing some of the guilt I felt for leaving Pam right in the eye of her emotional storm of loss and grief.

Mary went to the store for sandwiches, which threw her dog into another bout of anxious barking. I kept her distracted with a bowl of doggie treats. It took Mary longer than I expected, and the longer I sat, the more the stop felt like an interruption to my adventure. The catalyst for the pilgrimage was partly the feeling of being trapped by the ongoing needs of a dying church and denomination. As I sat waiting for Mary to return I became anxious, as if I had just allowed myself to get trapped in that world again, given Mary's advanced age and fragile body.

Mary drove up her driveway, her dog went into another barking frenzy, and my anxiety disappeared. For a full hour we enjoyed deli sandwiches, soda and oversized cookies while we talked about the things that really matter: life, death, grief, cancer, love, and family. It was the deepest connection we had shared since I'd met her the year before. I was glad I stopped. I hugged her and said, "My heart will be with you all on Saturday for Carley's memorial." And then I rode away.

The day's ride was completely uneventful, which was refreshing compared to the first three days of challenges. I pedaled easily through farm fields and large prairie lands. In the town of Prineville I bought supplies, so I could cook a meal rather than the easier "boil water, add contents, stir and enjoy" packages. I stuffed fresh broccoli and potatoes into my jersey pockets, along with orange juice, eggs, a morning pastry, bananas, Gatorade and more protein bars for the road. I left town with my jersey pockets bulging with staples and imagined what a strange sight I must have presented to the cowboy boot-wearing community of Prineville.

The ease of the ride also allowed enough emotional space for all kinds of thoughts and feelings to emerge. It was as if a reservoir of repressed feelings had built up and the pilgrimage was allowing me to suddenly acknowledge them, feel them, and name them. I wanted to remember everything I was thinking so I could share it in my blog and with the Church. I felt the pilgrimage was giving me the freedom and permission to say out loud what I and many others (like Christine) had felt for a long, long time. Too much was flooding my brain, and I finally pulled out a small notebook to write down thoughts that might end up as a blog topic sometime later in the pilgrimage. I scribbled single words and phrases as fast as I could: authenticity, congregational hospice, legacy, letting go, wilderness, smorgasbord spirituality, story rather than preaching, experience over belief, etc.

I arrived at the campground feeling fresh and enjoying the first signs of vitality and energy within since before the trip began. I was looking forward to fixing as close to a home-cooked meal as I could on the road using a backpacker's stove. Excited about all the thoughts and feelings flooding my mind, I wondered if what I had initiated with Christine was just the beginning of a "coming out." Was this my chance to speak to churchgoers about the shift taking place between religion and spirituality, a topic they often didn't want to hear on Sunday mornings?

I found a campsite overlooking Ochoco Lake that reserved a section for bikers and hikers. The campsite achieved a nice blend, retaining a primitive and natural state alongside modern enhancements. A simple picnic table was the only luxury in a grassy area that could have handled twenty tents if needed. Oak trees were sparsely scattered over the hillside that shielded one section of the campsite from another.

I picked a spot on the down side of the hill, where I could see the water some hundred yards in the distance. I was anticipating a rich evening. Quickly I unloaded my bike, separating camping equipment from cooking equipment and clothing from food. I concentrated first on the tent: unrolled it, slipped the poles through their slots, and then gingerly bent both the good pole and the amateurishly taped-together broken pole into place. Snap! The second pole broke in exactly the same place the first pole had snapped. I no longer had a tent—I now had an expensive tarp supported by two spindly sticks. I sighed and let out an oath no upstanding pastor would even think. I couldn't believe my bad luck, but I knew I would survive somehow.

While I did my best to set up the badly disabled tent, another cyclist walked his bike into the clearing a hundred feet from me. He had a pull-behind trailer for his gear in contrast to my rear wheel panniers and rack. Interested in his set-up, I wandered in his direction and we compared the experience of the two different methods of packing our gear. It was clear that the trailer gave him a greater feeling of stability on the road; the disadvantage was it was awkward to park because of its length. Something like the experience of trying to park an RV in a city environment, I imagined.

The cyclist was on a one-night excursion from Bend. He loved to take off in the morning, bring along some good food and wine and a book, and enjoy the quiet natural setting of Ochoco Lake before returning home the next day.

After we'd compared bikes and bike gear, I said, "By the way, I'm Brian."

"I'm Bob. So where are you going?"

"Riding through the West, visiting all the places I've lived."

"Yeah? Where you from?"

"I live in Portland." This might be the moment to describe what I thought I was really doing. "Actually, this trip is part of a project. I'm listening for the shift from religion to spirituality." I imagined I might get more of the story I was seeking.

He seemed vaguely interested. I went on, "The Presbyterian church where I'm pastor is about to close. As part of their legacy, they want to capture this story for other churches that are declining."

I had said too much. I saw the light go out of his eyes and felt the energy of the conversation sag. Hundreds of times before I'd experienced that same wall going up at the mention of my being a minister. Conversation would shift to anything but religion. It was disconcerting, but reminded me that his response was exactly what I was trying to capture. People like Christine are willing to share their changing spiritual beliefs and values. But there are a lot more people like Bob who prefer to keep their beliefs to themselves and are wary of anyone from the religious community. I had just trespassed on his personal life.

We parted company. I was sad that rather than connecting as two cyclists we'd ended on either side of an unnamed wall that rose up at the mere mention of religion. Why can't we talk about religion without it sounding offensive or people feeling it is being forced on them?

I remembered a prominent family in a church where I was pastor in Kelseyville, California. The parents were members of my church, somewhat moderate in their religious views, while their children and grandchildren were more conservative, almost fundamentalist. Still, they had a very close family and enjoyed trips together, backyard barbecues and family holidays. I asked them how they stayed so close despite their differences. Their answer—"In our house, we don't talk about religion or politics"—has stuck with me all these years. I could only think how unfortunate it is that the two most important and sacredly held parts of our lives—religion and politics—we can't talk about.

I am very aware of the separation of these worlds. In church, not only could I talk about religion, it was expected. Out in the community, I have to be careful what I say and to whom I say it. Religion is reserved for the pulpits and pews—that seems to be the rule. But it just isn't me. I don't want to live as if I had one life in the church and another outside the church; I want to be the same person in both places. I've often described myself as feeling spiritually schizophrenic and this experience with Bob had just accentuated it.

I enjoyed my boiled potatoes and steamed broccoli, and spent the evening eating chocolate and reading Harvey Cox's *The Future of Faith*. I may have ridden away from the church, but I was still digging into the dynamics of the religious world. Harvey Cox's thesis is that those of us alive today are living at the threshold of a complete paradigm shift. His belief is that we are at the end of a 1,500-year period he calls The Age of Belief, and that something new that could possibly be called The Age of Spirit is emerging. As I dug in to Cox's argument, I knew there was some relationship between his analysis and my awkward conversation with Bob. I imagined Cox's theory probably formed the basis for the invisible barrier that had gone up between us as I tried to engage Bob in this larger conversation.

I crawled into my down sleeping bag and looked out at the sky. A full moon splashed the lake and the surrounding hills in a soft, warm light. Despite the logistical challenges of the first few days and an almost non-functional tent, I felt pretty calm and confident. My interchange with Bob might have been disappointing, but it reminded me why I was on this pilgrimage.

DAY 5
Ochoco State Park to Dayville, OR
78 miles

I COULD NOT HAVE PREDICTED how deeply powerful this day would be. Somewhere between the physical beauty of the terrain I rolled through and my heart beginning to open up to the experience, I simply felt pure goodness all day. Even on the one brutal climb, the second of the day, I was overcome by how much goodness there was around me and how much goodness I have been afforded in my life. Much of the day I found myself reciting the Navajo Pollen Path prayer: "Beauty before me, beauty behind me, beauty above me, beauty below me, beauty all around me. I am on the pollen path." Years before in college I had taken a Native American literature class while immersing myself in a religion major. They were in different departments, yet I was struck by the parallels between Native American legends and the stories of the Bible.

I rode for miles along a crisp stream with just the sound of the wind and the water rushing by. It was wonderfully meditative and soulfully healing. Twice I saw, lying ahead, canyons with this same stream carving its way through the gorge. After the night at Ochoco State Park, I think my heart was still vulnerable from the magic of the moonlit night and the disappointment I'd felt over the lost connection with Bob.

There was more to it, however. I've had some rough moments in my life. As I recited "beauty before me, beauty behind me" I felt a softening toward the people and parts of my life that had deeply wounded and hurt me. For reasons I still don't understand (nor care about), my parents split when I was three years old, resulting in my birth mother leaving our family. Over the next several years, I only had contact with her a few times before she decided it was better not to see my sister and me until we reached adulthood. The feeling of abandonment runs deep in my soul and unfortunately was duplicated in my late twenties when my dad's second wife (a stepmother who later adopted us) abruptly ended our relationship. As if life comes in a series of repeated patterns, my wife of twenty-five years suddenly moved out one day with no warning.

Yet with all the pain those experiences and memories elicited, my heart felt big and expansive this day. I felt love and forgiveness for these people. I felt acceptance and forgiveness for myself for my contribution to these broken relationships. I could tell as I repeated the words "beauty behind me" that I wasn't just reciting them to convince myself that even such hurt could be beautiful. I was saying them, at least for that moment on that ride and that day, because even those difficult experiences were part of the gift of life.

The lens I wore that day clothed every experience in a thin veil of beauty and goodness. The terrain was softly rugged—inviting yet challenging. A young woman smiled and said hello as I rode by. White pelicans, larger than blue herons, took flight as I rode by a small, marshy lake. Headwinds sometimes slowed me to a crawl and tailwinds lifted me in flight as I emerged from the mouth of a canyon. Even on the most brutal hill (1,400 feet of vertical climbing in a short seven miles) the challenge, the strain, and the sweat streaming down my face all became part of the pure goodness of the day. I actually loved the pain and relished the feeling of the lactic acid building up in my legs. I felt alive.

I arrived in the small town of Dayville that evening after 78 miles of glorious and challenging riding. My heart was full and my mind active; I was opening up to the invisible hand of the pilgrimage as something grew inside.

I stopped at the local Presbyterian Church, which offered lodging according to my Transamerica map; a sign on the door directed me to a home just behind the church. The resident, a member of the flock, let me into the church, and showed me around. The entire kitchen was available for use, and donations from cyclists over the years had been spent on building a separate bathroom, shower room and laundry facility. A computer with internet hookup was available in another room. The only thing missing was a bed.

"You can sleep anywhere in the building except on the pews," my host said.

"Hah! The only time people are allowed to sleep in the pews is during the pastor's sermon!" I wasn't sure she appreciated the irony or my humor.

The mood of the pilgrimage had definitely shifted after crossing Santiam Pass in the rain. Maybe it was because I had not had any more logistical challenges and was now settling into a rhythm. Maybe it was because keeping my body going was no longer taking all my energy, leaving me room to think, reflect and feel. Maybe it was because the beauty of traveling through Eastern Oregon had finally directed my focus to a softer, more mystical place. Probably it was a combination of all three things. Whatever the cause, I felt I was starting to do some of the hard reflective work that the pilgrimage was calling from me.

That night I cooked steak and potatoes and finished the evening with a pint of coffee ice cream. It was refreshing to be able to sleep indoors, as my tent was barely better than a way to keep the rain off. I luxuriated in the extra time I had and the comfort of being able to sit at a table with chairs.

The awkwardness with Bob when the subject of religion had come up was still fresh in my mind. Before starting the pilgrimage, I felt I would need to work through this thing I have teasingly called "spiritual schizophrenia." People project onto me, as a pastor, who they think I am and what they think I believe. Sometimes I feel the need to challenge those projections, but most often not, especially if I am in a professional role and my presence is more about what others need than about how I want to be seen. But at the same time, I know there is often a wide gap between how others see my religious identity and how I think about myself.

I think I first recognized this awkwardness in 2007 as I sat down to create my Facebook profile. I had felt for many years a certain discomfort with being too closely aligned with the term "Christian." Not so much because I was ashamed of it, but because I had no idea what projection another person might assign to the label. The opportunity to fill in the blanks for a Facebook profile became kind of a gift I didn't expect. I made my way through the first few categories—birth date, gender, hometown, and current city—fairly easily.

It became a little more complicated when it asked for my political views. I am registered with the Pacific Green Party, but almost always vote on the Democratic ticket since my vote for Ralph Nader in 2000 resulted in the electoral-college victory of George W. Bush (some friends still have not forgiven me!). My idealism was quickly tempered by the real world effects of holding too rigidly to my puritanical views. It took a few hours, but I finally landed on "politics that support compassion and justice." This allowed me to name the values that informed my politics without feeling boxed in by any particular party affiliation.

Then came the next question. Religious views? Dang! One would think after completing an undergraduate degree in religion and a Masters of Divinity degree that I would have this pretty well worked out. But I knew immediately that this was going to be the most difficult question of the whole profile. If I followed the lead of the census survey I would have just written in "Christian" and left it at that. But I literally shudder when I think of calling myself a Christian in public.

In recent years a religious right has hijacked the term in the media and I want no part of being associated with a group that has come to be seen as intolerant, rigid, non-thinking, exclusive and homophobic. I am probably closer to the values of self-proclaimed atheists than I am to this particular Christian demographic.

I thought of distancing myself from the religious right perception by reporting that I was a liberal Christian or a progressive Christian. These terms felt more comfortable, but all it did was push me more to the left on the continuum of Christian beliefs. These terms didn't resonate with my soul and still felt too narrow, like trying to stuff myself into an undersized casket.

I don't recall now whether I left that line blank or whether I settled on "progressive Christian" for a time. I do know I spent the next six months working out a short pithy label that would capture both the depth and breadth of my constantly evolving religious views. It reminded me of the process I had gone through in seminary, when we students had to write our statements of faith: we were given a full nine months to shape them, receive feedback from our peers, and get approval from the ordination committee. That statement of faith was supposed to be the boiled-down version of everything we had learned and experienced up to and including our three years in seminary. This was no easy task! The only difference with the Facebook example was that I felt compelled to come up with a clear, concise label, rather than a 1,000-word explanation and defense.

In the end, I landed on "agnostic Christian mystic" and have been delightfully surprised at how well this label has both identified me spiritually and given me a religious label to live up to. If anyone dares ask me what it means, I tell them that this unique identifier leaves room for doubt and uncertainty, as well as places me in the camp of those for whom the experience of the Sacred is more important than an unquestioned, static belief in God.

I went to bed that night in the chancel area of the sanctuary, usually reserved for Communion and preaching. Three steps below me stood ten rows of pews split by one center aisle. My head was just below the pulpit and my feet in front of the altar. John Calvin would roll over in his grave if he knew what I was doing, but it was the only carpeted area, and the cushioned pews were off limits.

I lay there thinking how rich and rewarding the day had been. I allowed myself to digest the fact that I had been living two identities for a long time. I lived with, tolerated and sometimes even supported the projections people had of me as a minister—always kind-hearted, prayerful, and God-loving. I also had my Facebook identity where I used "agnostic" and "Christian" in the same sentence, which would shock any God-fearing Christian under my care. But there, on the pilgrim path where the soul is allowed to expand and distance softens perceived risks, I was able to say out loud in my public blog, "If I have to have a label, then I would be willing to say that I am an agnostic Christian mystic." If anyone had a problem with that they would have to chase me down on some remote road in the middle of nowhere.

DAY 6
Dayville to Austin Junction, OR
62 miles

I REALLY BEGAN TO FEEL THE RHYTHM of the pilgrimage as I left Dayville the next morning. My legs were tired, but strong. I was riding comfortably more miles than just five days prior, and feeling less taxed by the end of each day's journey. Thoughts and feelings that had lain dormant for months, if not years, literally flooded my mind in the hours I spent in the saddle each day.

My plan was to ride as far as Austin Junction, about sixty miles to the east through a series of small passes. Austin Junction represented a small fork in the road: Transamerica riders would be either coming from the north or taking a left turn to travel north to Missoula, Montana. However, I planned to stay on Highway 26 all the way into Idaho to visit my alma mater, the College of Idaho (the C of I) in Caldwell.

The college was just about three days ride away and I was looking forward to getting back onto the campus. The C of I played an important role in shaping my life and character, and inciting a love for religious studies. Thanks to a couple of professors who took a little greater interest in me, a rather timid freshman eventually discovered a more confident, bright and determined Brian who had remained hidden until that time. I could feel as I rode that Caldwell was my first real destination; stage one of the pilgrimage now felt like getting from my home in Portland to the college.

The day continued to mirror the pattern I had felt since drying out from the earlier rainstorm and leaving Sisters. I was in a nice, rich, deep meditative space. I had found a rhythm in my legs and a confidence in my strength that allowed me to focus less on riding and more on the terrain, both around me and in my head.

I enjoyed the rolling grasslands and prairies of Eastern Oregon. The terrain was therapeutic, with soft contours and a road that traced the sensual outlines of the landscape. I felt as if I had taken a mild sedative; my body and spirit had almost completely relaxed. I pedaled my way through a series of small Eastern Oregon towns, stopping only briefly in Mt. Vernon, a small town of just 500 residents that boasted at least ten churches to serve the wider rural community. I took a picture of the Mt. Vernon Community Presbyterian Church and thought about how much the church plays the role of community center in a town like this.

Next came the larger town of John Day. I had promised to stop there and talk with the brother and sister-in-law of Betty, another pillar of Eastminster Church. I met them at their real estate office, a quiet, two-room setup that felt more like a home than a business. We talked for the better part of an hour about the pilgrimage, about Betty, and about the challenges facing Eastminster due to successive generations opting out of church affiliation and participation. But I felt I was going through the motions of conversation. While they seemed glad I had made the connection, the issues that had propelled me to take the pilgrimage seemed to glance off their shoulders. It wasn't that the issues weren't pertinent to them, just that they had a casual, almost resigned approach to the changes affecting religious congregations. They spoke of the role of the church in the community, even as they acknowledged that younger generations weren't assuming the responsibility left by aging populations.

I understood the central role the church has played in communities like Mt. Vernon and John Day, where generations have lived, farmed, ranched, and called them home. I also thought about the tsunami-sized changes that seem to be coming our way, culturally, religiously, and spiritually. I left with conflicted feelings, fearing that communities like these will not have the internal flexibility to shift and adapt. It seemed to me that the church as they know it will die with them as their generation passes away. I felt sad. As much as I'd felt at home with Christine five days earlier in Silverton, I also grieved for these people who would watch the churches erode away as people like me either abandoned the church or demanded something different.

I could not have predicted that I would see this story played out in the next town along the road. Just as the mountains begin to rise again, Prairie City nestles in a wonderful little valley of irrigated farmland against the backdrop of Dixie Butte in the Blue Mountains to the south. There I took a picture of the Methodist Church, which was perfectly positioned directly across the green city center park, resting at the base of the mountain—built for the perfect camera shot.

What made this church different than any I had encountered up to this point is that it had a Closed sign out front. It's hard to know the exact story, but most likely the membership simply declined in this rural town until they could no longer afford to keep up the building and pay for pastoral leadership. I wrote this in my little notebook before beginning the climb back into the trees, heading toward Austin Junction just a few more miles down the road. From there on, I rode on some of the more inviting stretches of road up to this point—wide highways with little traffic, towering pine trees shading the entire road for a cooler afternoon ride—and relished the pleasure that courses through my veins whenever I settle into mountainous terrain.

I arrived in Austin Junction at the crossroads of two highways, where a lonely but inviting log cabin-style building was the only sign I had ridden into civilization. A couple of gas pumps were situated out front. Large doors ushered customers into a small gift shop with an ice cream stand, and a comfortable dimly lit restaurant and bar with tables constructed from wood right off the property. There was no motel, so I asked where I might be able to find lodging or a campsite for the night. They must have had numerous such requests, as the owner immediately said I could set up my tent on the property behind the business for a five dollar fee.

I wheeled my bike into the grove of trees, set up my nearly useless tent (it was getting embarrassing even putting it up) and unpacked my gear. I hurried back to the restaurant and settled into one of the tables for a well-deserved beer and dinner. It was the kind of place where it's easy to linger. I was halfway through my meal when a couple came in and sat down at a table within earshot. They were obviously locals, as they immediately struck up a conversation with the owner, Dottie, asking about other residents and talking about things only those who lived there would know about.

The conversation turned to a project that the woman, Melanie, was heading up. Apparently she was working with the town of Prairie City

to turn an abandoned building into a community and personal enrich-
ment center. "Dottie, what we're trying to figure out is what to do with
all the religious symbols in the building," she said.

"Can't you just get rid of them since it's no longer a church?"

"It's not that easy. Some on our committee feel that the church is a
historical landmark and we should retain some of the religious elements
as a nod to the contributions they made in the past."

"I guess that makes sense. But won't that make some people feel
uncomfortable in the building?"

"That's exactly what we are torn on. Some of us feel if it's a community center that's open to everyone, the religious symbols should be
stripped away."

I couldn't hold my tongue any longer. "Are you talking about that
Methodist church in Prairie City? I noticed the Closed sign on the
building when I rode through."

That's all it took. Melanie and Norm invited me to bring my dinner
over to their table and join in the conversation.

"What are you doing in these parts?" Melanie asked.

"Well, I'm riding my bike on a 4,000 mile journey." I hesitated to
say too much and maybe cross that awkward line with regard to religion.
Given that they were already flirting with the subject, I decided to go
on. "Actually, I'm studying the shift taking place between religion and
spirituality. I have a church that is dangerously close to closing in
Portland, which is why I perked up when I heard you talking about
that Methodist church."

We were off and running. Melanie and Norm were as close to aging
hippies as I could imagine. Yet Melanie, of the two, didn't appear to
hold deep counter-cultural values. She and I talked, while Norm listened
politely but with a slight lack of interest. I was struck by how much
Melanie understood the shifting world of religion and spirituality. She
was thrilled that the community center would occupy an old white

church with the traditional steeple. She had nothing against religion and felt that the community center would serve the purpose of meeting people's spiritual needs. In her imagination, the schedule included dance, yoga, meditation, and classes that fit under a broad umbrella of honoring body, mind and spirit. For Melanie, the center was simply the next incarnation of the church's mission to meet the community's spiritual needs.

Melanie was talking my language. I thought about what was happening in Prairie City and the thousands of churches that were predicted to close across America in the coming generation. The conversation continued energetically and suddenly I found myself being invited to Norm and Melanie's home for the night, to get a shower and sleep on what they called a nice, fluffy bed. I had already paid my five-dollar fee for the campsite, but given the condition of my tent versus the opportunity for more conversation, it was an easy choice. I rode the extra three miles to their home, which turned out to be a sort of do-it-yourself, multi-staged, oversized cabin situated next to a flowing stream. It was a lovely little spot, as idyllic as I could imagine. I walked through the front door, and Melanie greeted me with "Mi casa, su casa"—my home is your home.

I appreciated the hospitality, and our conversation continued late into the evening—but I was left with a nagging loneliness. The immediate connection, shared conversation, invitation to share dinner, and being welcomed into their home gave me a taste of what I longed for. I wanted to be among my people (that same feeling I'd had briefly with Christine), have a home, and be in an intimate relationship. I got just enough of it to accentuate precisely how little of that I had in my life at this point. I was glad for the story of the Methodist church/soon-to-be community center, and thankful for the hot shower and comfortable bed. But I sank into the fluffy pillows feeling very lonely.

How had I lost so much?

DAY 7
Austin Junction to Unity, OR
25 miles

I GOT AWAY EARLY AND TRACED my way back to Austin Junction. I needed to tear down my tent and get my gear re-packed and situated on my bike. The dinner at the café had been excellent, and I was looking forward to starting off my day with another hearty breakfast and a couple of cups of strong coffee. I was not disappointed. I ordered French toast with eggs and bacon; it was so good I made a mental note to stop there if I ever drove through this part of Oregon again.

Nonetheless, I was antsy to get on the road. Having climbed Dixie Pass the day before, I assumed I had come out of the eastern edge of the Blue Mountains and would start descending gradually toward the Oregon-Idaho border. Plus, it was time for a rest day: my legs were still pumping, but I could tell they had little to no snap. They needed time to recover and rebuild from the first week of riding. I planned to ride only as far as the town of Unity, just 25 miles out. Technically I couldn't call it a rest day if I was riding, but the shorter distance would give my legs a much-needed respite.

I rolled away from Austin Junction for what I thought would be a casual two-hour jaunt into Unity. I descended a short hill, curved around a bend—and came face-to-face with an unexpected and significant climb.

During the first six days of riding I'd been following an Adventure Cycling map of the Transamerica Bikeway that displayed elevation gains on my route. Before each day even began, I was able to create a strategy based on how many mountains and how many vertical feet of climbing there would be. But at Austin Junction the Transamerica Trail turned north, while I went southeast, so I'd resorted to my AAA map that was great for showing distances and displaying the names of towns along the way, but showed no topographical information. That I had to guess at. I had guessed wrong.

I dug in and started propelling myself up the mountain, not knowing just how much of an ascent I was facing. Nearly an hour later, I crossed the summit of Blue Mountain Pass at 5109 feet.

As I reached the top, a song started playing in my head. I grew up in Colorado and John Denver's *Rocky Mountain High* was the first album I ever bought as an adolescent. His song, "Sweet Surrender," played in my mind now as if stuck on a particular verse: "Lost and alone on some forgotten highway..." As I repeated the words, the lyrics almost carried me down the road. "There's a spirit that guides me, a light that shines for me, my life is worth the living, I don't need to see the end." I felt lost and alone and lonely, but I trusted the future unfolding ahead of me.

After the surprise climb the ride was short. I was settling into the prairie land of eastern Oregon. A wide sweeping turn from south to east deposited me in Unity, a town about a half-mile long with no cross streets, and consisting only of the handful of businesses and homes that line Highway 26. I chuckled at the brief thought that the residents might call themselves Unitarians, a reminder of a religious tradition I had some experience with.

It was still early, only noon when I arrived. It was the first day I would have the luxury of enough time and space to do more than just set up my tent, get dinner, buy supplies for the next day, write my blog post and allow some brief recovery time. There was one motel in town: a very cheap one that was priced appropriately. The bed was uncomfortable and the faucet leaked, but it was still a step up from crawling into a sleeping bag in a sagging tent. I took care of laundry, enjoyed an impromptu nap, and settled into one of the most luxurious evenings of that first week.

I ate at a restaurant just a short walk from the motel, one of those western-style buildings constructed completely of pine wood. A few people were seated around tables: judging from their attire, they were mostly tourists passing through town, with a few local residents seated at the bar. I enjoyed a steak-and-potatoes meal that was heavy on portions and light on quality. But that was just fine with me; I needed lots of calories.

Then I pulled out the Harvey Cox book I had been reading, *The Future of Faith,* and ordered a piece of apple pie with a hefty scoop of vanilla ice cream. As I held the book in my left hand and ate the over-sized dessert with the spoon in my right, I was overcome with emotion—the pie and ice cream opened up all my senses. Cox was busy describing the passing away of church institutions. The night before, I had shared the story of a church that was closing, but being resurrected in another form, followed by riding through a day feeling very aware of the loneliness and lost-ness of my life. I felt sad and grateful all at the same time: sad for the world that seemed to be passing away, and grateful for what was emerging. It was the same feeling I'd had after my mother-in-law died, sad for her passing, but grateful for the richness she had brought to my life.

The pilgrimage was doing its work. I was becoming more vulnerable, opening up to the pain and possibility of my life. And it came courtesy of an academic book and a piece of heavenly pie.

DAY 8
Unity to Ontario, OR
71 miles

BEFORE I LEFT ON THE PILGRIMAGE, one of the most common questions (might I even say concerns) was where I would stay each night. I told people that, since I was cycling, I couldn't imagine how I could plan any more than two or three days ahead. For one thing,

I wanted the flexibility to go as far as I felt able each day. I didn't want to feel tied down to a certain distance, only to discover that either my legs didn't have it in them that day or that I wanted to take advantage of a delightful tailwind. Of course, a tailwind can just as easily be a headwind, depending which way I'm going. Things like rain, excessive heat, biting cold, and detours to avoid heavy traffic can suddenly add an hour or two of unexpected riding.

I had only been riding for a week, but already I was learning to trust that I could find a place to sleep as late as the afternoon of each day. The only days I had planned my night's stay on the trip were the first night in Silverton with Warmshowers hosts, Rod and Laura, and my second night in the campground at Detroit Lake. And remember that I almost didn't make it to Detroit Lake given the onset of leg cramps just a few miles into the ride. The third day I rode into Sisters sopping wet and cold and found a motel. The fourth night I'd planned on reaching Ochoco State Park; arriving with no reservation, I had still been able to enjoy that lovely site in its bike-and-hike section. The next night I set my sights on Dayville, relying only on a note on my Adventure Cycling map that the Presbyterian Church would host cyclists. Dayville was followed by Austin Junction, where I first pitched my tent behind the café/store and then received a better offer from Norm and Melanie to stay in their guest bedroom. It had all worked out.

I left the motel in Unity unsure if I would end up in the town of Vale, 65 miles out, or Ontario, 85 miles out. Quite honestly, it didn't matter to me. I was comfortable with riding until my legs gave warning signs and then finding a place to stop in the next few miles. Rolling grasslands early in the day's ride transitioned into the flatter, irrigated wheat and hay fields of eastern Oregon. Once again, the landscape allowed me to fall into a meditative state as I didn't have to anticipate major climbs or worry about traffic hazards. There were a few cars on the road, but most gave me plenty of room as they passed.

My thoughts were also with Pam's family as the memorial for her sister was being held that day. The rhythm of my pedaling alternated between soft and easy as I grieved with them, and hard and desperate as I expressed my anger over the double tragedy—Pam's sister had lost her only son, a high school senior, who died by drowning shortly before her own death. Painful, painful, painful.

The nearly flat terrain suited my body. I am strong enough to climb mountains, but not particularly fast. However, when I hit the flats my strong and heavy body acts like a train that has gotten up to speed. Thirty years before I had ridden in the National Championships, on terrain like this, in races called time trials. I had covered the 65 miles to Vale by early afternoon and decided to shoot for Ontario for the night: it would be no more than two hours of riding. Tub (as he is fondly called), an Eastminster member, had given me the phone number of one of his extended family. When I called I spoke to Tub's sister-in-law and asked where I might stay for the night. I thought she would either point me to a campsite or allow me to set up my tent in their backyard.

"Well, you know," she said in a friendly voice, "Tub is here right now. Let me put him on." I had to laugh—Tub was visiting for a family reunion of sorts. They invited me to stay the night in an extra bedroom and join them for the reunion and a barbecue dinner later that night. The hardest decision I had to make was accepting a ride from Tub in his four-wheel-drive truck. I insisted that I really needed to ride all the way into Ontario and not cheat on any of my miles. Remember, I do have a fairly active ego! Tub explained that they would all need to drive across town for the barbecue and if I rode all the way in I would likely miss the carpooling and the dinner. In the end, I used my better judgment, accepted the ride, and swallowed my pride.

After dinner, Tub and his family asked what I had discovered so far on the pilgrimage. Tub, I was sure, was especially interested as he knew that Eastminster was teetering close to closing—he would jump at any juicy discoveries I might have made that could save the church. I told him about meeting Bob at Ochoco State Park and how the conversation died after he discovered I was a minister.

Tub shook his head. "But Brian, you're one of the easiest people to talk to that I know."

"I know, Tub," I said, "but Bob didn't know me. Obviously, he was wary of anything that smells like proselytizing."

"I don't get it," Tub said. "I still say you're easy to talk to."

Once in my cozy room, lying in a comfortable bed, and still full from a great dinner, I felt grateful. But I also felt I'd taken a detour back into the church world. I had felt safe with my own thoughts after being gone for over a week, but that evening I found myself being slightly careful about what I said and aware of the need to explain things in a way that Tub and his family could hear them. How free I'd felt expressing my agnostic Christian mystic leanings, and chatting about churches becoming community centers! Cox was introducing me, in his book, to the possibility of a new world emerging after a 1,500-year dynasty of orthodox belief. I was flirting with crossing over into a whole new world, yet that evening I'd been pulled back into the old world like a child suddenly being woken from dreaming.

I wasn't ready to come back to the real world. I liked the dream I was having.

DAY 9
Ontario, OR to Boise, ID
70 miles

THIS WAS A DAY I'D LONG ANTICIPATED. I was returning to the campus of the College of Idaho, an institution and community that had a major influence in shaping the direction of my life. While each day on the pilgrimage had its own integrity, Caldwell, where the college is located, was my first real destination point. Caldwell may be a dusty, manure-smelling town, but the college sits on the western edge of town on what feels like an oasis of 36 square blocks. Across the street are the stockyards, and just beyond them the freight trains noisily clank their way through town, blowing their whistles to warn motorists of their dangerous presence. Despite this—maybe because of it—I'd felt very much at home at the college. I grew up on the front range of the Colorado Rockies in a small town. Three blocks away, trains would noisily blow through town, and just outside the city limits cow pastures and red barns graced much of the land to the east.

I was first introduced to Caldwell in 1979 after making one of my most important decisions as a young adult. I had taken a year off after high school before entering college, largely because I'd burned out on school my senior year and come dangerously close to not graduating. My composition teacher gave me the gift of a D-minus grade so I could graduate. A year of working as a saw man in a mobile home factory convinced me that I wanted a college education. At the factory, I'd worked alongside forty-year-old men who were still bragging about their weekend drinking parties. That was a future of which I wanted no part.

I applied to two colleges: the College of Idaho in Caldwell and Whitworth College in Spokane, WA. I was more impressed with the campus of Whitworth than Caldwell, quite honestly, as well as the city of Spokane and the mountainous, pine-covered landscape surrounding it. But my best friend from Loveland, Dave, was a student at Whitworth. For the first time in my life, I realized I needed to establish my own identity. I had lived very much in the shadow of Dave who, it seemed, was always one rung higher than me in almost every respect. He was president of the National Honor Society whereas I was a mere card-carrying member. He played varsity tennis, while I had to settle for junior varsity. He was the salutatorian (second-highest grade point average) of our class while I was further down in the top twenty percent. We both were Eagle Scouts (the highest award of the Boy Scouts), but he received his long before I got mine.

So despite my deeper attraction to Whitworth I decided on the College of Idaho, where I would be able to carve out my own identity and finally emerge from Dave's shadow. It was a good decision. Over the next few years I discovered my own unique interests; met my future wife; made a lifelong friend. I began to believe in myself and, as is often said, finally came into my own.

It was during my college experience that I discovered what I'm most passionate about. Before college, I'd imagined I would end up in engineering. My father was a mechanical engineer and, like him, I excelled in math and enjoyed the world of numbers and their relationships. By the time I entered college, I'd chosen political science as a major, holding some far-off dream that I might serve as a U.S. senator at some point. But some of my most interesting classes were in the department of religion, and I discovered a strange fascination with Biblical literature and the inner psychic spiritual world to which it points.

In the fall of my first semester, I watched a half-hour television program that highlighted cyclist George Mount as he trained for the 1980 Olympics in Moscow. As fate would have it, our country didn't participate in those Olympics because of our boycott over the U.S.S.R.'s involvement in Afghanistan. But that didn't matter to me: that half-hour program opened up a drive and a passion inside me. I decided right then and there that I would leave college after the winter term to try my hand (well, actually my feet) at bicycle racing.

This wasn't completely impulsive. I grew up riding my bike just about everywhere. My mother (my dad's second wife) introduced me to 15–25 mile rides in my early teens. Later, my friends and I often took rides of 25–35 miles on the weekends. On one such ride, a few racers passed Dave and me; we quickly caught up with them and rode for a few miles. At a stop, one of the racers raised his eyebrows and said, "You two young chaps are really strong!"

Some months later, I entered a short bicycle race. Clearly, I was in a different league: I was at least twenty percent faster than the rest of the group and put a considerable space between me and them in the first half-mile. Unfortunately, I was also grossly inexperienced—taking a corner too fast and too sharply, I crashed out of the race. But the image of that gap between me and the other racers, and the reminder from local racers that I was strong, were stored away in my head. When I watched that television program in college, those reminders surfaced and I made my decision right then: I would spend the next stage of my life racing bicycles and trying to get to the Olympics myself.

Over the next three years I raced competitively, winning many of my early races. As I rose to the more elite level my winning days ended, but I still qualified for the National Championships in both my second and third years. During this time, I married the woman who had become my best friend at the college; after three seasons of racing, Lisa and I returned to finish our degrees.

Back at college, it was soon clear that political science was no longer my driving passion. I still loved the world of politics and political theory, but I was concerned about the effect a political career would have on family life since I was now married. I threw myself into three areas: religion, physical education and choirs. While I kept my involvement in choir consistent, I couldn't decide between religion and P.E. for my major. I first declared a religion major with a P.E. minor, then shifted to the opposite. I felt equally attracted to both, and went back and forth until finally choosing to complete a double major in religion and the newly created major of sports and fitness center management.

At the College of Idaho, I felt most authentically myself. I was involved in the activities and areas that most intrigued me and mirrored the passions I felt inside. There, our first child was conceived. The

College of Idaho had it all for me: religious studies, singing, cycling and physical education, establishing my own identity, marriage, friends, and the beginnings of a family.

Now, on my loaded-down bicycle on a pilgrimage born (I thought) out of a desire to resurrect a religious career, I cycled slowly around campus. I felt very much at home even as a nagging sense of grief ran through my veins. I'd always imagined how perfect it would have been to pursue a chaplaincy position on the campus—but the chapters of my life hadn't allowed that. Coasting around the sidewalks of the campus, I grieved over how much of the life I had craved was now gone. My marriage to Lisa ended in divorce near our 25th anniversary. The delightful days of coaching my children's soccer teams were long past. And the passion that I'd felt for religious studies had been tempered by the harsh realities of church politics and ongoing congregational decline.

I meandered around the campus reflecting on that little idealistic slice of the world—and how different the real world was. I sat outside the humanities building where so many of my favorite classes had taken place. Dressed in my cycle-touring clothes, I leaned against my loaded bike bearing its reflective panniers and the message of adventure, travel and challenge. With the bike under my hands and the humanities building looming above me, I recognized that, at least for this moment, my two college majors had finally come together. I was following my two greatest passions—athletics and religion—and living them out on the bike.

I left the college early in the afternoon with plenty of time to reach Boise, where I was anticipating a rest day in the home of another couple belonging to Warmshowers. It was an enjoyable ride. I rolled through farmland familiar from 25 years earlier. I still recognized the pungent smell of onion crops interspersed with hundreds of acres of growing mint. I stood up on my pedals and passed lumbering tractors, glanced in my rear-view mirror for approaching semi-trucks, and braced myself against the blowing dust and heat of the valley. The road was flat and straight, and I recalled the days when I used to train on this stretch for time trials—essentially a race against the clock, where strength and one's ability to ride through pain are a rider's best assets.

Just before reaching Boise I received a call from Multnomah County in Portland, asking if I would interview for a position as the interfaith director for the county. I had begun college studying political science and moved to religion, and discovered that in many ways they were close cousins. This position was tailor-made for me; it would allow me to act as a bridge between the religious community, and civic and government agencies. I was already deeply engaged in local government in Portland as an alternate to a county commissioner, co-chair of the East Portland Action Plan (a visioning committee), commissioner to the City Charter, and member of the Portland Plan Advisory Committee, working on a 30-year vision for the city. I'd expected to get this call sometime during my pilgrimage as I had sent my resume in weeks before my departure. I'd already thought about my response.

Phone in hand, I swallowed hard. "I would love to, but I've already committed to this pilgrimage and at this point I need to honor that." I hung up.

I felt it was the right decision, but had the call come before I left I'm sure I would have followed it up. I couldn't believe I would let this position get away from me under any circumstances. Yet I had.

After recovering from some momentary regret, I arrived in Boise. I was slightly dehydrated from the heat and dry conditions and lost no time in following the directions to my host's home. I was glad to be back in the Treasure Valley, a place Lisa and I had seriously considered making our permanent home. With nine days of riding behind me, a tent in need of repair, and a head full of memories of a life once so full of promise, I stopped to rest.

DAY 10
Boise, ID
Rest Day , 0 miles

I WAS THANKFUL FOR the day off. My body needed it, but I also needed to allow my emotions to catch up. Each day had brought new challenges, conversations and experiences. With the tight schedule of riding each day, getting oriented to a new town or location each night and securing a place to sleep, there hadn't been much time to process the depth of the experience.

By the time I got up, Rachel and Patrick, my hosts, were already off to work. Rachel had left a loaf of freshly baked cranberry applesauce bread, coffee beans, and a note telling me to help myself to the contents of the refrigerator. With the luxury of not having to pack up, I enjoyed breakfast out on their deck. It was then that I saw the Eden-esque setting I'd been invited into. Rachel and Patrick live on a two-lot plot of land in a three-story home that Patrick has built almost completely by hand, starting with a simple one-story house that had been neglected over the years. The current home is spacious and has personal touches that display their personalities and interests. Outside, the large remaining lot is densely planted with trees, flowers, ferns, shrubs, and a garden with a small creek running through it. They have designed the flora to provide a natural canopy for birds and butterflies. As I sat on their wood deck drinking strong coffee I was in paradise.

My thoughts turned to the unique community of people called the Warmshowers network. With no prior knowledge of me at all, except for my profile on the website, Rachel and Patrick had trusted me with their home. The truth is, I also trusted them; I was sleeping in the house of people I had never met before. In this age when people appear so separated and cautious, Warmshowers seemed like a throwback to a more innocent time. Maybe it's actually a foretaste of a new and more trusting time. Shouldn't the world be more like this, where strangers share stories and don't hesitate to take care of each other?

The morning slipped away lazily. I finally decided I couldn't waste any more time putting off my tent issues. I called a college friend, Bret, who still lived in the area and was good enough to chauffeur me around town while we caught up. He'd been a groomsman at my wedding and I returned the favor two years later at his wedding to Jill, Lisa's best friend in college.

As we neared the REI store, I began preparing my case in my head, arguing that their tent had been defective. I'd had the tent two full years, but had only used it on two separate one-week tours. I hoped they would replace the poles at no charge, since it seemed to me they should have held up for much longer than two weeks. But companies have a way of finding loopholes and, quite honestly, I'm not much of a fighter for things like that. With the next REI located five hundred miles away in Bozeman, it was more important that I walk out with a functioning tent than insist it was their error, not mine. I needed the tent more than I needed my pride intact.

I shouldn't have worried.

"Can I help you?" asked the clerk at the customer service desk.

"Yes," I said. "I'm doing a 4,000-mile cycling trip and both my tent poles snapped during the first week."

"Let me see." The clerk eyed the damage. "It doesn't look like we have replacement poles for that tent since it's an outdated model."

My heart began to sink. Here we go, I thought. The script has already started and I'm going to end up having to buy new poles.

"Can you wait a minute?" she asked, and disappeared through a door at the back.

I fidgeted for a few minutes, running through scenarios in my head. What could I say to convince them I hadn't caused the breakage through any error on my part?

The clerk returned with a chipper smile on her face. "We'll just replace the whole tent with a brand new one of equal quality."

I was stunned. Just like that it was done. She showed me the tents that qualified, and I picked one I liked even better than the original. There was a twenty-dollar difference in price, so I threw in a couple of freeze-dried meals for the road. I left the store feeling giddy, imagining how I might develop some great partnership with REI, where they would sponsor my next tour in exchange for enthusiastic endorsement and promotion!

After an afternoon of visiting with Bret, he dropped me off back at my hosts' home. Rachel and Patrick had prepared a meal for us out on the same deck where I'd spent my luxurious morning. We drank beer and talked about biking; Rachel and Patrick were the real thing when it comes to bike touring. They'd met while cycling through New Zealand on separate multi-month-long tours. Since getting married, they've cycled through Tibet, the Himalayas, Thailand and Vietnam, and told me they were planning a tour around the world.

Before retiring for the night, I pulled out my maps. Arriving at the college and Boise seemed to signal the end of the first leg of the pilgrimage. I had much history in this area because of college, my now-defunct marriage, and life-long friends. The next place I had history was Bozeman, Montana, where I was born and where memories of a distant, painful past were still buried. I was returning to the town where my never-ending wrestling match with abandonment began.

On the way I would need to contend with two major mountain passes that would test my legs and my determination. There were 500 miles still to cross, including the jagged Sawtooth Mountains and the Continental Divide that separates Idaho from Montana. Patrick had warned me that freezing temperatures were still being reported in the town of Stanley, little more than a hundred miles away. It was time to gear up for the next stage of this adventure. Patrick asked if I had stopped at the Anne Frank Memorial as I rode into Boise. I'd ridden by it, but hadn't taken the time to stop, as I was working on directions to their home while fighting dehydration.

"Definitely don't miss it on the way out," he said. "Your riding reminds me of the Alice in Wonderland comment, 'I'm late, I'm late, I'm late for an important date.' I keep wondering what you're late for. Stop at the memorial this morning and look for any number of hot springs on the way to Stanley. You shouldn't miss these!"

PART TWO

Entering Sacred Territory

July 20 – July 28

The Salmon River flowing from the Sawtooth's.

DAY 11
Boise to Ten Mile Creek Campground
53 miles

I HAD NO IDEA WHAT I HAD so quickly passed by two days prior. Having coasted back down the hill, I rode into the Anne Frank Memorial and parked my bike next to one of the memorials where I could keep an eye on my gear. I was greeted by a quote from journalist Judith Miller: "We must remind ourselves that the Holocaust was not six million. It was one, plus one, plus one..." That made me pause. Then I sat down to read the forty or more quotes chiseled into the stone slabs encircling the park-like setting. Twenty-five years before, I had written my senior honors thesis on the "Protestant Response to the Holocaust." For the first three months of research I cried, as I read story after story and hundreds of accounts of Jews innocently and unsuspectingly marching off to their own deaths. As I read the quotes at the Anne Frank Memorial I was equally overwhelmed.

Yet I felt an undeniable spirit of hope as well. Lined up next to each other were quotes from Jimmy Carter, Eleanor Roosevelt, Alice Walker, Moses, Helen Keller and many more—all speaking to the issue of justice, peace and human dignity in their own unique ways and words. I sat on one of the semi-circular stone benches, silently meditating on the words and experiences that gave rise to this memorial. Others milled about, reverent and silent. The structure and arrangement of the pew-like benches made the stone slabs seem like an altar of sorts. The energy of this outdoor space naturally drew me inward to where silence, prayer and meditation became the only appropriate response. I left that sacred space feeling as if I had just worshiped more deeply and authentically than I had for years in church.

A few miles out of town, I stopped for water at Lucky Peak reservoir. While at college I had worked one summer for the YMCA, and had spent a few lazy afternoons supervising youth at the water's edge. I used the facilities, filled my water bottles, and mentally prepared for the little bit of climbing I faced that day. Just then two women, not too much younger than me, cycled up. I found some excuse to talk to them, and after a short conversation I took off feeling rather full of myself as the women seemed impressed by the sheer size of this pilgrimage challenge. I pedaled up the road to the top of the dam and could feel their eyes still locked onto me. I rode all the harder, milking the opportunity to impress them further. I felt like a teenager showing off for the girls and laughed at myself.

By early afternoon, Boise was many miles behind me and the rugged mountains were staging themselves before me. After a brief late lunch in Idaho Falls, I circled the town looking for a place to set up my tent for the night. There were plenty of options, but I was particularly choosy after my Boise accommodations—spoiled by the luxury of a bed and the Eden-esque surroundings at Rachel and Patrick's place.

I decided to make my way up the road a little farther. I knew there were long stretches of forest along this road with virtually no towns, but I felt a little adventurous. Would this be the night I would have to find a flat spot off in the trees, hidden from curious drivers on the road? To my surprise, I happened upon Ten Mile Campground, exactly ten miles from Idaho City. Only one other family was camped in the area; I found an isolated spot next to the creek and hidden from the other campers. It was as luxurious as the home I had left in Boise, if raw and wild.

I unpacked my bike, set up my new tent, and prepared my sleeping quarters for the night. With an eye for order, I set the picnic table as if it was my little home. I pulled out my stove, cooking utensils and the night's meal, and set up a makeshift kitchen. At the other end of the table, I opened my laptop and placed my tiny notebook within hand's reach as I prepared to write a blog post about the day—a ritual that had become routine. I wouldn't have internet access, but I could at least use the juice in my computer to write that night and send the post at the first opportunity next day.

Next came bodily hygiene. I can certainly ride from one day to the next without a shower, but after a day of sweating, heat, and blowing my nose farmer's style (you know, shut one nostril with a finger and then blow, leaving a trail of snot on the road, my sleeves and shorts), a shower is almost essential day-to-day. I had the perfect place. I walked over to the stream and dabbled my feet to feel how cold it was. Yes, my guess was confirmed: this was icy snowmelt coming off the peaks more than 6,000 feet above me. I stripped down completely, got out a wash cloth and bar of soap, and sat on a rock just a few feet into the stream. There I reveled in the fresh, frigid water as I doused myself with as much of it as my nerves could handle.

Afterwards, I felt clean again. But more than that, I felt alive. Really alive. More alive than I had in a long time. Above me, towering pine trees reached to the sky, allowing intermittent ribbons of light to filter down. It reminded me of the effect of stained glass windows in a glorious cathedral. I had my own makeshift home with a creek that served as a bath, a picnic table that was both kitchen and home office, and a tent to retreat to as darkness fell. At home I had a car, a fifth-floor, two-bedroom apartment overlooking the city of Portland, a job that paid a decent salary, and a reputation as a particularly determined community leader. Yet in that simple campsite I had everything I needed.

Like that morning at the memorial, I was in a sacred space—a sanctuary of trees, water, and the light of dusk.

DAY 12
Ten Mile Campground to Stanley, ID
83 miles

THE FOLLOWING MORNING I AWOKE ready to put my legs and determination to the test. I stretched for a few minutes to work out any kinks from the day before. I breathed and tried to stay calm, knowing that this day would require every bit of energy I had. I'd had a full rest day two days prior and the 53 miles traveled the day before had not been taxing. My legs had some snap to them for the first time on the trip.

The problem was that the town of Stanley was 80 miles away and my route crossed three mountain passes on the way. The highest pass, Banner Summit, peaked at 7,200 feet and was 2,000 feet higher than any pass I had crossed thus far. I knew Stanley was probably 15–20 miles farther than I should be trying to tackle, but I was itching to see if I could get all the way there. I decided to ride as far as Sourdough Lodge, 36 miles out, and then decide whether I should prepare for another night of camping along a crisply rushing stream, or load up with just enough food to get me over the summit and roll into Stanley.

The first miles were stunningly beautiful. I followed a number of creeks and then the lovely Payette River for a while. Most of the time the water cascaded therapeutically through the gorge, only to enter steeper sections where it violently erupted. I passed numerous hot springs, but with my mind set on riding long and hard, I rode by each one with only a twinge of regret. By the time I reached Sourdough Lodge, I had crossed two of the three passes and my legs were beginning to feel the effects of all the climbing. As I sat in the restaurant contemplating my options, someone yelled across the room, "You know, Stanley is having live music out in the street tonight." That was all I needed to hear. I loaded up on enough Gatorade and Cliff Bars to get me over the summit. I was just about ready to pay for my supplies when I stopped, turned, and went back for a container of Noodles in a Cup and some trail mix. I was determined to conquer the pass, but caught myself thinking, *I'd better be prepared for a night in the woods. Just in case.*

It was one hell of a climb up to Banner Summit. I was pushed to my absolute limit on several occasions, and found myself numbing out in order to push the pain into deeper recesses of my brain. I found myself on long stretches of Tour de France-like ascents—steep, unrelenting, and torturous. Even on the ascent over the Cascade Range the week before, the incline had been steady and long, but not so steep; I just had to keep a good consistent pace. On this pass I found myself counting pedal strokes. "C'mon. Fifty more revolutions," I'd say, and when I hit fifty I would assess my strength again and tell myself, "C'mon. Just twenty-five more." For nearly an hour I played that game, taking the mountain in stretches measured by small increments of pedal revolutions.

I was sweating profusely, sweat literally running down from my head to my torso and cascading over my legs. On flatter sections the breeze usually evaporates any sweat, keeping me dry. But here I wasn't going fast enough to create a breeze. Even my biking gloves became saturated in sweat, creating an uncomfortable recipe of grease, sweat and snot all blended together.

Just as I was wondering if the mountain had beaten me, I rode up on a small trickle of water, no wider than my foot, cascading over rocks and hidden underneath yellow and purple wildflowers. I didn't want to stop, concerned that I might not get my legs churning again, but I couldn't pass up this surprise gift. As I dismounted carefully so as not to cause a sudden cramp, I nearly started crying. I removed my toxic gloves, soaked them in the rivulet of water, and wrung them out. I refilled my water bottles with ice-cold mountain water and poured it over my head and my overheated leg muscles. God, that felt good!

I experienced a beautiful humility. There I was at the edge of complete exhaustion on this climb, yet this small stream left me feeling I lacked nothing and had all I needed for the day—and, as a metaphor, for life. Pain and goodness were dancing with each other.

I reached the summit, cornered a traveler to take my picture at the 7,200 foot Banner Summit sign, and prayed that last 25 miles into Stanley had no more ascents. My legs were completely shot, my mind numb, but my soul felt full.

I was glad I made the decision to push myself into reaching Stanley. I knew the Sawtooth Mountains had a reputation for spectacular beauty, but I was not prepared for how stunning and breathtaking they were. The valley reaching into Stanley is a blanket of lush green meadows parted by winding, quiet streams, set against the backdrop of the jagged, rugged, snow-capped mountains—they're called Sawtooths for a reason.

I set up my tent in an underused and completely empty park a half-mile above the town. That evening I walked back down the gravel road to find the main street blocked off for a party. The band were setting up their stage, and beer and brat stands were opening up as people slowly converged on the center of town. Impatient to get a full meal, I walked a few more blocks to Maui Waui Pizza, and sat outside enjoying a Canadian bacon and pineapple pizza, a mug of beer, and the thousands of acres of lush green meadows and dark green mountains before me.

Overhearing a conversation at the next table about treks into the wilderness for pictures, I butted in. Michael, Keith and I were soon talking about our adventures: my grand circular pilgrimage around the West, and their hiking into the mountains for unique and never-be-fore-seen shots of waterfalls for a book project. We parted and Michael offered, "May the road rise to meet you; may the wind be always at your back." I knew the quotation. It's a popular Irish blessing attributed to St. Patrick that cyclists often share. Michael meant it as something of a joke; we had talked about how my journey was circular in nature, so the wind could not always be at my back. It was a true blessing, however, because that comment and his intended touch of irony showed that he really knew what I was doing. He "got" me—it felt good.

The promise of street music and a festival had provided the final push I needed to get myself over the mountain. But by the time I'd finished dinner and was droopily relaxed by a couple of good beers, I didn't have enough energy to enjoy the party. I walked back up the hill to the park, where my tent was the only sign of civilization for miles to the south and west.

I crawled into my sleeping bag with nothing but the majesty of the mountains in view. My aging body was tired, but I relished the unusual strength and perseverance I had discovered during the beautiful, punishing ride. As I drifted off to sleep, I was struck by the thought that the day properly deserved the title, "Beauty and the Beast."

The first week had been marked by various—and continual—logistical challenges, but now I had experienced two consecutive days where I felt I'd entered sacred territory. The terrain had shifted, but so it seemed had my heart.

DAY 13
Stanley to Challis, ID
59 miles

I AWOKE EARLY IN THE MORNING just before the sun would sneak up over the mountains east of my tent. Though plenty warm in my down sleeping bag, my nose was cold: I knew immediately it was a chilly morning. I tend to like lazy mornings back home—a couple cups of coffee, sitting in my man chair, reading the paper and finishing a crossword puzzle before tackling the day—but on the bike

I feel forced to organize myself a little more quickly so as to beat the afternoon sun. Lying there in bed, I committed to walking down to the town, eating a hefty breakfast of pancakes, eggs and bacon, and quickly returning to my campsite where I would disassemble everything and pack it up for the trek along the Salmon River.

I pulled on some long pants, a long-sleeved jersey, and a jacket. The air was cold and it took a couple of minutes before my clothing warmed up to my body temperature. I opened the front flap to my tent. Damn. Damn. Damn! My rear tire was flat. I don't know why it deflated me so much (pun unintended!), perhaps because it's so unusual for me to feel motivated in the morning. Having pushed myself to tackle the day before sunrise only to find that a flat tire was going to delay me, put me in a sour mood. So much for the shifting of my heart. I was back to logistical issues.

I followed through on my plan of walking back to Stanley, and ate at the same pizza place as the night before. The restaurant was busy already, and I had to wait a few minutes for a table. A bank sign across the street flashed the time and temperature—38 degrees, meaning it was probably close to freezing when I'd first got up.

After a lumberjack-sized breakfast, I did what I had to do. I returned to my camp, spent a half-hour fixing my flat tire, and ran through the morning routine of tearing my tent down, repacking it, loading my panniers, and making sure the weight was even on both sides of the bike. Off in the distance, just above one of the jagged Sawtooths, shone a large, wide rainbow that was severed at top and bottom like a multi-colored winner's ribbon. On both sides hung thick, dark sheets of rain, and above me, blue sky. I wasn't sure if it was a warning or a gift.

By the time I was ready to ride again, much of the morning had slipped away. But though the day started with the challenges of an icy morning and a flat tire, Michael's blessing of the night before then seemed to take over.

For the entire 59-mile ride that day, I felt I was being gently pushed along by an invisible hand. Unlike the steep passes on the way into Stanley that had required a gritty, angry determination, I pedaled effortlessly all day, following the path of the descending river. In my rear-view mirror rose the ragged, snow-capped Sawtooths. To my right, the crisp, inviting Salmon River brought up images of the movie *A River Runs Through It*, and the temptation to stop and trade in my bike for a fly-fishing pole. A few rafts filled with water adventurers floated by. In the trees above me, hawks and ospreys expressed their curiosity and anxiety about my invasive presence in their home territory.

The day wore on and the terrain slowly transformed from the rugged Sawtooths to the just as rugged, but barren, Lost River Range. Pine trees and craggy hillsides were replaced by sagebrush and velvety brown hills with softer contours. A small herd of Bighorn sheep quietly grazed alongside the road, hardly noticing me. I came to a stop and casually took a picture trying not to spook them.

I rolled easily into the town of Challis, found a cheaply priced motel room, and sorted my clothes for a run to the laundromat. The day started off with the minor challenge of a flat tire, and ended with minor frustrations about laundry. The coin machines weren't working in the laundromat, so I spent twenty minutes in search of quarters and laundry soap. I bought more soap than I wanted or needed, and returned to the laundromat to discover I had less than an hour before the facility would close. At six p.m. of all times! I washed my clothes, dried them as far as possible in the time remaining, and left the extra laundry soap there for the next traveler. Despite the minor challenges, it did feel like a day of grace.

But another feeling was easing its way into me. In the lead-up to my pilgrimage, people had shared stories of others who had embarked on similar journeys. I'd heard the story of one man who simply hit a psychological wall during the second week and abandoned his ride.

He made an attempt again the next year and rode with an iPod plugged into his ears, which apparently saved him on his second try. Another man told me he'd nearly abandoned his trip during the second week, but gritted his way through it and discovered a new world after a number of psychologically scary and dark days.

I was finishing my second week and wasn't feeling anything like that sort of a wall hitting me. More than anything, I was sobered by the sheer size of this adventure. It was coming home to me that I had completed less than one-fifth of the journey, and had already been on the road nearly two weeks and ridden over 700 miles. I still faced at least eight weeks covering more than 3,000 miles, the expansive Wyoming high prairie, the challenging Rocky Mountains, and the terrifying Nevada desert. Even if I did hit a wall at this point, Boise was 140 miles behind me and Bozeman was 350 miles ahead of me. It was clear that the road was my new reality.

DAY 14
Challis to North Fork, ID
82 miles

I WOKE UP IN THE MORNING feeling sluggish. It was hard to drag myself out of the comfortable bed. Per my usual routine I headed into the bathroom to pee—almost nothing. I had become dehydrated. I was surprised. I'd had a very easy day following the graceful descent of the Salmon River the day before, but I must have gotten lazy about keeping up my fluids and electrolytes due to the easier pace.

I ate my usual breakfast at a nearby family restaurant and tried to ply my body with juice, water and coffee. But as I mounted my bike, I still felt sluggish and in a melancholy mood. I don't know whether the depression led to my sluggishness, or my sluggishness led to the mild depression. I did know I was having a hard time turning the pedals.

I found myself singing. But unlike the "Lost and alone..." song that kept repeating in my head in Oregon, impromptu sacred songs emerged from my lips. I started singing simple little ditties with sacred words: "The goodness of the Lord is all around me. The beauty of God is in me." I repeated these songs over and over again, trying to convince the depression to melt away. This was so unlike me. I get enough of sacred music at church; elsewhere, I tend to prefer the music of U2 or David Gray or Brandi Carlile, to name just a few. Yet my soul seemed to know what it needed, and after ten miles of Gregorian-like chants the depression eventually lifted, my legs felt lighter, and the bike was gliding again.

I rode by a small plot of farming land just off a lagoon, probably no more than five acres. As I approached I startled a hawk that flew off as I rode by. Moments later, a deer bounced off into the trees to seek safety from this strange creature on two wheels. As I watched the deer flee, she bounded right by three wild turkeys who seemed oblivious to the commotion around them. I stopped to take a picture. As I remounted my bike, a great blue heron with a wingspan of prehistoric proportions burst from the lagoon and flew right across the path not twenty feet in front of me. Any one of these experiences would have put a smile on my face and a sigh in my heart, but their occurrence in such rapid succession turned the field and lagoon into a sacred place, a sanctuary of goodness and beauty.

Not far down the road, I passed by a home with a large front yard abutting the lonely pavement I rode on. There in the middle rested an isolated statue of a woman sitting in the grass, her arms wrapped around her knees as if bringing them into her chest. Her face was nestled into the space between her knees and her chest. Was it grief? Prayer? Gratitude? I didn't know, but it suddenly turned the lawn into a place for holiness. Rather than being just a green showcase for flowers, that lone figure created in the garden a sacramental quality of grace and softness.

I rode through the town of Salmon and located the Presbyterian church. Being that it was a Saturday, I contemplated staying overnight and attending the Sunday service next morning. I tried to locate the pastor, but members who happened to stop by told me she was out riding horses. I looked at the signboard in front of the church advertising her Sunday sermon. It read, "Wherever you go, there you are." That sign was all the push I needed. It reminded me that God or Life or Sacredness is with us wherever we are—I didn't need to be in church to find it. I continued my journey.

As if I had put on different-colored glasses, I began to look for that sacred quality all around me. It wasn't long before I came across a white-steepled church seemingly in the middle of nowhere. It felt like a relic of a long distant past. I knew churches like this probably had a precarious and uncertain future. It symbolized for me how we ministers feel, as the culture becomes less reliant on our profession and our skills.

Yet as I rode by the church and thought about its history and place in the community, I felt a softness in my heart for it. Like the lone woman on the lawn a few miles before, this white church building was probably a living symbol to the community of so much that the people held dear. How many times had the community gathered in this place to bless and baptize children and grandchildren? How many of the local residents could point to this building and say, "This is where Pastor So-and-So married us 50 years ago." How many of them were hoping that, when their lives ended, this was where their closest friends and family would gather around home-cooked dishes and tell stories and laugh and cry together? I knew I was looking at a building that represented the past more than the future. I also knew that the soul of the community likely resided there.

Just a few miles down the road the north fork of the Salmon River veers off to the west, while my route headed north up and over the Continental Divide and into Montana. At this junction sat the so-called town of North Fork, the only sign of whose existence was the combination motel/restaurant/convenience store/gas station. Nevertheless, it was a perfect place to stop for the night after a wonderful day of gradual, almost imperceptible descents following the Salmon River.

The motel appeared to be not much more than a few boards slapped up, nailed together, and painted. But inside, the room had just the right combination of rustic, modern and feminine touches: a replica wood stove with gas heat stood against the wall at the foot of the bed; pine window frames and doors gave it a wonderful western feeling. And despite the tight quarters, a love seat made you feel you could relax as if in your own living room. Once again I felt I had entered a sacred space of some sort—just what I needed for preparing to tackle another mountain pass the next day.

DAY 15
North Fork, ID to Wisdom, MT
53 miles

THREE PANCAKES, TWO SCRAMBLED EGGS, four slices of bacon, a large orange juice and a bottomless cup of coffee: that had become my routine breakfast, especially on a day when I anticipated some strenuous cycling. Today was one of those days. There was only one way to reach Montana at this point—over Chief Joseph Pass and the Continental Divide. In addition to this particularly difficult challenge, there were no towns between North Fork and Wisdom, my evening destination. It was only 53 miles away, but a day spent in the saddle climbing requires an unusual amount of calories. I was hoping that the pile of food before me would at least carry me to the top, and I could rely on Cliff Bars and bananas the rest of the way.

I'd been told I should expect to begin ascending immediately after leaving North Fork, and was prepared for as much as four hours of mountain climbing. Cycling the first miles, I knew I was climbing, but for a full seventeen miles I wondered when the real climb would start. The grade was not nearly as frightening as I had geared up for.

Finally the grade increased significantly, and for ten miles I had to dig deep, forcing myself to keep the pedals moving one revolution at a time. I settled into this numbing rhythm fully expecting it to keep me preoccupied for most of the morning. While I inched along at a snail's pace, I was suddenly attacked by a swarm of horseflies who decided I was easy prey. Horseflies are not something to take lightly: they are like regular flies on steroids—the Arnold Schwarzenegger version of the common housefly with a needle for a nose. Being bitten by a horsefly is as startling as a nurse missing your vein when searching for a blood sample: "Holy hell!" you may well exclaim.

On those steep portions of the climb my rate slowed to six miles per hour. Sweat poured out of me like a sponge being squeezed. This seemed the perfect combination for the horseflies—yummy, smelly, salty sweat, offered at a speed where I could not out-pedal them. I spent the next few miles trying to survive. On my left, big vacation trailers and RV's chugged up the pass; on my right were steep forested mountains. I did my best to hold a straight line, swat at the damned creatures, and escape from what felt like an insect version of Hitchcock's movie, *The Birds*. I won the battle, however: three of them stuck their needle-like noses in me, and six were left flattened on the ground for birds to clean up. I didn't even feel remorse!

Suddenly I was cresting the top of Chief Joseph Pass at 7,241 feet. I was completely surprised I had reached the top so quickly. After the climb into the Sawtooths where I had been pushed to my absolute edge, I'd spent two full days psychologically preparing myself for another knockdown, drag-out fight over this pass; after all, I was about to cross the Continental Divide for what would be the first of many times on the trek. I spent a couple of minutes spinning in a circle looking for clues that there was more to this mountain. But this was it. I had reached the top a full hour ahead of my original estimate. I sat down on a log feeling almost deflated, like a boxer who prepares for a prize fight only to knock out the opponent in the first round.

The climb of nearly 30 miles was followed by a gradual descent through the forest. I relaxed on my bike and let gravity do the work. I recognized this land—high mountain meadows with small streams running through them; tall grasses and wildflowers; pine trees mixed in with currant berry shrubs. And the occasional deer grazing on the far side of a clearing, a safe distance from cars, humans and bicyclists. I was born in Montana and grew up in Colorado; this felt like home. As I entered more deeply into the Montana landscape, I was no longer just an observer. My heart reminded me that I was a resident. I belonged to this land.

About halfway between the summit and the town of Wisdom, I arrived at the Big Hole National Battlefield. I was inclined to ride on by and get into Wisdom on the early side, but an inner voice told me here was something I needed to do. I wasn't disappointed.

Panoramic paintings recreated the scene of the Battle of the Big Hole of August 9 and 10, 1877. I looked out over the rolling hills and imagined the atrocities and shame that took place there. In a surprise attack by the 7th Infantry Regiment on the fleeing Canada-bound Nez Perce, nearly ninety Nez Perce and thirty-one soldiers died in a brutal and bloody battle. Just as I felt that I belonged to this land, I also recognized this was my history. I am a child of the West and a descendant of those early settlers. We had learned about this history in public school, and played Cowboys and Indians on the dirt mounds where suburban houses were being built by the dozens on old tribal lands. What had felt like innocent childhood games was exposed as replaying genocide.

I grabbed a Coke from a vending machine to give me one last burst of energy and hopped back on my bike. I carried both elation from the successful climb and grief from the battlefield in my heart. Both the mountains and the shame of my ancestors' past are part of me.

I arrived in the small town of Wisdom (I wanted to embody that name!) in early afternoon with plenty of time to orient myself, get some food, and find a place to sleep. I had a late lunch. As I ate, I noticed across the street a trio of three young, fit, male cyclists parked at the local bar enjoying what one usually enjoys at a bar. I was delighted. After setting up a campsite, I planned to join them.

A quick survey of the town led me to believe the city park on the west side of town was the best camping spot. I was busy setting up camp when two more cyclists wheeled their bikes into the park and began erecting their tents. Before I was done, three young women passed the park on their bicycles, heading into town just three blocks away. I put on some civilian clothes and pedaled to the bar where I'd seen the first three cyclists drinking beer. By the time I arrived, at least a dozen cyclists had plopped on the railing and the chairs in front of a line of $3,000 bicycles. Given the Montana location and the rustic nature of the bar, it looked like a hitching post—except instead of horses there were bicycles, and instead of cowboys with hats there were cyclists wearing helmets and tight, shiny spandex. But all of us were doing what people did at a bar in the Old West: sitting there drinking beer, talking about the day's ride and how well our modern horses had held up.

In all, nineteen cyclists had arrived in this little three-block town for the night. I asked the bartender if this was a common occurrence.

"No," she said. "It's not unusual to have two or three of you in town at a time, but we've never seen this many all at once. It's bizarre!"

Unusual, but perhaps not that surprising, as the Lewis and Clark

Bicycle Trail is routed through Wisdom, and the town also sits at an intersection that connects two legs of the Transamerica Trail.

I was in heaven, and spent much of the evening sitting at the bar trading stories. I met KC, who was on a similarly-themed pilgrimage—he was slightly older, working through some personal issues and blogging about his experiences. The three fit males were recent college graduates, who had decided this was their one chance to embark on an adventure together before they found themselves committed to careers, spouses and children. A father, son and daughter-in-law were taking a trip not too long after the younger couple had married. I was immediately jealous of them and the bond they were creating with each other, as I grieved the loss of my marriage and in-laws. The three women were stopping at organic farms along the way, educating local children about the benefits of natural food. Among the rest were two friends from Yorktown, Virginia, who had the freedom to travel in semi-retirement, and the strength and will to complete a cross-country trip together.

And of all the places for this unlikely convergence of cycling pilgrims to happen, it happened in a little western village called Wisdom. You couldn't script it better than that!

DAY 16
Wisdom to Dillon, MT
61 miles

WHEN I WOKE IN THE MORNING, one of the men across the park was busy packing up his tent and organizing his gear to mount back on his bike. I lay in my sleeping bag an extra few minutes. I couldn't believe I had to pull up my tent stakes again. Day after day, I'd gone through the routine of arriving in a town, getting oriented, finding groceries, checking out the restaurants (or restaurant, as was often the case) and securing a place to sleep. For a few hours each evening I got to call that home. But as I nodded off to sleep, I knew the next time my eyes were open I would have to say goodbye again.

This morning I felt it more acutely than ever. I'd felt I was riding into home territory as I crossed the Montana border. Not only was it my birthplace, but my heart had immediately recognized the terrain. Added to that, I'd ridden right into a whole herd of cyclists in Wisdom and enjoyed a full evening of conversation, stories and laughter among people who knew me despite having never met me. I didn't want to leave this. I didn't want it to end. But I knew it had to, a fact made easier to accept by knowing every one of the other eighteen cyclists would be packing up and making their way to their next destination as well.

I also recognized that this feeling of wanting to put my roots down, even if only for an extra day, had its origins in the reasons for the pilgrimage. I'd felt rootless for a long time. Even during my marriage, we had lived in six different states during the course of our slowly eroding relationship. I had quickly gone through three significant romantic relationships after the divorce. And I worked in a profession that often required me to pick up and move every few years. I was tired of having to pull up my tent stakes over and over again. I'd found some people I liked and a piece of land that called to me. Yet again I knew this was not—and could not—be home.

Over my routine breakfast at the one restaurant in town, I prepared to say goodbye to Wisdom. Only two of the cyclists who had stayed in town that night were going in the same direction as me. The young, ambitious couple took off while I enjoyed another cup of hot coffee, true to my pattern of enjoying leisurely mornings whether at home or on a bike.

I would be riding through the Big Hole Valley and eventually crossing the Big Hole Pass at 7,200 feet. But by now that number was not so frightening, as the valley floors hovered around the 6,000-foot mark. I no longer had to climb 4,000 feet in order to reach one of the many summits in mountainous Idaho and Montana. Now, 7,200 feet represented just a good, hard hill climb that might tax me for an hour or less.

I caught up to my two cycling friends as they stopped to take pictures and have a snack. I carried on riding, as I got the feeling they were enjoying each other's company and didn't need an old man dampening their riding experience. Not too far after that, major road construction was under way. It was clear that a bike could not pass easily over this section: they had just laid a thick layer of gravel that would be near impossible to negotiate. In addition, crossing would take five times as long on a bike, leaving me vulnerable to the trucks and tractors working on the road. I parked my bike in the line of other vehicles and considered my options.

My two friends came up behind me. They were as perplexed about what to do as I was. While we were surveying the scene and freaking out just mildly, the driver of the truck ahead of us hopped out of his vehicle and asked if we needed help. We sure did! Ten minutes later our three bikes and gear were loaded up in the back of his truck-bed, and we were crammed into the cab of his vehicle for the three-mile ride across the torn-up pavement. I felt I was cheating a little bit—that I was supposed to complete this trip completely on my bike. But this was only the second time I'd accepted help, and I allowed my rigid idealism to take a vacation.

I spent much of the day in the Big Hole Valley that nestles between the Continental Divide to the west and the Pioneer Mountains to the east. There is something about the way the valleys are bordered on all sides by mountains that makes the sky feel like a large, baby-blue blanket stretched out over the entire state. You would think that having reached the boundary of one mountain you would leave this bowl-like environment. But as soon as you cross one peak, you descend right down into another mountain bowl. Having grown up in the Rocky Mountains of Colorado and more recently the Cascades of Oregon, I'm used to mountains serving as a clear wall separating one terrain from another. In this part of Montana, the mountains seem to come in waves and the sky seems unusually large, which is why it is called the Big Sky State.

I crossed the summit and began to descend. My bike picked up speed and I was soon racing down the mountainside at 45 miles per hour. A little cross wind pushed on my right side and I kept a firm grip on my handlebars, leaning slightly to the right to counter the force of the wind. Suddenly a good gust grabbed at me, throwing my bulky load to the left. It took me a few seconds to get the bike back under control and a few minutes more to slow my heartbeat. This surprised me—I've cycled at speeds exceeding 60 mph before. But I had made a rookie mistake, and placed all fifty pounds of gear over my back tire rather than spreading it out over the two tires. I pledged to address that as soon as possible.

After successfully negotiating road construction and getting over Big Hole Pass without crashing, my mind turned toward the days ahead. The town of Three Forks was a little over a hundred miles away. As a child, I had spent some very precious time there with my great-grandpa. I didn't know him well, but whatever it was about him and our time together, he owned a piece of my heart. Just fifty miles beyond that was Bozeman, the college town where I was born. When I say the name out loud it's with a sense of pride and fondness—yet Bozeman is really a mystery to me. Our family broke apart there when my mother left. And kindergarten was the only year I spent in school in Bozeman.

I imagined I was riding toward a town where I'd arrive and say, "Trick or treat?" completely unsure of which I would get. But that was still over a hundred miles from Bozeman; first, a night in the town of Dillon.

DAY 17
Dillon to Three Forks, MT
96 miles

I SET OFF FROM DILLON, a town at the cross-section of three highways and Interstate 15. Immediately I was pushed along by a strong wind, like some invisible paternal hand had grabbed my seat and was guiding me down the road. It lifted my speed so much that I began watching my speedometer and odometer carefully. I was adding at least three miles per hour to my average speed. My original intention was to get to the town of Three Forks, where my great-grandpa had lived. That was 85 miles out, which on most days would have been about the maximum I should realistically expect of myself. But three hours into the ride I had already covered fifty miles and was toying with the idea of riding straight into Bozeman, 120 miles from my starting point.

The highway was reasonably flat with only minor grades up and down. The wind pushed me along consistently. The only difficulty was the Texas-sized rumble strips on the right side of the white line—they were the worst I'd seen. They were probably great for cars, as drifting onto those two-inch-deep ruts would wake a sleepy driver with a start. On a cycle, however, I had to grip and strain with all my might to keep from being bounced right down to the pavement. There was only a thin edge of pavement—often of varying widths—to the right of the rumble strip. I decided the safest place to ride was just to the left of the white line in the lane of traffic. Better that than taking a tumble on the strip and falling either into the overgrown ditch or the passing traffic. When large trucks came up behind me I was able to see them in time to negotiate my way across the rumble strip and onto the narrow, smooth pavement next to the shoulder.

It didn't always work. In my rear-view mirror, I watched a large timber truck barreling down on me. There simply wasn't enough room on the shoulder to risk crossing the rumble strip. Riding in the rumble strip was a surefire way to throw my bike across the lane in front of the truck, so I rode a nice, straight, consistent line as far to the right as I could. The monster of a semi didn't ease up on the accelerator one bit. In fact, it didn't budge an inch as far as I could tell. As it blew past me, the force of the wind nearly knocked me over. I could have sworn that the large logs sticking out beyond the width of the truck passed right over my head and the gargantuan truck tires just missed my handlebars by a few inches.

I kept riding, but my breathing was shallow, my hands were shaking and I was pissed off that the truck driver hadn't even attempted to show a little grace for my vulnerable position. As I continued on my journey, my anger turned to sadness. I knew there was nothing I could do to change the possibility of being hit by some inconsiderate asshole, short of abandoning the trip—and that was not going to happen.

After I recovered from the near miss, I reassessed my progress on this wind-aided day. If that invisible force kept up I would be able to ride all the way into Bozeman by late afternoon and have a beer while smiling to myself at the ego-boosting accomplishment of having ridden 120 miles in one day. I reached the town of Whitehall and wandered into the grocery store for a few snacks, a pint of whole milk and Little Debbie donuts (a new favorite on the road). My map indicated a longer route to Three Forks south of the freeway that I was trying to avoid. I asked the clerk about my options: she told me that a frontage road would take me through the canyon next to the freeway where I could avoid the longer route and a bit of climbing. I thanked her and quickly downed my snacks, still in hopes of reaching Bozeman by the afternoon.

Unfortunately I missed a turn and, like a typical man, even when I knew something wasn't quite right I refused to ask for help and kept riding further and further away from my destination. Supposedly, I could avoid a major climb by taking the frontage road through the canyon. I kept looking for the canyon and climbing hills, and still refused to turn around and correct my mistake. I knew I was making my situation worse. I just kept turning the pedals, thinking there would be some road somewhere that would help me get my sense of direction. Finally, over twenty miles later, I came to a T-junction in the road with a sign that set me straight: to the right I could ride into Yellowstone National Park; to the left I would eventually find the town of Three Forks. I had given back the miles the wind had given me. In the end my attempt to reach Bozeman failed, not from lack of ability, but because of a stubborn streak. That stubborn streak had its roots in Bozeman, I was quite sure. Twenty-seven miles later I limped into Three Forks totally spent.

Rather than the rent-by-the-week, shabby, paint-peeling places, I picked the one motel that seemed to cater to people passing through town: a two-story building with expensive four-wheel-drive trucks and comfortable sedans lined up in front of the rooms. It looked so busy I was worried they might not have a room.

I walked gingerly through the front door and was greeted by a tall, leathery-looking gentleman whose face held a lifetime of hurt and pain and adventure.

"I see you're riding your bike through here," he said. "Where ya headed?"

"Right now, Bozeman. But I'm actually on a long trip, visiting all the places I've lived."

"Where all ya going?"

I started to list the places I had already visited: Portland, Caldwell, Boise. Then I went on to my future destinations. When I got to Colorado he brightened. "Oh, that's God's country. I've spent a good deal o' time there."

At that I decided to get a little more specific, and announced I would be riding over Trail Ridge Road before entering Utah and then Nevada.

"Trail Ridge Road? Damn! That's ambitious," he said, his face lighting up.

Of course—that's why I said it. I have a deep humble side, but I also know what sounds impressive to folks and I don't mind stroking my ego on occasion.

"Yes. I've ridden up Trail Ridge twice before, but I was thirty years younger and wasn't carrying fifty pounds of gear back then," I said.

"I'd be afraid of the damn RV's going up the pass."

"Actually, I feel pretty safe on the road. The ones I worry about are the Texans who crawl along and drive down the middle of the road, afraid to get within five feet of the edge. Coloradans aren't real fond of Texans."

He lit up again. "People who don't belong in the mountains shouldn't be there. They're my mountains and if people want to go there they need to honor them. All these damn tourists who take over and crowd us out. They should know better."

He was shifting from being interested in my ride to being a little scary. I tried to inject some reason into his comment, saying, "Well, I think everyone has a right to be there. I was just saying that it's annoying to get behind an out-of-stater who slows everyone else down."

"Let me tell ya. Couple years ago an acquaintance from Ohio asked me about seeing the Rockies. I told him if he wanted the real experience he should drive over Trail Ridge. When he got here I asked him, so, whadya think of the Rockies? You know what he said? 'It was okay, but nothing special.' I fuckin' kicked him out right there and told him never step foot in my state again."

I smiled insincerely, grabbed my room keys, and snuck out of the office. I wondered how he felt about cyclists taking up part of his road—I wasn't sure I wanted to find out.

DAY 18
Three Forks to Bozeman, MT
47 miles

I WAS EXPECTING TO MAKE a quick visit to my great-grand-pa's old house, but Three Forks wasn't the way I remembered it. I recalled a dinky little town with the majority of houses lining the one existing street. Three Forks had grown more than a town should be allowed to grow. I recalled a small hill behind great-grandpa's house—just big enough to have a good sled ride down. I remembered it because of the time we walked up the hill when great-grandpa was trying to catch a pestering skunk. The cage had done its work. Thankfully, I don't remember what great-grandpa did with the skunk.

But Three Forks didn't have a hill anywhere in sight—it was flat as a pancake. I asked a few locals if they'd heard of the Ambersons and if they knew of a hill somewhere in town. I must have appeared a little loony. The people were polite, but I can't help wondering if they were thinking, "Look around, buddy! Do you see a hill here?" Instead they said, "Name doesn't ring a bell. And Three Forks is pretty flat all over." I rode in circles around town trying to make a connection between Three Forks and my great-grandpa. On the main road not a full block from my motel was a sign: "Willow Creek—7 miles." It finally hit me. He'd lived in Willow Creek. My father had always said Three Forks because it was the nearest town of any substance that a stranger might recognize.

The detour into Willow Creek would only add about two hours to my day. I only had a fairly short distance left to Bozeman, where I would take at least one rest day. So I headed down the road to Willow Creek, which was flat and straight, running along farmland and irrigation ditches busy with cattails and little birds flying in and out of the lush growth. As I neared Willow Creek a warm feeling ran through my body. I could see the grain elevator that was always the first signal we were getting close to great-grandpa's house. We'd lived there for a few months after my parents divorced and my mother left, I know, but I have no memory of it. I remembered the grain elevator from those every-other-year trips we took after we moved to Colorado. As I rode into the town, I was transported back to my childhood and the excitement I'd feel every time we returned.

Willow Creek is small, very small. The population is listed as 210 and may be only slightly larger than it was forty years before, when we were visiting. I followed my instincts, cycling down Main Street and keeping my eyes open for the familiar hill where I expected to find my great-grandpa's house. I found it, but it wasn't exactly as I remembered. In fact, it seemed a lot smaller. The house my great-grandpa had built was no larger than a shack or a one-car garage by today's standards. Yet it looked right.

I just wanted to confirm it. Next door, a neighbor was busy on his front sidewalk with a measuring tape and tools; he was getting ready either to widen the sidewalk or put in permanent flower beds.

"Excuse me, sir," I began, "I'm cycling through the area. This house may have been my great-grandpa Amberson's place. He died in 1986. A long time ago—but I wondered if you might have any information."

"Amberson? Yep, that name rings a bell," he said, stretching his back. "I believe he built the place, right?"

"That's him. I was pretty sure this was the place because I remembered the hill behind his house."

He gave a wry smile. "I understand he was quite the character."

"I don't know that for sure," I said, "but I do have some pretty fond memories of him. He used to put my sister and me to bed at night and give us a pill 'to help us sleep.' We really thought he was giving us some special medication. Only later did we discover that the thing he called a pill was actually a chocolate chip."

He cracked half a smile at the image. "You're pretty loaded down there on the bike. Where did you ride from?"

I told him about my need to reconnect with the places and people of my past, following a divorce and the slow, painful erosion of professional ministry.

John, as he'd introduced himself, opened up. "That sounds tough. I'm recently divorced too. A few years ago my wife and I lost a child. Then I got a neurological disease that's slowly disabling me."

I could see its effects on his face and arms where his skin was marbled and broken in spots.

"It was just too much for my wife. She finally left a couple years ago. Now I'm just trying to survive and fight the bitterness."

I watched him as he continued to work on his project, whatever it was, on the sidewalk. It seemed to me that he was trying to build a little beauty and structure into his disappearing world.

I realized I was playing the role of chaplain: listening, helping him process the feelings of grief, loss and bitterness that seemed to be companions to his triple dose of cruel loss.

"The biggest thing I am learning, Brian, is to accept life on life's terms," John said. "I'm working on letting go of the expectations I had for my life so that I can enjoy the actual life I still have left."

I nodded. "In some ways, that's what this pilgrimage is about for me too. I'm not sure yet whether I'm trying to beat back my losses or learn to accept them. Three weeks ago I thought it was the former, but now I'm not so sure."

"Do you believe in angels?" John asked.

The question surprised me, but I took a stab at being as honest as I could. "Well, I don't know if I believe in actual angels, but I do believe there is a loving presence that exists in the world."

"I'm not sure what I believe, but since I've been sick I feel like I'm turning my life over to something bigger than me. I'm not sure what it is, but this doesn't feel like the end."

We talked for nearly an hour—him on his knees on the sidewalk and me straddling my bike. Strangely enough it didn't feel like a one-way conversation, as if I was the chaplain and he was the parishioner. I listened to him talk about his broken world, and he allowed me to explore my grief over the losses I'd had and continued to experience.

But it was through our attempts to accept apparently difficult futures that we really connected. He was trying to come to terms with a disease that, so far, had only one outcome—increasing disability and death. I was trying to come to terms with a profession that seemed to be dissolving away just when I was hoping for more stability and security as I entered my fifties.

I strolled back around the corner to my great-grandpa's shack-like house. I took a picture of it, the hill rising in the background the way I remembered from four decades prior. The lingering fondness for my great-grandpa, coupled with my conversation with John, somehow linked my distant past with my present identity and my future fears. They were part of one unfolding story.

I rode away saying to myself, "This is who I am. This is what I do. This is where God wants me." I had left Eastminster church three weeks before, but my identity as a minister was sitting on that bike as surely as if I was riding a tandem with my identity in the back seat. I love being a minister and I grieved then that the role and institution that had supported my work were fading away.

I followed the same road from Willow Creek back to Three Forks and continued on my route to Bozeman, just a short 30-mile hop. It was nice to have a day when I wasn't feeling pushed physically. I was looking forward to what would emerge as I crossed the small span of land from Willow Creek to Bozeman, from the clear memories of great-grandpa to faded memories of my first years.

The ride was not the reflective, contemplative, look-at-the-scenery ride I had hoped for. After making my way back to the main route, I soon encountered busier roads nearing the university town of Bozeman. The roads were narrow with little to no shoulder, but not overly trafficked. As long as I kept in a straight line, watched my rear-view mirror for approaching traffic, and didn't get distracted, I felt reasonably safe. Yet I was also aware that I was passing makeshift roadside memorials every couple of miles—more than I'd seen any other day.

When I got within ten miles of Bozeman I chose the frontage road that paralleled the freeway. Freeways have broad shoulders, but are often littered with broken glass, and little pieces of metal and debris that can result in a flat tire or a quick swerve to avoid a hazard. The frontage road was an obvious choice.

I funneled from the county road onto the frontage road and soon discovered this wasn't the normal frontage road that only drew the occasional car to local businesses. Signs for the Bozeman airport were posted along the side, and large dump trucks repeatedly passed within inches of me and turned into several entrances to gravel pits. There was no shoulder at all. The white line was painted right on the edge of the pavement next to a one-foot-wide dirt and gravel shoulder that dropped off quickly into a ditch. I'm a very experienced cyclist and have ridden thousands of miles in city traffic, down steep mountain passes and along narrow canyon walls where a misjudgment can be one's last misjudgment. But I have never been as unnerved as I was on that stretch of road.

The frontage road was crowded with traffic, with little pause between cars as they passed in both directions. I could feel the frustration of the drivers; they were either hurrying to the airport or felt that I had no right to slow the normal flow of the day. Mud-clumped dump trucks, dark brown UPS trucks, and local delivery vans raced by me as if I were invisible. More than once, as I glanced in my rear-view mirror, I jerked my bike off onto the twelve-inch gravel space to let one of those devilish, monster-like dump trucks overtake me like a charging buffalo ready to trample a rabbit.

What unnerved me more than anything was the feeling that I was considered expendable out on the road. It wasn't the road itself, but that the vehicles gave no indication they were going to make it any safer for me. I could hear them thinking as they squeezed by, "If you insist on taking some of our road then what happens is not our responsibility!" I thought back to the timber truck that had blown by me two days before, and then to the motel owner in Three Forks. Maybe I'd entered an area where I was considered a foreign threat. Did they not know that I was a native of Montana? For the first time on the trip I honestly worried about being squashed by something bigger than me. Could it be that my life would both begin and end in Bozeman? I prayed not!

I cycled into Bozeman and recognized nothing. I'd arranged to stay with Elizabeth, another Warmshowers host who had offered her lawn for my tent, a kitchen to cook in, a hot shower and laundry facilities. I followed the directions to her house, giving my nerves time to calm down from the harrowing ride. Dozens of bike racks packed with bicycles lined the streets. Despite its still being summer, college-age students meandered through the streets, and the buzz that comes from having a university in town was palpable. I felt this was the kind of place I could call home, more by virtue of the person I had become than by the fact of my start here.

I arrived at Elizabeth's a little early and settled onto her back deck to enjoy the warm summer sun while listening to the faint buzz of this small city. One of her neighbors noticed my presence and came over.

"Hi! I see you're touring. I'm Ralph."

"Brian. Yeah, I'm staying at Elizabeth's for a couple of days. Are you familiar with Warmshowers?"

"Oh yes," Ralph answered enthusiastically. "My wife and I are cyclists ourselves. Warmshowers is great. How was your ride into Bozeman today?"

"Actually—it was a little rough," I said, deciding to be frank. "I only came from Three Forks today, but the last ten miles into Bozeman scared me half to death. I rode in on the frontage road."

"Oh no." He cringed. "That's a terrible road. That's the route to the airport. Gravel pits all the way along."

"Yes, I know. I found that out." I tried not to sound bitter.

"There are much safer routes. Let us know when you're leaving and we'll help you find your way back out of Bozeman."

He waved goodbye as Elizabeth pulled into her driveway. "You must be Brian," she called out. "I'm glad you made it safely."

I smiled, deciding to wait to tell her the full story. Elizabeth gave me a quick tour of the house, showed me where I could set up my tent, and gave me a few minutes to shower while she transitioned from work to home. We agreed to have dinner together at a Thai restaurant, a cuisine I hadn't eaten since Portland. Together we walked through the bustling downtown, and settled into an attractive, modern-looking restaurant situated among dozens of downtown businesses, including a corner bike shop that I took notice of.

"How did you decide to do this long pilgrimage?" Elizabeth asked, once drinks were in hand and orders had been placed.

I told her about the losses, the impending church closure, and the shift taking place between religion and spirituality that was threatening my livelihood.

"How did you decide to become a host for Warmshowers?" I asked, turning the conversation back to her.

"I did a cycling pilgrimage last year too. Not as ambitious as yours," she added hastily. "But I did the Camino in Spain by bike. It was an eleven-day trip."

"Really? I had a church member attempt that last year on foot. Unfortunately he had health problems and had to return. Are you Catholic?"

"I am, that's how I knew about it, but I can't say I went with any particular religious intention. I just thought it would be a really neat thing to do on a bike," she said. "I can't wait to do something like that again."

I was happy inside. Like the evening in Wisdom when a whole flock of cyclists had unexpectedly shown up, I was sharing time with someone who understood this strange world inhabited by those who call themselves pilgrims.

DAY 19
Bozeman, MT
Rest Day, 0 miles

I HAD A SOMEWHAT RESTLESS NIGHT out in the tent. Most of the nights I slept in the tent were slightly restless. I think my 51-year-old body is not as pliable and forgiving as it once was. I woke up feeling a little as though I'd reached a fork in the road. I had a full day before me to rest, take care of some internet issues, send home a few unneeded items, and enjoy what Bozeman had to offer. Yet I also felt a little anxious that I was getting behind schedule. I had planned a six-day-on, one-day-off schedule. Now I felt I needed to take the time necessary to regroup, as if to prepare myself for the second stage of this journey. I pictured the week from Portland to Caldwell/Boise representing one leg, and the ten days from Boise to Bozeman representing another leg. Bozeman being my birthplace made it seem like a perfect transition point. But I still felt the need to push on, despite the emotional significance of this place.

I expressed my wrestling to Elizabeth. I was concerned that if I didn't stay on schedule I wouldn't make it back to Portland and Eastminster church within the ten weeks I'd been allotted.

Elizabeth looked at me, puzzled, her brow furrowed. "What? You can't email them and ask for more time if you need it?"

"Quite honestly, it never occurred to me," I said. "They were gracious enough to give me ten weeks and I feel I have to honor that."

I immediately thought of Patrick in Boise, who had teased me with the Alice in Wonderland quote of riding like I was running late for something.

I hated to admit it, but I knew Elizabeth and Patrick were right. I needed to slow the pace down, take care of issues that arose, consider my safety, and allow enough space for my soul to catch up with the miles. I'd traveled from my partly staged interview with Christine nearly three weeks before, to my honest conversation with John the day before in Willow Creek. I'd admitted then that I wasn't sure if I was trying to outrun my losses—beat them back by sheer grit and determination. I was no longer sure I knew what this pilgrimage was really about.

I arranged for a much-needed ninety minute massage. It was luxurious. I hadn't done the ideal amount of training before I left on the pilgrimage, so those first few days of long miles—with the extra fifty pounds of gear I didn't take on my training rides—had come as quite a shock to my body. It wasn't until that day heading toward the Sawtooths, when I climbed three mountain passes and covered 83 miles, that my body really felt like it was getting used to the daily mileage. By the time I lay down on the massage table I was feeling really strong, but I also felt like a coiled spring. I was rock solid and felt like a walking statue, as my muscles were set to one position and one task only. The therapist did her best to loosen up my taut body, and also warned me that my muscles were showing signs of dehydration.

That was one of the issues I planned to attend to. I knew I'd be hitting stretches in Wyoming where I wouldn't have access to water for sixty to a hundred miles, meaning I needed a way to carry an extra four liters of water on my bike. Also, that nervous moment not far from

Wisdom, where the gust of wind had nearly toppled me as I flew down the mountain at 45 mph, reminded me I needed to transfer half my load over the front tire for more stability.

But first I had an important connection to make: my Uncle Max and Aunt Shirley were expecting me. My birth mother had given me their contact information and I'd set up a time to visit them on my day off. Truthfully, I was doing this out of a sense of obligation to my pilgrimage, to my mother and to them. Although Bozeman was my birthplace and the site of some formative experiences, I was surprised that I felt very little emotion for or connection to the place. When my uncle drove me around town, I recognized nothing. I told him about the red-and-green painted married student housing we had lived in when I was a child, but I remembered the buildings looked old and tired even in the sixties. He drove me to where he thought they probably used to be and showed me the new modern townhouses that had been erected in their place. It wasn't until we drove by the three-story red-brick elementary school that I finally connected with a memory. Uncle Max took a picture of me standing on the concrete stairs out front. I remembered sitting on those same stairs waiting for a taxi to pick me up and deliver me home, while my dad was in classes and my stepmother was working. A wave of embarrassment shot through me as I recalled the time in kindergarten when I'd needed to use the restroom, but was too scared I'd miss the taxi if I went back inside. I couldn't hold my bowels and got into the taxi with a mess in my pants. The driver had said nothing. I wondered if he still remembered that ride as clearly as I did.

I expected there to be more story here; here my eighteen-year-old mother gave birth to me. My sister was born two years later. A year after that—under circumstances I'm still vague on—my parents divorced, my dad got custody of us kids, and my mother left. Was my lack of connection to this place because it all occurred before I had much memory? Or because I'd learned to repress the emotion, pain, and hurt that had come with feeling abandoned?

I had learned early in life that I was pretty much alone in the world; depending on others had not served me well. The stubborn streak that had led me off my path two days earlier had its origins here. Sure, I could have asked for directions when I got lost, but I had a long history of figuring things out on my own. I'd have accepted help if it was right in front of me, but I wasn't going to search for it.

It was strange to be in this town that had all the attributes I might look for in a place I could call home. Yet I felt like a visitor, with very little emotional connection to it. Maybe I had just gotten really good at repressing memories. Either way, my childhood experience in Bozeman had shaped me and my relationship with the world for good or for bad.

PART THREE

Facing The Enemy Within

July 29 – August 11

The Yellowstone River in Yellowstone National Park.

DAY 20
Bozeman to Livingston, MT
32 miles

I AWOKE AND ALLOWED MY SENSES to adjust to the day. I felt uneasy and anxious, a feeling I immediately recognized: the day before the pilgrimage began, nearly three weeks earlier, I'd had the same feeling. Whatever the origin of that uneasiness, I took it as a sign that I was about to embark on the second stage of this journey. Whether it was putting Bozeman behind me or anticipating Yellowstone and the lonely terrain of Wyoming, I wasn't sure. But something was stirring in me and I felt myself girding my loins.

I did commit not to leave before feeling completely ready. I enjoyed a wonderful meal at the Nova Café, one of those bustling little breakfast places where one often has to wait for a table. The restaurant was full, but I was able to secure a small table. My French toast, eggs and bacon were rich with butter, syrup and fat, and I enjoyed the energy of the people as much as the food. I liked Bozeman even if it didn't bring back a fondness for my childhood.

I sent a few small items home totaling exactly a pound—well, actually it was one-tenth of an ounce less than a pound, but who's counting? They included a broken pair of glasses, two small manuals for my camera and digital recorder, and receipts I'd been saving for the purposes of professional expense reimbursement. Next, and most importantly, I got my bike into the shop to add another set of panniers. Luckily, they had two new front panniers and a front rack that I liked. Bike shops in the summer often are booked days ahead, but since I was on the road and purchasing nearly two hundred dollars in equipment, they found the time to get me back on the road, which I appreciated.

It was 2:30 p.m. before everything was ready. I had a decision to make: should I stay one more night in Bozeman or take off that afternoon and cover some of the distance between Bozeman and Yellowstone National Park? It might have been wiser to stay, given that I would be leaving during the heat of the day—it was already 93 degrees. But I couldn't ignore the itch to get back on the bike. Having taken care of these various issues, I couldn't wait to start making my way toward Yellowstone and see what this next stage of the journey held. I was anxious. I was nervous. I was sobered by what lay ahead of me, but couldn't put my finger on the source of my foreboding.

Back on Elizabeth's deck, I hailed Ralph next door.

"Okay, I want to get to Livingston tonight," I said, "but I really don't want to get caught in traffic like I did coming into Bozeman."

"I have the perfect route for you," Ralph said. "Keep north of the freeway—it's a fairly short thirty-mile route that'll take you over a couple of easy hills and avoid almost all the traffic."

"That would be great." I breathed a sigh of relief.

"The reward at the end is a downhill section into Livingston that feels like you're landing a plane! It's really fun."

He was right. The back route out of Bozeman to Livingston was free of traffic and beautiful. The only thing I questioned was the description of "easy" hills: one was particularly steep and required me to gear down to my smallest gear. But it wasn't particularly long, and at the top I saw the fifteen-mile descent he'd referred to. It was as deliciously delightful as he'd promised. The gradient allowed me to coast at a consistent 30–35 mph without the need to pedal or brake.

As I rode down the hill, my nervousness began to turn to excitement. Whatever was out there waiting for me, I was ready to face it.

After three nights of uncomfortable tent sleeping, I treated myself to a night at the historic Murray Hotel right in the center of town, just across from the old train depot. The sign above the clerk's window said, "Guns must be checked at the front office." I wasn't sure if this meant I was safer or more at risk. I asked for a room. When I hesitated at the price, the clerk immediately knocked off ten dollars, saying, "I think we can give a guy on a bike a break." I stayed in an antique-style room and slept in a poster bed with a deep fluffy comforter—bliss!

DAY 21
Livingston to Gardiner, MT
57 miles

I EXPECTED A FAIRLY CASUAL DAY of riding to the town of Gardiner, right on the Wyoming border at the entrance to Yellowstone National Park. It was a 57-mile stretch with a mild ascent, as it followed the Yellowstone River to its origins in the mountains. The park itself promised some serious climbing, and I was hoping to save my legs for the challenge.

I left the historic Murray Hotel in Livingston and found a nice depot diner next to the train tracks, where I consumed my usual pancake, eggs and bacon breakfast. The trek south of town was delightful. The road was lined with woodstove-burning log cabins, a few rustic motels, fly fishing shops, and the river carving its way through the canyon, providing a close-to-God experience my imagination couldn't better. Past the canyon the landscape opened into a valley, where small farms, a country school, and a lazier life seemed written into the terrain. An adult and two baby osprey eyed me from a nest perched on top of a telephone pole. I rode through a couple of small towns, but only knew it by the green signs indicating their names. One was the town of Pray. I stopped and took a picture of it, relishing the irony. Was this a not-so-subtle message to me?

The truth is, the nervousness I felt on leaving Bozeman had returned. I might have been projecting myself 200 miles ahead to the high prairie lands of Wyoming that float in the air between 5,000 and 7,000 feet. But my more immediate concern was Yellowstone Park itself. One of the things my research on the park had made clear was that reservations for lodging and campsites are recommended weeks—even months—ahead of time. Since I was cycling, there was no way I could predict exactly when I would arrive, nor how long it would take me to get through. I was riding into the park relying solely on trust. This made me very nervous. The distance between the north entrance and the east entrance where I would exit was 85 miles, and included two imposing passes of 8,500 and 9,000 feet. Moreover, I wanted to enjoy the park rather than power my way through it without relishing its other-worldly manifestations.

Even though I was learning on this pilgrimage to trust that something would work out, I began to imagine the possibility of finding myself in the park at dusk with many more miles still to go. The idea that I might have to ride late into the evening with lights sounded terrifying. The idea that I might need to pull fifty yards off the road into the forest was bone-chillingly scary. Half-seriously, I imagined the local headlines: "Pastor Rides Over Cliff Under a Mystical Moon!" or "Grizzly Bear Attacks Pastor Defending His Last Cliff Bar." Maybe that sign at Pray really was meant for me.

I was just a few miles beyond Pray when this supposedly casual day eroded into a battle. Emerging from the flat valley, I began tackling the twenty miles of rolling hills that led to Gardiner. A nasty headwind met me. The combination of gradual ascents and ever-present headwinds suddenly made me feel I was grinding my way up a ten-percent-grade pass. I had the strength to do it. But psychologically it left me feeling slightly defeated and increasingly worried.

Despite my growing nervousness about what lay ahead, I had a truly enjoyable and illuminating evening in Gardiner. I found a campsite at an RV park on the north side of town. There I was able to shower, do laundry, and enjoy a little writing at my own personal picnic table right at the edge of the Yellowstone River. For all my complaining about headwinds, risks, and traffic, I had to admit that I had it good. While others back home were going to work, getting their oil changed, and complaining about all the crap on television, I was sitting by a high mountain river, typing away on my laptop, breathing in the fresh air, and between nervous sighs feeling very grateful to be living out of four bags on two wheels. I had no other responsibility but to enjoy, survive, and appreciate what was right before me—and what was right before me was quite magical. The river flowed by just fifteen feet below my tent. That wind I'd fought earlier now felt refreshing. And Yellowstone was just the other side of this small resort town.

Once I had my campsite under control and my gear ready for another day, I meandered into town for dinner. I chose a cheap Mexican take-out place, staffed by the usual college students who descend on resort towns in the summer. There I met Julie, one of the staff, and had one of the most illuminating conversations I'd had in months.

Julie was about the same age as my own daughter, also called Julie. We hit it off immediately. I discovered she was about to enter her senior year at the College of William and Mary in Williamsburg, Virginia, majoring in world religions.

"I majored in religion in college too," I told her. "And now I'm a Presbyterian minister."

Julie laughed. "My father's a Methodist minister, but I doubt I'll end up like him. His idea of religion is very different than mine."

"I think I know what you're saying," I said. "This trip is all about wrestling with and getting a handle on the changes taking place around religion and spirituality."

"That's right." She gave another chuckle. "My dad teases me." Adopting a mock-male voice, she said, "'Julie, you seem to change your religious orientation every semester!'"

"What does he mean?"

"Well, he thinks I should choose a religion and stick with it. But every semester I study a different religion—Buddhism, Shintoism, Islam, Native American traditions, Jewish mysticism, and, of course, Christianity—and I get excited about each one."

"You know, it's not just young people like you. I have minister friends I graduated with twenty years ago who now call themselves Buddhist Christians. A lot of us are blending Christian beliefs with other religious beliefs and practices."

As quickly as the conversation grew deep it ended. Julie nodded. "Yeah. I get it. What do you want in your burrito?"

I enjoyed my meal out on the second-floor deck, thirty feet above the Yellowstone River. Our conversation left me feeling full and hopeful. I had an irresistibly strong notion that I had just seen the future of religious leadership in America. I was struck by the irony that Julie was, in many ways, following in her preaching father's footsteps. But I'd bet my life savings that she'll never wear a preacher's robe or orate from a wooden box in a church despite her future degree in world religions. I was excited for the world I saw emerging through Julie; at the same time, she confirmed the grief I felt.

A new world was coming—one I wanted to help give birth to. Yet I still belonged to the old world that would eventually pass away, along with the role that had been the source of my livelihood.

DAY 22
Gardiner, MT to Bridge Bay, Yellowstone Park
69 miles

I DON'T TEND TO BE MUCH of a morning person, but I got up early enough to take down my tent, pack up and get to the gate at the park entrance by eight a.m. I wanted to assess my camping options for that night, and have as much of the day to work with as possible. I felt I was gearing up for the challenge of my life, depending on what the rangers had to say. If my worst fears were realized, I might be able to reach the east entrance by six p.m. if I didn't stop at all the turnouts and had an unusually strong day.

I rolled up to the window, and paid my park fee. "I haven't reserved a campsite," I told the young park ranger. "What do I do if I simply run out of steam before I make it to the east entrance?"

He wasn't sure and yelled over to another, apparently more experienced ranger. "Hey, this guy wants to know what he should do if all the campsites are full and he can't ride any further."

She said the words that brought me close to tears. "If you're a hiker or a biker, you will not be turned away!" That one sentence melted away my two days of anxiety, allowing me to relax and enjoy the adventure through the park.

The ease with which my concerns were handled reminded me of Elizabeth's comment in Bozeman: "Can't you just tell the church you need more time?" I was still carrying leftovers from my childhood, it seemed. My mother (my father's second wife) could be unmercifully rigid. One of the rules in our house was to close the gate to the back yard. We had no animals to run off, but it was still a rule. The few times I forgot to close the gate, I was quickly marched off to the basement to stand in the corner with my nose pressed up against the concrete for half an hour. It was enough of a reminder to be obsessive about the rule and I rarely forgot it.

But I internalized that rigidity. The night our Boy Scout troop camped in the mountains, the scout leaders asked us to get our sleeping bags out before they locked up the trucks. I got distracted, as fourteen-year-old males are prone to do. I missed the window of opportunity, and rather than risk the shame and punishment of asking them to unlock the truck, I accepted the consequences. I spent the night outside by the campfire, doing my best to keep from freezing. In the morning the scout leaders discovered me, and asked why I hadn't asked them to get my sleeping bag. I said matter-of-factly, "It was my fault. You asked us to get our bags and I got distracted. I missed my chance."

I'd brought the vestiges of that world to Yellowstone.

The day was full of rich experiences. I first stopped at the Yellowstone Hotel for a tasty buffet brunch, since I'd skipped breakfast earlier that morning. A herd of elk meandered across the green grass outside the windows. Signs warned us not to approach them too closely. I imagined they were tame enough to tolerate our presence, but not so tame that they trusted us to touch them.

I followed many of the same cars throughout the day, as we all stopped to hike up to a geyser or peer over a boiling cauldron of rotten-egg-smelling ooze seeping from the earth. One of the highlights was seeing a bull elk that put me in mind of how it must feel to see royalty up close. His antlers were easily six or seven feet across. Standing in the grove of trees away from gawking tourists like me, he seemed confident enough to let those of us watching be a temporary annoyance, but also wild enough that he wasn't interested in lingering around us too long.

The riding was difficult—and blissful. One moment I'd be sailing through lush, green meadows, then sweep around a corner only to find myself upon another moon-like landscape, with steam and bubbling pots of witches' brew escaping from the earth's belly. Then I would test my legs again as the earth turned skyward and I climbed another steep pass, towering peaks flanking me, while a rushing frigid-looking stream carved its way through narrow canyons next to the road.

The highlight of the afternoon was standing on the overlook for Lower Yellowstone Falls. I nearly wept at the stark beauty and raw power of the water as gravity forced it over the rocks and sent it crashing down hundreds of feet. I had the strange experience of wanting to lean into the energy of the falls, to feel its power and soulful, violent movement, as if it wasn't enough to observe it from a distance. Of course, I knew I couldn't, as a few feet more toward the edge would have sent me torpedoing toward the bottom, like the water. I would have gotten the experience, but not lived to tell the tale.

I remembered the first time I had that experience, in Racine, Wisconsin. (Racine was one place I was not visiting on my pilgrimage to places lived. It was just too far and would have made my circle more of a triangle. Theologically I like the circle better, even though some would point out that the triangle represents the Holy Trinity. I believe God is found in the circle of life rather than a side of a triangle these days!) My wife and I lived in a house one mile west of Lake Michigan. I often took walks over to the lake and along its rocky beaches. When it wasn't too cold (and it often was!), I would head over to the edge of the lake in the winter. The waves were often three, four, even five feet high, and would come crashing in against the rocks and blocks of ice that had formed. I had that same strange yearning to jump in and allow my body to be carried by the crashing waves. I wanted to experience what the waves were experiencing. At the time, my thoughts unnerved me a little. Did I have a death wish? Was my longing about wanting to die?

Years later I discovered the language of the mystics that described this longing to be one with all of life—the ocean, mountains, lovers, family, food, dance, and work. I've had that same feeling many times since and know now that it is not a death wish, but simply a desire for union and communion in its deepest form. Now I meditated on the falls before me, felt gratitude for its sublime beauty and power—and greedily yearned for more, much more.

Shortly after I left the falls, a younger cyclist rode up on my back wheel. Tim was on a cross country ride, like many of the cyclists I met. He'd started in New York City and was making his way to San Francisco. We rode together for a few miles. Suddenly, a violent thunder and lightning storm erupted with practically no notice. Wind gusts and cold rain caught us both by surprise, and we darted as fast as we could to Yellowstone Lodge just a couple miles away. We both had our sights on finding campsites, but we agreed that, given the violence of the storm, we'd share a room if we could find something under a hundred bucks. The hotel only had one room available with a queen bed for the steal of a price of $217. We were pretty desperate, but not that desperate. Tim seemed a nice enough kind of guy, I mused, but we couldn't share a bed on our first date.

We went our separate ways, and I pushed through the rain to the campsite I was shooting for originally. True to their word, the park official confirmed what the earlier ranger had said. Though the site was full, she drew me a map and directed me to a hike-and-bike site, saying I could camp wherever I found room.

Only one other biker was there, set up already and doing what I was about to do—find a way to dry out my clothing and gear. Matt and I were both tired, but we talked just long enough to discover we had something in common: we were both on Portland to Portland treks. Mine was a big 4,000-mile circle beginning and ending in Portland, Oregon. His was a 3,000-mile-plus ride across America beginning in Portland, Oregon and ending in Portland, Maine.

The traffic through the park that day had been accommodating. Like Montana, there were virtually no shoulders to ride on and cars, campers and RV's constantly streamed by, like a line of ants looking for a food source. Yet unlike my terrifying frontage road experience in Bozeman where I thought I might get squashed, in Yellowstone the message seemed to be, "There is room enough and time enough for everyone." Cars either gave me a wide berth or slowed down until they could safely pass. Even oversized RV's followed this kinder, gentler rule.

Two campers had already warned me to be cautious—a grizzly bear had been spotted making her way through camp just a few minutes before I arrived. I was tired, but my heart was full and I was grateful to have a safe place for the night. I settled into my normal post-ride evening routine of cooking, cleaning, and planning for the next day.

Yet I couldn't get that one line out of my head: "You will not be turned away." It struck at the core of what this pilgrimage was about. I experienced early abandonment when my young birth mother left, and that abandonment was repeated in my divorce and the deaths of my mother-in-law and stepmother (my father's third wife). At some level, this pilgrimage was rooted in the fear that Mother Church was also about to abandon me.

My whole life I have carried a deep desire to belong somewhere, to have a place to call home, a place where I know I'll be safe and taken care of. I have spent much of my life learning to accept the realities of early abandonment, and the need to survive emotionally without the support of others. I assumed that the world is rigid and cold and unforgiving, even as I longed for something more graceful. Maybe that was the attraction of religion—to find that divine Mother I'd always longed for.

I went to bed grateful. At least for that moment, the world seemed a little softer and more forgiving.

DAY 23
Bridge Bay, Yellowstone to Cody, WY
81 miles

I WOKE EARLY, determined to get a good start on the day. I hoped to get to the town of Cody just over 80 miles away, which meant a tough twenty miles to reach the summit of Sylvan Pass at 8,350 feet on the east side of Yellowstone Park. I would be rewarded with a gradual 60-mile descent into Cody.

As I left camp, the clouds over the pass looked a little dark and ominous. I rolled into the visitor center to get a report on the weather, anticipating a game of cat-and-mouse with the rain clouds. I needed to decide whether to make a run for it or stall for part of the morning. My request wasn't receiving speedy service; finally, they referred me to another building. I crossed the street and saw what I thought was a break in the clouds. Impulsively, I turned my bike east, and started cranking to get my butt up over the pass.

There was no precipitation at all. Instead, my hard riding was interrupted by an unnerving obstacle that had to be overcome. Five minutes away from the visitor center, a large bison (well, they're all large!) meandered onto the road just as I rode by. I stopped and waited patiently to allow him to choose his path. But apparently I was right in his path. He didn't charge, just kept deliberately and slowly making his way toward me. I didn't want to turn my back on him, but I certainly didn't like the feeling of him inching toward me. Eventually, three cars also arrived on the scene and slowly tried to make their way around the stubborn beast. The cars' occupants were more interested in taking pictures than protecting me, and I began to get nervous that they would just drive off and leave me alone with this hairy creature.

The driver in the first car yelled, "Be careful!"

Duh! was all I could think. That was not the kind of help I was looking for. Finally the same driver positioned his car between me and the bison, and together we made our way around him, the car acting like my personal bodyguard. I would have loved to get a picture, but I was concerned that in my fumbling it might be the last photo I ever snapped.

The clouds began to send down a very light sprinkle of rain. I had learned my lesson in the Cascades: the road edged right up to the western shore of Yellowstone Lake, where I stopped and slipped into my rain gear. At worst I would have to ride in a little rain, but I would be dry and warm. I propelled my bike up the steep grade and the rain progressed from steady to hard. I was still fine. I was getting wet, but with a little determination I could ride through it. Not too far from the summit the sky simply opened up, as if a bulging plastic bag full of water had burst, letting loose a torrential downpour. There was no place to stop and get cover. Even the lodge-pole pines didn't have enough limb width to deter the flood from the sky.

I was already as wet as I could be. There was nothing else to do but keep riding forward. After the summit, it wasn't just rain that was a problem: the downpour was so violent it caused golf ball- to base-ball-sized rocks to cascade down the mountains and litter the highway. Small streamlets of muddy water ran across and down the road, creating little gullies on the shoulders. My brakes were minimally functional, as the pads could not grip the wheel rims through the water. Seeing became a near impossibility. I switched back and forth between wearing my glasses (which I couldn't see through) and removing them, necessitating shutting my eyes to protect them from the stinging rain.

I reached the bottom of the pass at the east entrance to the park. There at the convenience store/gift shop/restaurant were seven other cyclists holed up, drinking coffee and waiting out the storm. They too were drenched. All of us had hung our clothing and gear on our bikes and over railings, to let it dry as much as possible. The downpour also taught me the difference between waterproof panniers and water-re-sistant panniers. In the light rainstorm I'd encountered in Oregon, the gear in my panniers stayed dry. After this storm, my handlebar bag and two panniers in the front (the water-resistant ones) had over an inch of water in the bottom. Maps, money, phone, and a few pieces of cloth-ing were completely drenched. My sleeping bag had soaked up the water like a sponge—I still had not learned to put it in a plastic bag! I'm an experienced racer, but I had a few things to learn about touring.

The one gift I took from the experience was a picture of the stream just a few hundred yards from the coffee shop. The storm at the top of the pass had produced near flash-flood conditions down below. The river looked at least double its normal width and quadruple its depth. It roared through the valley in a thick, red, muddy mixture of water, earth and tree limbs. I was relieved I had a picture to accompany my story in later years, so friends and family wouldn't dismiss my sto-ry-telling as fanciful exaggeration.

After passing through the east entrance, there was still a 2,000-foot descent into the town of Cody, named after "Buffalo Bill" Cody, the American scout, bison hunter and showman. Despite still being soak-ing wet, I enjoyed the ride. For 50 miles I followed the North Fork of the Shoshone River that bulged and raged from the morning's outbreak of violent weather. Canyon walls towered above me on both sides of the road, and rock chimneys greeted me around many of the river's bends.

Given the condition of my gear, I was determined to find a motel in Cody rather than a campsite. I stopped at the Super 8 on the west side of town. Drenched and miserable, I asked the tall male clerk if they had a single room and how much it was.

The man looked at his computer screen. "I think you're in luck. We have one room left for $136."

It was twice as much as I wanted to pay, but I was desperate. I didn't want to go hotel shopping and discover I'd lost the only remaining room in town.

"I'll take it," I said, fretting at how much it cost.

I dragged my bike and gear into the lobby; it would take three trips to get everything up to the second floor. As I unloaded my gear from the bike, a couple came into the lobby.

"Do you have a room for the night and how much is it?" they inquired.

The clerk looked at his computer screen once more. "You're in luck. I have just one room left for $136."

I turned and glared at him. He caught my piercing stare and a hint of shame crept over his face.

Up in my expensive room, I spread out my gear: sleeping bag hanging over the shower bar, clothes draping the chairs, money laid out flat on the desk, and my phone in a bowl of rice, trying to save it from near certain death. I was exhausted. I'd gone into the wilderness to be tested, discover myself, and maybe even come face-to-face with God. I was as close that day as any to getting everything I had asked for.

DAY 24
Cody to Meeteetse, WY
33 miles

IN THE MORNING, it was obvious that I had to do more to address my soaked clothing and equipment. Most of it hadn't dried enough to make me comfortable with stuffing it back into my panniers, where it would start to stink. Worst of all, my down sleeping bag was still wet and the feathers had formed into little clumps. I was frustrated. Patrick's comment, "I'm late, I'm late, I'm late for an important date," filtered through my mind again. Something was driving me; unplanned obstacles annoyed me. I wanted to keep rolling.

The town's laundromat turned out to be just a couple of blocks from the type of family restaurant where you can expect generously portioned meals. Three hours later I'd eaten a hefty breakfast, washed the sand out of three loads of clothing, dried them, and been rewarded with a fluffy, warm, down sleeping bag. It was 3:30 in the afternoon and ninety degrees out.

I hadn't given up on staying on the schedule in my mind. I had anticipated getting to Thermopolis, a 90-mile ride that would end at the world's largest natural mineral hot springs—hence the name. I'd been averaging about 12 miles per hour (without stops) and estimated that I might be able to push into Thermopolis by 10 p.m. with the use of night lights. Local residents in Cody told me there wasn't much between there and Thermopolis, except for one convenience store in Meeteetse. I was left with three choices: stay another night in Cody; ride hard and into the night to Thermopolis; or ride as far as I could and then pitch my tent someplace off the road between two rises, amidst the dry sagebrush and rattlesnakes.

I set out southward, making a quick stop at a grocery store so I'd have enough staples for the entire trek to Thermopolis or for a night out in the sagebrush. I mounted my bike, steeled my nerves for the challenge, and began pedaling. Almost immediately it was clear that my ambition was way ahead of my strength and endurance. There was only a minor elevation gain in the first thirty miles, but it came in a series of three-steps-up, two-steps-down waves, and I quickly felt the effects of that, the heat, and the lingering sluggishness from the prior day's battle with the mountain and the storm.

Around dinner time I rode into the small town of Meeteetse. The warning that there was just one convenience store was way off. It had two motels and two eating places—a restaurant/bar and a breakfast café. The first motel, the Oasis, offered a sprawling grassy area next to a large barbecue picnic area meant for family reunions and other such large group affairs. I set up my tent on the soft grass, rolled out my now fluffy, air-dried down sleeping bag and wandered over to the open restaurant/bar to enjoy what was left of the evening.

I ordered a Fat Tire beer at the bar, partly because I like it and also because it has a picture of a bike on the label—you'd think I could diversify my interests some. Two seats to the right of me was a thin man close to my age, with slightly disheveled hair. He was leaning over a Coors and quietly watching a ball game on the TV above the bar.

"Do you know if there are any services between here and Thermopolis?" I asked, pretty sure I already knew the answer. I just wanted to talk.

"No, there isn't much between here and there." He glanced at my casual summer clothing. "Are you the guy that came into town on a bike?"

"Yeah. I'm camped down at the Oasis on their lawn."

"This is pretty barren country here. Where you going?"

I went through my usual explanation about visiting all the places I'd lived and trying to come to terms with the demise of the church. When he discovered I was going to be traveling through Nevada and California, he perked up.

"I'm from California, but I moved up here to take care of my aging parents. They have a sizable piece of property that takes most of my time. Did you say you were going to travel through Nevada?"

"Yeah, I'll be riding through the desert on what they call the Loneliest Highway in America before entering California."

"You know, I'm a major Burner," he said promptly.

"A major Burner? What does that mean?"

"Have you heard of the Burning Man Festival? I try to go every year."

"Oh yeah, the Burning Man. I've heard of that," I said. "It's a big deal, I understand."

"Attracts over 50,000 people every year."

"I heard it was started by a man who just wanted a way to ritualize his divorce," I said.

At that the conversation took off: he wanted to talk about Burning Man and I wanted to talk about the importance of rituals. For over an hour we probed the changes wrought in the religious landscape as other loosely formed spiritual communities have taken over the role that churches once assumed was theirs. We talked about the growth of new kinds of communities and experimental egalitarian models.

I left my companion at the bar, and walked the few blocks back to my campsite. I stopped on the bridge overlooking the Greybull River that split the town—I was sad. The conversation had been intellectually stimulating. But I thought of how radically different Burning Man was from our churches, and despite what the church could learn from the Burning Man experiment there was little chance I could describe, in positive terms, how a group of 50,000 people descend on the desert every year to stand around a 100-foot wooden statue and watch it burn. It only confirmed the spiritual schizophrenia I'd felt for so many years.

DAY 25
Meeteetse to Thermopolis, WY
60 miles

I WOKE UP READY for a more casual day than I'd had since leaving Bozeman. I was fairly certain I could reach Thermopolis, having ridden a short distance the day before: it was only 60 miles south and 1,000 feet lower in elevation.

Thermopolis was one of the handful of destinations that held part of my story. As best as I can put the story together, after my parents divorced and my mother disappeared from my life, my father was left scrambling to care for his two young children. For a few months, the three of us lived with my uncle and aunt in Thermopolis, along with their four daughters. I have very little memory of it, just a steep hill behind their house and the small movie theater a few blocks away. I was itching to see how I felt about the place.

I ate my usual biker's breakfast at the small café, listening to a tableful of men talking politics, farming and hunting. Noticing one of the men seemed curious about my biking outfit, I weaseled my way into their conversation.

"Good morning," I said. "Good day for a ride."

"We'd join you on our tractors if we thought we could keep up," he said, obviously teasing me about how different our lives must be. "What the heck are you doing? There isn't much out here in the middle of Wyoming."

Once again I described my pilgrimage, choosing to highlight the shift taking place in the church. I'd overhead them talking about how America was changing.

"You know, young man, it's not just the churches slipping away; it's the Elk clubs, the Moose lodges, and the Granges. We're watching the passing away of a whole culture."

"I think you're right," I said. "Where I live in Portland, all those service clubs that were thriving after World War II are begging for members and at a loss about how to connect with a younger generation."

"It's not just in the big cities. Even out here, where we have nothing better to do," he smiled at his own self-effacement, "those organizations are dying away."

I wished them a good day and paid my bill, musing that these overalls-wearing men, their boots caked in mud, sounded more like sociologists than farmers.

I left Meeteetse thankful for the respite and services I hadn't expected when I left Cody. I remounted my bike and was immediately given a gift—a strong tailwind that grabbed me from the back and nudged me along. The terrain was rolling hills, but I could feel gravity working in my favor.

Generally, I tried to get to my evening's destination between four or five in the afternoon. That day the wind just kept pushing me along, and I arrived in Thermopolis in time for a late lunch. I surveyed the area and settled on a burger joint called Dairyland. You know the kind of place—where the burgers and shakes are made the way you remember them from the good ol' days, before fast food chains started blending chemically simulated shakes.

I was enjoying my all-American meal of cheeseburger, extra-large fries and chocolate shake when a couple leaned over my table.

"Is that loaded down bicycle next to the tree yours?" the woman asked.

"Sure is," I said proudly.

"You mind if we sit with you?" she said. "We're cyclists ourselves. We don't see too many of you coming through. Thermopolis isn't exactly a biker's paradise, what with the heat and long dry stretches between towns."

They joined me. Chris and Jennifer were both medical professionals who had done well for themselves in that small town. When I said I was from Oregon, they told me they make a trip to Oregon every year to ride their tandem for a week or so. Finally, like my dinner mates at Austin Junction, Chris asked, "Do you have a place to stay for the night?"

"No," I said, "but I understand there are mineral hot springs. If I can find a camping spot close to them, I'd love to do that."

They understood, only reiterating that if I needed a place I could just pop in on them and make myself at home.

After lunch, I pedaled the short distance to the hot springs and locked my bike against the outside fence. I enjoyed a luxurious bath in both the warm swimming pool and the hotter soaking pools. There

I fell asleep for a few minutes, drifting off into worlds only one's mind can conjure up. I hadn't allowed myself to relax that much since long before the beginning of the pilgrimage.

Having dried and dressed, I made a brief survey of places to stay: the campsites were crowded and the motel was too expensive. I rode back through town and found Chris working out front on his driveway. Taking up their kind offer, I set up my tent on their perfectly manicured, thick lawn. I shared dinner with them and their two children and we had a perfect biker's meal: pasta and meat sauce, salad and garlic bread. They concluded the evening perfectly with Oregon's finest—Tillamook marionberry ice cream.

Over ice cream, Chris turned pensive. "You know, Brian," he said finally, "we had another cyclist come through a few weeks ago. I'm thinking I could set up a social networking site for touring cyclists that would work a lot like couchsurfing.com."

I let him continue, though I was pretty sure he was describing what Warmshowers had already done.

"Cyclists could be guests when they're touring, but act as hosts when they weren't. It would be like a national cycling community based on trust and a shared interest in touring."

Now my smile was too broad to hide.

"Isn't that a great idea? You'd participate, wouldn't you?"

I was almost laughing by this point. "Warmshowers, Chris. You just described Warmshowers. I've already stayed five nights with their hosts on this trip."

"I love it! We're signing up!" he exclaimed. "I had no idea."

That settled, my thoughts wandered to the next leg of my trip. I was a little concerned about the lack of services between Thermopolis and Casper, over 130 miles away. I knew the town of Shoshoni was 33 miles away—that part was easy. The question was how to negotiate the hundred-mile stretch after that.

"Do you have any suggestions about how best to get to Casper from here?"

Chris and Jennifer stumbled over each other trying to speak first. "Get to Shoshoni first," Chris said. "You can either stay in a motel or camp in the public park downtown. Then gear up for a Herculean effort the next day. You'll need enough water to cross the full hundred miles, but if you leave early from Shoshoni you might make it."

"Or you could do what our friend did," Jennifer said, not to be outdone. "He wasn't excited about having to ride a hundred miles, so he just rode on through Shoshoni and got as far as he could toward Casper. When he got tired, maybe fifty or so miles away, he stopped and camped fifty yards off the road."

"It sounds like either choice is going to have some risks."

"I think you need to be prepared for that," Jennifer confirmed. "At one time there was a little dinky store in the town of Hiland, between Shoshoni and Casper, but I don't think that place has been open for years."

I knew immediately which option I would lean toward. I felt more confident in my strength and determination to get where I was going, than in my ability to stay calm in a tent on a treeless prairie with rattlesnakes and gun-toting cowboys guarding their land. I would ride to Shoshoni, stay the night, and make a hundred-mile dash across the hot prairie next day.

I slipped into my sleeping bag early in the evening and let my mind wander. I was relaxed from an easy, wind-aided day of riding, and the soak in the hot springs. I was also steeling my nerves for what I expected to be a significant challenge two days hence. But I noticed a subtle sadness.

I knew very little of Thermopolis except that we had lived there during a chaotic part of my early life—but it held a chapter of my story. Shouldn't the place bring up some emotion? Delight, or if not delight, pain? I'd had the same experience in Bozeman. I was less troubled by what I felt, than by what I didn't feel.

Whatever I was looking for on this pilgrimage wasn't showing up in Thermopolis.

DAY 26
Thermopolis to Hiland, WY
74 miles

I WOKE IN A CLOUD of melancholy. My sleeping pad had sprung a leak during the night, and despite the soft grass my body was sore from being in too direct a contact with the earth. A homey and delicious smell wafted from the kitchen. I entered the back door of the house and saw that Jennifer had left out some freshly baked cinnamon rolls. She and Chris had already left for work, and their children were involved in summer activities somewhere in town. I had the house to myself.

I showered in their large, expensively tiled shower in a bathroom easily three times the size of anything I've ever had. It wasn't melancholy I felt—it was jealousy. Chris and Jennifer had everything I'd wanted and worked for in my life: good, stable jobs, a beautiful home, and the ideal family. Plus they cycled! How perfect could it be?

I'd put myself through college and achieved a master's degree on my own. I'd worked hard to assemble a career around ministry and community service. I had raised children and made the sacrifices parenting naturally requires. Yet here I was divorced, living in subsidized housing in Portland, and anticipating that my job would soon end. Where had I gone wrong?

I left Thermopolis in a foul mood. Was there something I was supposed to see—or feel? What had I missed?

I rode toward Wind River Canyon with no sense of anticipation, although I was entering one of the great geological marvels of the West. Signs pointed to layers of rock, some as recent as 200 million years, others as ancient as 800 million years. The steep canyon walls above Wind River rose at least 1,000 feet above the rushing water. Time and erosion had carved out numerous natural sculptures, such as the famous Chimney Rock.

Yet with all that natural beauty inviting my gaze, I pushed my feet round and round and round. My thoughts followed suit. *What the hell am I doing out here? What good is it going to do to ride my bike 4,000 miles? How will that make one whit of difference in my life and in the future of the Church?* I couldn't find an answer. I was truly out in some kind of psychological wilderness.

I was too far from home to back-track. If I had thoughts of quitting, it was at least a five-day ride to the closest airport in Bozeman or Laramie. Ahead lay a 100-mile stretch with no reported services, and I was still asking, *how did Jennifer and Chris end up with such a roomy, comfortable home and an enduring marriage while I'm struggling with past losses and impending losses, and living out of four bags on my bike?* I was riding through one of the most beautiful acts of Creation, missing it all because of feeling sorry for myself.

At a small convenience store and bait shop on the river, I stopped to refill my supplies. The storekeeper, a pleasant woman, greeted me. "Do you want me to fill your water bottles?"

The kind gesture cracked my sour disposition just a little. "That would be great," I said. "What a beautiful area this is."

"Yeah. It sort of surprises people who drive through thinking there isn't much to see in this part of Wyoming."

The human contact was softening my mood. "My dad was born in Worland. He would mention the Wind River Canyon when we visited here. But I didn't have any memory of it. I'm really glad I'm riding through it," I said, hoping that would become true at some point.

Back on the bike, I buried my swirling grief a little more with each pedal stroke. I would force myself to enjoy this section rather than regret it afterwards. Plenty of time to feel sorry for myself later, if I still needed to.

The canyon opened up at the southern end and spat me out into Shoshoni. I arrived in early afternoon planning to follow Chris's advice: stay in Shoshoni for the night and then dig deep the next day for the 100-mile Iron Man challenge across the dry, windy prairie to Casper. The map confirmed that a place called Hiland did exist—at least on the map—but neither my hosts of last night nor the clerk by the river could say if there would be services available. Jennifer had mentioned a little store in that stretch, but thought it might have closed. I decided that staying the night in Shoshoni made the most sense.

Shoshoni, it turned out, had three motels, but two were boarded up and weeds climbed above the windows. Only one motel still operated, and it was completely full and booked for the summer. A new oil field had been discovered close by, and crews were making Shoshoni their home for the summer. That left only one option: sleeping in the narrow, one-block city park at the T-junction where two highways meet. That decided it. If I had to sleep outside then I might as well shorten the distance to Casper by as much as I could, and sleep outside closer to my next day's destination.

I wheeled over to the combination convenience store/gas station/ deli, ate a large deli sandwich, bought food for the night, and strapped an extra four liters of water to my bike with all-purpose bungee cords. I took a big breath. For the first time on the trip, I fully expected to have to stealth camp somewhere out on the barren prairie. I was now truly in the middle of the wilderness—physically, psychologically and spiritually. I wasn't scared. I wasn't confident either. I was just resigned to my situation—no motels and a 100-mile no-man's-land before me. It was what it was.

I set off and rode in solitude for forty miles, with only the occasional four-wheel-drive and semi-truck passing me. It was a very barren area,

Hiland being the only dot on the map. Seven miles before I reached that dot, my legs started to complain. I needed to settle down for the night soon. I would push myself to Hiland and see if it might be more than the ghost town I was expecting.

Before long, I saw the faint outline of a building in the distance. Something still existed there, but whether it was still inhabited was another question. I neared the building; out front were two pick-up trucks. That looked promising. I parked my bike under a sign that read, "Bikers welcome!" I knew it was meant for the leather-wearing Harley biker type, but I didn't care. It had my name on it and I would take it.

Surprisingly, Hiland was twice the size I'd first imagined—it had two buildings instead of just one. The larger of the two was another bar/restaurant/store combination. The phone rang. Standing behind a nearly empty glass case that had at one time offered snack food, the clerk picked it up and answered, "Hiland. Can I help you?" I nearly burst out laughing. Imagine picking up my phone back home and simply saying, "Portland"! I loved being in this other world, where my assumptions about life were swallowed up by another reality.

The other building? I was in luck. It was a ramshackle series of five rooms and five doors in what they called a motel. It was good enough for me. I'd thought I was going to be sleeping in the sagebrush with rattlesnakes. I've never been so thankful for a one-star room.

There wasn't much space—I couldn't even fit my bike in and had to lock it up outside, which usually made me nervous. Out there in Hiland though, I couldn't imagine what use anyone would have for a Cannondale touring bike. I stripped off my sweaty clothes, took a shower (the best part of some days), and donned shorts and a t-shirt, planning to head over to the bar for drinks and dinner.

I walked out the front door. Two more cyclists, a couple, had just arrived and were setting up their tent on a small flat area just behind my room. Seeing me, the woman nearly shrieked, "This place just saved us!"

"Yeah, me too!" I agreed. "I was just about ready to camp out in the sagebrush when I discovered this little oasis."

"That's what we thought. The headwind was awful. We were about ready to give up," she said. They had come from the opposite direction, starting in Casper and were hoping to make it to Shoshoni, the same 100-mile stretch I was trying to conquer.

I walked over to the bar to get rehydrated (read, drinking beer and lots of water—or is it drinking water and lots of beer?). The couple, Jamie Lee and Aaron her boyfriend, soon joined me. I ordered a Coors, the best choice they had. Coming from Portland, I've been spoiled by the sheer volume and diversity of microbreweries. It's hard for me to call Coors beer anymore, even though I grew up in Colorado where the stuff is brewed with "Rocky Mountain Spring Water" they promise.

"We'll have the same. Two more Coors please," yelled Aaron. Turning to me, he said, "You're on your way to Casper, right?"

"Yeah, I plan to get there tomorrow night."

"Well, the good news is that Casper has a bar downtown that serves one-dollar pints of microbrews. You'll have to check that out."

I liked the sound of that.

We opened up our menus and my eyes grew wide. When I was a kid, our family would go to a restaurant and my father would embarrass us all by saying loudly, "I wonder if they serve Rocky Mountain oysters here?" Then he would lick his lips and we'd have to ask, "What are Rocky Mountain oysters, Dad?" He would just smile and we returned to our menu-gazing.

"I think I'm going to order the Rocky Mountain oysters," I said, wanting to lick my lips as my dad had done, but not having enough courage in front of my new friends.

Aaron ran down the menu until his eyes locked on the description. "Oh gawd, you've got to be kidding me! Deep-fried sheep testicles? That's insane!"

"You know what? I'm serious. My dad taunted and teased us for years about loving them. This is my one chance. I have to at least give them a try."

Jamie Lee cringed a little, but her face bore a hint of curiosity.

Aaron looked at her. "No way. You're not going to try them too, are you?"

"No," she said. "I don't want to order them, but if you do, Brian, I'd be willing to have a bite."

Aaron kept shaking his head.

I looked for ways to make him even more uncomfortable. "You know, Aaron, Rocky Mountain oysters are really humane." He stared back, disbelieving. "If you eat lamb they have to kill the poor creature," I said. "But oysters just require a wave of the razor and it's over."

Aaron was done. There was no sense taking it any further.

While we waited for dinner, we dived into the kind of conversation I imagine takes place in French street cafés. Politics, religion, education, paradigm shifts, and the erosion of hierarchical systems found their way onto our table. Like the sociologist farmers back in Meeteetse, we agreed that whatever was happening wasn't just about church—it was a radical transformation of American (and probably Western) society.

"One of the things I find interesting is how rigid most Protestants are about their beliefs," Aaron said.

I asked him to elucidate.

"My grandfather loves the Torah, and shows up most weeks at the synagogue to study with his friends. But he calls himself an atheist Jew. And that doesn't seem to be a problem for him or his friends. In fact, I think even his rabbi is fine with it."

I listened with interest.

"I just can't imagine a Protestant doing the same thing. To say you're an atheist and a Christian would be an oxymoron."

"You're absolutely right," I said. "I think most Christians consider those to be opposites. If you don't believe in God, you're an atheist. And if you do believe in God you're a Christian."

"I like my grandfather's approach better. It seems more honest. He loves being Jewish, but he isn't sure that the evidence supports the existence of a god."

A wave of relief came over me; Aaron was talking my language. "When I was asked my religious views on Facebook, I ended up with the description, 'agnostic Christian mystic.' I love how those words feel when I say them. But if I went public with something like that, some Christians would try to burn me at the stake!"

Our dinner arrived. Aaron had a ground-up cow-flesh burger nestled between two halves of a bun. Jamie Lee had the juicy loins from a pig covered in gravy. And I had eight round sheep testicles, deep-fried until perfectly tender and crispy. Jamie Lee took the plunge, nibbled on one, and gave a thumbs-up. Aaron held his ground.

I licked my lips and gave thanks to four rams who had escaped the altar, but not the knife.

DAY 27
Hiland to Casper, WY
62 miles

JAMIE LEE, AARON AND I took pictures of each other before heading off in separate directions.

"How about we toss a coin to see who gets the tailwind today?" Jamie Lee offered.

I didn't bite as I knew already it was in my favor. They had the Tetons just ahead as their carrot to keep motivated, while I only had the promise of one-dollar happy hour pints at the end of the day. We said our farewells.

I felt lucky that Hiland had basically erased what I had thought of as a difficult and risky challenge, but the stretch after Casper—a 90-mile jump to Medicine Bow—had no towns whatsoever, not even a dot on the map. I wanted to be ready for that. So a rest day in Casper was in the plan.

Just a few miles down the road, I came across a sign for a viewpoint. I'm not one to stop at too many viewpoints because I enjoy the actual cycling so much. And I really did have a marvelous tailwind that pushed me along rapidly, but this particular sign caught my eye. I could see a break in the terrain that seemed odd for the dry, high prairie landscape I'd gotten used to. As I neared the viewpoint, I read the sign fully: Hell's Half Acre. I rode up to the edge of a miniature Wyoming version of the Grand Canyon of Yellowstone, with painted rocks, jagged walls, and caverns carved throughout its rough, scraggly terrain.

Before I'd finished looking, a couple of bikers of the Harley variety pulled up. They were intrigued that a cyclist would be out in this no-man's desert. I chose from the variety of explanations I had used already, since I wasn't even sure what this pilgrimage was about anymore. I settled on the losses I'd experienced in recent years, assuming motorcycle riders wouldn't have much interest in church or spirituality.

Their interest seemed genuine. "Actually, I'm the pastor of a church that's facing eventual closure," I went on. "Part of their legacy to the community is to capture this story of the shift from religion to spirituality."

That was where I'd lost Bob way back at Ochoco State Park in Oregon; these two, by contrast, couldn't wait to follow up.

"Glenn here comes from a whole line of ministers—his grandfathers, father and siblings," his friend said.

Glenn took up the story. "I have a brother who's the head pastor of what's called the 'emerging church' in Sydney. Now it's a mega-church."

"I know all about those," I said. "I helped a church start one in California fifteen years ago, but when it grew to ninety people the church got scared and fired me."

"Damn. That's why I belong to the world ecumenical movement," Glenn said. "The church is crazy!"

I smiled. I wasn't about to argue. "It sounds like you practice your faith in the world without the headaches and politics of church."

He smiled back, and raised his eyebrows. "Yes, that's it. You know, though, I don't know what I would do if I couldn't serve somewhere. Gary and I design hospitals for communities. It feels like our calling. I learned that in the church and never lost it."

We looked at each other with an immediate recognition and gratitude for having crossed paths. We had only spent ten minutes together, but parted knowing we were kindred spirits—me on a bicycle serving God in the church and they on Harleys serving God in healthcare. We were like brothers who'd gotten separated at birth and been given this one little opportunity to reconnect. Our souls recognized each other, though our lives were being lived out in different worlds. Despite the likelihood that our paths would never cross again, the encounter was written onto my heart.

I still had over fifty miles of riding to do, but the wind was slightly in my favor, and the terrain was largely flat. Pronghorn antelope were scattered across the land in small herds to left and right of the road. I remembered counting them as a child as we drove through Wyoming. I started to do the same and quickly became bored.

My mind floated back to the question that had popped up the day before: What the hell am I doing out here? It had less energy and angst to it now. Somehow the conversations with Jamie Lee and Aaron, and the coincidental (or destined) meeting with Glenn and his friend had left me with a sense of purpose. I didn't know what the hell I was doing, but I was connecting with people who understood both the struggle I had with ministry and the passion I felt to serve.

The wilderness didn't seem quite as imposing. I didn't feel quite so lost and alone.

In Casper I found a reasonably priced motel after some searching. I slipped out of my cycling gear and enjoyed a good hot shower—seriously, about the best part of every day. I was looking forward to tracking down this microbrewery that served one-dollar happy hour pints. It wasn't hard to find: right there on the main drag was Sanford's, a large marquee under its name proudly proclaiming, "HOME OF THE $1 PINT BEER."

The beer was quite good (much better than Coors), but I found myself sitting next to a guy who was recently divorced, had ended up leaving his daughter, and was looking for work in Casper. I swear sometimes people just feel pastor vibes emanating from me, like too much garlic. He wrested from me that I was from Oregon, like him—now we had a common bond. I'm sure he had already spent five dollars on one-dollar beers before I got there. He had good reason to be a little drunk, but I had good reason not to want to sit and hear his whole story. I listened for a while and offered some pastorally comforting words. Eventually, however, I decided to go to another restaurant where I could eat in privacy. He offered to come along. I finally drew the line with some excuse that wasn't true, but served its purpose. I could have used another beer, but the price had become too high.

Days before, John and I had talked as he worked on his sidewalk and I hadn't felt the need to scurry off, but with this struggling gent I couldn't wait to find an escape. John hadn't leaned on me like an overly dependent child; we were just two adults digging together in the dirt of life. This guy wanted to be taken care of and I didn't need that on my pilgrimage. I needed time for me.

DAY 28
Casper, WY
Rest Day, 0 miles

I WOKE UP IN A COMPLETE BRAIN FOG. I had trouble forcing myself to sneak out of the warm covers. There was no reason for me to race off into the day, but I felt sick to my stomach—not the virus type of over-active intestines, but that uneasy feeling you get when you've done too much and your body yells, "Slow down! Slow down!" Plus, on those hot summer days in Wyoming I probably should have been drinking more water and less beer; dehydration may have played into that sickly sluggishness.

I had a number of logistical issues and errands to address on this rest day. The first was to get cash. There was no Bank of America in the area, but I found a bank with an ATM. I got my cash, but left my card in the machine. When I returned a half-hour later the card was gone, more than likely swallowed by the ATM when I didn't retrieve it quickly enough. Bank of America ATM's typically spit my card out before giving me cash. This one did it afterwards, and I probably walked off as soon as I had my bills, as usual. I was forced to spend the next two hours on the phone trying to get another card while on the trip. This was Saturday—I didn't want to wait until Monday to see if the local bank could retrieve it.

After a number of transfers to various bank employees and staying on hold for most of the morning, the bank and I had formed a plan. I would reach Loveland, Colorado, in four days, where I would stay with the parents of my childhood friend, Dave. A new card should be waiting for me.

I spent the rest of the day doing laundry and setting up potential Warmshowers hosts for the next week. A young couple in Laramie, three days out, responded and I looked forward to the potential for more contact that I couldn't get camping or staying in motels. In fact, I noticed a subtle shift in me: for the first time in four weeks I thought about going to see a movie that night. I didn't, but the fact I'd even considered it was significant and an indication that, maybe, I was ready to enter the world again. During the first two weeks, I'd gone completely within myself and couldn't get enough solitude; now I was starting to yearn for more connection.

The rest day had another effect, allowing my thoughts to catch up to me. Images that had resonated with me in previous weeks started to take on meaning. Two were especially poignant, and formed powerful symbols in my mind for the issues that had prompted this pilgrimage.

The first was a strange picture of a forest in transition in Yellowstone Park. The park suffered devastating wildfires in 1989 that turned much of it to burned embers. I had driven through in 1992 and was struck by the starkness of many of the hills, but also by the wildflowers and small saplings that were springing up at the base of charred barren poles that had once been trees. Now, twenty years later, I was riding through the same area. Those saplings I'd seen in 1992 were now ten to twelve feet high. It was strange to see some of the shorter burned trees still standing a good twenty feet higher, with a thick under-layer of green supporting hundreds of spindly dead trees in its folds. It was obvious we had the remains of one forest and the emergence of another. I couldn't help but think about the Church, and how that image perfectly reflected the need for one religious culture to give way in order for another spiritual culture to emerge.

An even more powerful image re-surfaced for me that day. In every state thus far—Oregon, Idaho, Montana, and now Wyoming—I had ridden by dozens of gracefully sagging structures on what must have been homesteads, farms and ranches from generations past. They were beautiful in their own way. The passage of time, the pull of gravity, and the natural cycle of life had caused them to buckle from their original upright position. Yet as I rode by, it was easy to imagine in these same structures the whole histories of families who had pioneered the land, endured repeated hardships, survived cold and harsh winters, shared in harvests, and rejoiced at the birth of children even as they buried loved ones. It was easy to hear the faint echoes of children laughing, dogs barking at wild critters, and to smell the rich aroma of fresh-baked bread through the broken windows. Riding by these relics of the past felt a little like coming upon an old King James Version family Bible: outdated in many ways, yet emanating a soulfulness and rich beauty, like a portrait of great-great-grandparents.

But as much as I cherished the spirit and ghosts of these old buildings, I felt and knew something else—that my calling and purpose was not to go into those sagging structures and try to prop up old beams to keep the roof from completely falling in. As I rode by, I could hear the spirit of the buildings saying, "Your energy is not here. Others will carry the burden and the grief of the dying church. But it won't be you." I felt sad for those who had invested a lifetime in the institution of the Church. And I felt freedom and clarity as the voice coming from the buildings advised me, "This is not your burden. This is not your story."

I had woken up in a fog, but closed the day with an unusual sense of clarity.

DAY 29
Casper to Medicine Bow, WY
94 miles

AFTER THE GOOD REST DAY and a sinfully delicious caramel pecan French toast breakfast at a bustling café, I was ready to continue my journey. I was looking forward to—and a little nervous about—the day ahead. I tried to trick myself into pretending it would be good preparation for the Nevada desert. My map told me it was 90 miles to the small town of Medicine Bow, and that the only sign of civilization between Casper and there was a single state-run rest stop about half way. Theoretically, I needed to carry sufficient water for the whole trip in case the rest stop didn't have drinkable water. Instead, I compromised. I took six liters of water, enough for 70 miles of riding, and if the rest stop didn't have water I would have to crawl the last 20 miles into town dehydrated, but alive.

I first needed to negotiate the four-lane street where McDonald's, WalMart, 7-Eleven, and Jiffy Lube had set up business. The strip was crowded with flashing business signs and intrusive billboards. One of these caught my eye; large, yellow, it shouted its message to every car, truck and semi passing by. Bearing a picture of a Bible in one corner, the sign read, "Holy Bible. Inspired. Absolute. Final." If that wasn't enough to get you to bow down immediately in the sagebrush, a helpful phone number was offered: Call 855-FOR-TRUTH.

I would have just passed by, acknowledging my own internal annoyance and whispering, "God, I hate this shit!", but another sign, fifty feet in front of the obnoxious billboard, now caught my eye. This one was a bright red square with clean white letters spelling out: WRONG WAY. With a devilish impulse goading me on, I crossed over into the median between the two one-ways and positioned myself. Having found just the angle I wanted, I framed the picture so that the overly reverent Holy Bible billboard stood front and center, and the ironically prophetic "Wrong Way" sat in the bottom right hand corner, like a commentator's revealing footnote. I snapped the picture, gloating like a chess player about to say "Checkmate."

Don't get me wrong. I too have reverence for the Bible; I consider it one of the great treasures. We have the writings of people two thousand and more years ago, as they wrestled with what it meant to be human, their moral obligation to their brothers and sisters, and the nature of their relationship to that which is most sacred, even divine. But inspired, absolute and final? Those sound like the words of a parent whose best answer to every childhood question is, "Because I told you so!"

I rode away priding myself on my cleverness, and angry about a religious right that has so co-opted the Christian name that I shy away from disclosing it in public. I have a deep, complex and rich faith. But I very rarely get to share that in public due to the immediate association of the word "Christian" with things like that billboard.

Immediately after I left the sign behind, I faced a gradual and taxing ascent. A stiff headwind also greeted me, making it feel like I was riding on foam rubber. Right away I questioned my decision not to carry enough water for the full ninety miles, worrying that I would run out. But now I also worried that the conditions would keep me from getting all the way to Medicine Bow.

I rode consistently, just knocking off one mile at a time. Near the fifty-mile point, nestled cozily at the foot of two mountains—the one I was descending and the other I would begin climbing soon—was a full service rest stop, with clean bathrooms and a drinking fountain. No vending machines, but water was all I really needed.

Having refilled my water bottles, I mounted the bike again and relaxed. The gently rolling hills and rocky outcroppings deserved more attention, but my focus was my own thoughts. Now that I had enough liquid to take me another seventy miles, the worries evaporated. I entered a phase of manic euphoria, suddenly grateful that I'd been given—and taken—this opportunity to ride across the Wyoming prairie. I tackled the next hill feeling everything was right with the world, even as my legs and my lungs told me I was being over-ambitious.

I reached the plateau and began a long stretch across the prairie, settling into a quiet, reflective and thankful rhythm. Not fighting anything. Not worried about my safety and survival. Feeling no need to prove anything. I was enjoying the moment, the solitude, and the dry heat and wind. I wasn't leaving home or going home. I felt very much at home right then in my body, on the bike, clicking off the miles one by one.

Suddenly, a van stopped abruptly on the other side of the road and I heard very clearly, "Brian!" After a full month on the road, it took me a moment to wake up from my pilgrimage-induced stupor and recognize my childhood friend, Kathy, from Loveland, where I expected to be in three short days.

"Oh my gosh! What are you doing out here?" I asked, baffled by her presence.

"I was really concerned you might not have enough water. It's dangerous out here, Brian."

"Kathy, I'm fine—really. I got water at the rest stop about ten miles ago."

"I know it's crazy, but I just decided to see if you needed help. My family thinks I'm nuts. I didn't know if I would find you, but I decided to drive until the gas needle hit the halfway point and then turn around. It had just got there when I saw you come over the hill."

This is my pilgrimage! You can't just show up and try to rescue me! My brain screamed objections. I couldn't hide my displeasure.

We talked for a few minutes, but I was itchy to get back on the bike and return to the exercise-induced euphoria I was feeling. I gladly ate a number of the homemade ginger snaps Kathy had brought, pocketed the rest, drank some of the Coke (my stomach couldn't tolerate more than a few sips), and took a couple of pictures, before agreeing to meet again when I arrived in Loveland.

It was true that I might have run out of water, but I didn't. Even if I had, I would have figured it out one way or another. I was annoyed: it seemed her need to help me was stronger than my need for help— remember, I'm pretty self-reliant. But I was troubled by my reaction.

Had a stranger offered help, I would have gladly accepted and filed the experience away as some sort of new age, the-Universe-always-seems-to-provide lesson. The fact I couldn't accept the generosity of a friend with equal grace gnawed at me.

Not too many miles later, I slowed down to take in the view of endless miles of soft green prairie. With the exception of the occasional car, I had ridden completely out of civilization. On all four sides, dozens of miles into the distance, there was not a single building or sign of people—just this lonely road splitting the prairie in half. I began to cry softly. The gratitude I'd felt earlier just welled up and finally seeped out. I knew this was not an environment in which to linger too long, as there was nothing and no one to depend on. Yet I didn't feel abandoned or alone. Rather I felt a deep sense of belonging, as if the road and hills and prairie were the invisible hand of my family and my community. I had everything I needed in this barren land.

The ride continued to be hypnotic as I traversed another expansive valley that felt like riding through brushed corduroy. It is not the lush green of the Willamette Valley of Oregon, but a soft hue, like the fuzz on a green tennis ball. Along the way, I startled a magnificent six-foot timber rattlesnake, who warned me with her rattle not to come any closer. I circled around, inched my way close enough for a picture, and then left her in peace. Before entering Medicine Bow I saw the first signs of civilization: ten-story-high wind turbines pierced the landscape for many miles. I felt I was riding across a massive landscape art canvas.

I pedaled laboriously into Medicine Bow completely spent from the long ride and heat, but satisfied and content with where I was. I was able to stay at the famous Virginian Hotel, the setting for the novel *The Virginian* by Owen Wister. Built in 1911, it was a gathering place for cowboys, railroad workers and business people. My favorite part of the hotel was the sign behind the bar that read, "Closed for Hanging!" I wasn't sure if it was a marketing gimmick or a relic from the past, but it certainly outdid the "Keep Portland Weird" bumper stickers I was fond of.

I drifted off to sleep only to be startled awake by massive, tear-inducing cramps in my legs. The 94 miles, the near 100-degree heat, the early headwind, and the altitude gain had finally caught up with me. My body was begging for mercy.

DAY 30
Medicine Bow to Laramie, WY
60 miles

KATHY WAS ON MY MIND when I woke up. I was still mad at her for trying to rescue me and still puzzled by my own reaction. I massaged my legs, as the cramp in my right leg had left it as tender as if I'd been hit by a rolling car. I walked from the hotel room to the restaurant and ordered the usual massive meal I'd become used to and now expected. I wrote a few notes, trying to jar loose the emotions related to Kathy, but all I came up with was that I was mad at her.

I would be seeing her in two days, so I finally let it go and got down to the business of packing my bike again for a much shorter ride into Laramie. I was motivated to get going. Loveland, my childhood home, was likely only two days away and it was pulling me forward. Thank goodness the 100-mile dry stretch was behind me.

I mounted the bike, said goodbye to the historic Virginian Hotel, and pointed my bike toward Laramie. I was in luck—the prairie wind was pointed in the same direction. It was squarely at my back, and I felt like a sailboat lightly skimming the surface of San Francisco Bay on a windy day. What should have been a six-hour ride started to look more like four hours.

I was flying along so well that I took extra time for lunch at Rock

River, not twenty miles from my starting point. I usually like to ride pretty much straight through, stopping only for refueling, visiting the occasional overlook or historical marker, or to follow up on an interesting conversation with a stranger. I prefer to ride hard all day, enjoying the pleasure of my body in motion, and then reward myself in the evening with a hot shower, good food, a beer if I can find one, and time for reflection and writing.

The wind was pushing me along so quickly that I scheduled a leisurely picnic into my day. I stopped at the local convenience store, placed a ready-made sandwich, cheese sticks, Gatorade, an apple and cookies in the basket. The clerk was checking out another person, the two teasing each other with the kind of bite that only comes from a little love and knowing each other well. I wondered what she might have in store for me.

"Well, you're quite the sight today," she said, eyeing my completely out-of-place wardrobe. "We don't see much of your type around here."

"Yeah, I'm starting to get that message. I've only seen one biking couple in the last three hundred miles," I said.

"Sounds like quite the trip. Where did you start?"

"Back in Portland. It may sound nutty, but that's also my destination. I'm riding in a big circle, visiting all the places I've lived. My church has given me ten weeks off to do this."

"Oh, you're a church person?"

Damn, I thought. Did I just say too much?

"I attend church occasionally, but I don't talk about it too much in these parts," she confided. "I'm a Religious Scientist."

My eyes must have doubled in size. "Seriously? Out here?"

"Yeah. There's just two of us, but we spend lots of time reading and talking theology. Martin Buber and Jurgen Moltmann are a couple of our favorites."

I was stunned. I hadn't heard those names since seminary over twenty years ago, and here they were being dropped by a feisty clerk at a convenience store in a dusty, don't-blink-or-you'll-miss-it town in Wyoming.

We talked for a few more minutes about feeling out-of-step with our religious communities; she obviously knew she had a safe ear in me. "You know," she said, "my friend and I have decided that when Judgment Day comes, the two of us would rather be in hell calling bingo numbers than in heaven with some of the self-righteous people we come in contact with every day."

I laughed, and immediately thought back to the Holy Bible billboard I'd seen on leaving Casper. If heaven is made up of those people I'm not sure I want to be there. Of course, as a pastor I could never get away with saying that, but this lady and I shared the same sentiment. If judgment, intolerance and self-righteousness is God's way, I think I'll go searching for a more palatable God.

I wheeled myself and my picnic supplies over to the small park. A large gazebo was situated right in the middle and not a soul was around. I had permission to completely relax—no pedaling, no conversations to nurture along, no planning and packing.

Kathy re-entered my mind. Still trying to find the source of my annoyance, I edged just a little closer. *I have to do this on my own, I have to do this on my own*, repeated over and over in my head. I wasn't sure why I had to do it on my own, but the words felt true. I felt my legs stiffening as I sat there, but I didn't really care. The day was short; I could handle it.

I continued to enjoy the easy, wind-aided push into Laramie after remounting my bike. Behind me, I heard a whistle and the rumble of a train slowly overtaking me a hundred feet to the right. My competitive juices kicked in. I started cranking faster and harder to see how long I could ride before the train completely passed me. One mile, two miles, three miles—I still couldn't see the back of the train. Four miles, five miles, six miles... Finally, at seven miles, the caboose went by and

I waved at the man on the back, acknowledging that I was conceding the train's victory. He waved back in a gesture of mutual respect. I imagined we were two grown-up men who hadn't outgrown their childhood toys—me on my bicycle and he on his oversized toy train.

I arrived in Laramie a full two hours ahead of the time I had scheduled to meet my hosts. I stopped at what looked like a high-end bike shop, the type that caters to racers and serious cyclists like myself. I replaced my nearly bald rear tire, and had the mechanics use an air pressure hose to blow through my frame pump. It was still leaking water from the Yellowstone rainstorm. When they put the nozzle right up to the pump, sand and guck came spraying out. The pump had been unusable, but I hadn't known it. I was fortunate not to have needed it on one of those lonely stretches.

I'd had the first signs of wanting to return to civilization while in Casper; the urge reoccurred in Laramie. In exchange for a bed, a roof, and a shower, I treated my hosts, Kennedy and Evan, to dinner. They suggested a popular Thai restaurant close to the university campus. The food was good, but I really enjoyed the energy. While I couldn't prove it, the restaurant seemed full of university staff and professors, a few students, and engaged people from the community. I imagined them discussing ideas, sharing philosophies, and wrestling with political issues. That's one of the reasons I enjoy preaching: every week I'm asked to have something pithy, inspirational and challenging for my congregation that helps them make sense of and understand the world in which they live. While I wouldn't call my sermons political, I don't shy away from talking about how our spiritual values can and should inform our political participation. Politics and religion are first cousins in my book—part of the same family, but living in separate houses.

I loved being on the road, but I was also longing for meaningful connections and ways to engage with people again.

DAY 31
Laramie, WY to Loveland, CO
78 miles

THE DAY I SPENT getting from Laramie to Loveland was one of mixed emotions; I could write a book just about the story behind this ambivalence. I was excited to get to Loveland and at the same time felt anxious. I had spent the first half of the pilgrimage anticipating this monumental day. Finally leaving Wyoming, I could put the effects of the nasty Yellowstone storm behind me, and exit the barren stretches of prairie I'd found both soothing and unnerving.

I rode through a difficult stretch of road construction, where I had to negotiate narrow ribbons of pavement between hundreds of orange cones, the persistent rumble strips, and occasional debris fallen from dump trucks. Twice I hit large orange cones hard with my front right pannier, jarring me almost into a fall.

The last stretch out of Wyoming is wide open, and advertises long, winding climbs miles before reaching them. They are steep enough to make you dig a little more deeply, but so long that, by the top, you have to just spin out your legs to let the lungs catch up and the heart to settle back into a more sustainable rhythm. I wasn't too concerned about them, however, because I felt the spirit of Loveland pulling me along: history, family, connections, and past pain were drawing me there. I knew I'd have reserves to call upon that wouldn't be there on more routine days. Unlike Bozeman and Thermopolis, where I expected to feel something but didn't, Loveland was inevitably going to open up a whole reservoir of conflicting feelings.

My last image of Wyoming was standing in the belly of a fireworks store close to the Colorado border. I obviously wasn't going to buy any as I didn't need the extra weight, but I used the excuse of buying a cold drink to browse this store that would be illegal in all but a handful of states. I had missed out on real fireworks as a kid, but I couldn't believe anyone would pay $149.95 for sixty seconds of colorful explosions.

As I continued toward Colorado, a wave of nostalgia swept over me. I was on the same route our family had taken many times, returning home from vacations or fishing and camping trips. I recognized the northern edges of the Rocky Mountains and the softer-contoured foothills leading to them. I knew I was nearing home (or at least a deeply familiar place) as the terrain evolved from barren sagebrush to a landscape where large scattered boulders lay peaceful among an increasing number of pine trees.

I stopped at the wooden "Welcome to Colorful Colorado" sign marking the state line. I couldn't believe I was there—nor how good it felt to be there. Crossing the border into Idaho, I'd only registered a faint feeling of transition. Riding into Montana was a little more revealing, as I was returning to a place that was part of my story, but about which I knew little. The Wyoming border had stirred a nagging anxiety, as I had only images of long, boring car trips that left me either sleeping or counting antelope. But entering Colorado was wholly different. I had a long history and a love affair with this state. I stood at the sign, took a picture, and lingered for a couple of minutes to relish the unnamed swirl of emotions that suddenly made their home in my body.

I planned to stay about three days in the home of my best friend's parents. My mind also turned to my mother (my dad's second wife, who sometimes took me on bike rides), still living in the house I'd grown up in. We had been estranged for more than twenty years—I found myself wrestling with whether to see her while I was in town. I had made numerous attempts over the years to heal our severed relationship; now, as I neared town, I wasn't sure I wanted to reopen that chapter in my life, only to be rejected yet again.

As I neared Loveland, I began to feel more and more anxious. My body was tense, as if I was preparing to hear a yea or nay from a job interview. Would I be accepted or rejected? I toyed with the idea of calling my hosts and telling them I planned to stay in a motel. Why? Because I wasn't ready to face the stew of complicated emotions that would arise in Loveland. I didn't know whether staying in their house, a house that had really served as a second home during my awkward teenage years, would bring relief or accentuate my feeling of home-lessness. My thoughts had "running away" written all over them, but I knew I'd regret not taking time to revisit my old life.

I picked a route to my hosts' house that would take me by my old home. Quietly, I rolled past the house, not sure if I hoped my mother would be outside, or dreading the possibility that she might. There was no sign of her, and I rode the final four blocks to Dave's parents' house.

It was great to see them—my anxiety immediately melted away. It was as if nothing had changed in thirty years: they were a little older, I was a little grayer, but we were still family. I didn't live here, but I felt at home. It was a relief.

I had yearned for this feeling when I stayed with Jennifer and Chris in Thermopolis, but there I was only a passing visitor; it left me aching and feeling sorry for myself. I'd had brief encounters with that feeling of home as I rode through the College of Idaho campus and descended into Big Hole Valley in Montana. But as I sat on Dave's old bed, the tightness in my chest relaxed. This was where Dave and I had shared sleepovers, a few teenage spats, and raced through dinners with his parents and brother. No matter how much time and distance separated us, this place still felt like home. Dave's parents, Mel and Betty, were still my surrogate father and mother.

DAY 32
Loveland, CO
Rest Day, 0 miles

I WOKE UP FEELING READY to spend a full day getting reacquainted with this town that held so much of my story. Kathy, my overly concerned, Coke-delivering friend, offered to chauffeur me from place to place. It had been many years since I'd spent any real time here, and I wanted to see what remained and what had changed. I knew, too, that Kathy and I needed to address her surprise attempt to rescue me. My annoyance was still with me, but I was ready to discuss what had happened so that it didn't come between us.

First, I wanted to call my mother. Being in Loveland and departing without an attempt to connect would only add to the grief I felt over our broken relationship. I should at least give her an opportunity to talk or meet, and hope that time had softened the emotional barrier between us. I called; she wasn't home. I left a message saying, "Hi Mom, this is your long-lost son, Brian! I wanted to let you know I'm in town for a couple of days. I'm cycling through on a long trip and would love to see you, if you're available. I'm staying with Dave's parents. Call me and we can get together. Love you." I hung up. My shoulders slumped and I immediately felt I'd opened up the old wound. I may have done the right thing, but I wasn't sure it was the best thing. Inside I was aching, despite the overly cheery voicemail that hid my pain.

Kathy picked me up, and we walked in the regionally famous sculpture park that hadn't been there when I left. We saved the conversation we knew we needed to have until lunch. Kathy took me to a new restaurant, in a strip mall that was also new, on the outskirts of town, a place I remembered as buried in corn and cows.

We ordered.

"Okay," Kathy said, "you were pissed off at me for driving out to help you, weren't you?"

"I was."

"You didn't hide it very well."

"I know," I admitted. "Honestly, I'm still not sure what that was about. Thinking about it, if a stranger had stopped to help me I would have welcomed it, and considered it a gift of the pilgrimage."

"So, what? You can't let your friends help you?" A little frustration crept into her voice.

"I know it doesn't make any sense," I said. "I don't know what to say. Except that after you left, I kept saying to myself, 'You can't just show up to help me. This is a pilgrimage!'"

"I'm sorry, but I really was worried about you. That's a nasty stretch. I couldn't stand the thought of you getting stranded out there without water."

I softened my stance some; I knew her motives were good. I still didn't completely understand my reaction, but there would be time to work that through. "Well, I have to admit the home-made ginger snaps were pretty darn good," I said. "You can only eat so many Cliff Bars before you start seeing them in nightmares."

She accepted my weak apology for not being more gracious. It was all I had in me. We changed the subject and continued talking about Loveland and all that had changed. She asked for the tab and went to the restroom.

I checked my phone. Still no call from my mom.

That night, Dave's parents took me out to dinner at the restaurant owned by their younger son, Tim. It was a lively place; Dave's parents were clearly part of the restaurant family.

"Brian, this is Marlene and Bill," Mel said, introducing two people who stopped at the table to say hello. "I think their two sons graduated just a couple of years before you."

"Oh hello, nice to meet you," I said, not recognizing them or the names of their children.

This happened a couple more times; it was clear I'd been gone a long time. Thirty years ago, I would have known most of the people going in and out of that restaurant. The town was familiar, but my people were gone.

Sitting around the dining room table back at their place, Betty said, "What do you want to do tomorrow? If you want, you can borrow our car."

"That would be great. I'm planning on having dinner with my step-siblings. You remember that my dad married Alice? She died two years ago during a heart valve replacement procedure."

"I'm so sorry to hear that," Betty said. "I didn't know."

"Yeah, it was pretty rough. Most of her children still live in Loveland or Fort Collins, and we're getting together. It'll be the first time I've seen them since the funeral," I said. "Plus—I really want to visit the old church." I was referring to Mountain View United Presbyterian Church, which had had a deep and profound influence on my life. In some ways, it was as much family as my immediate family.

Mention of the church ignited a question from Mel, almost as if I had pressed a light switch. "Brian, what are we going to do about the loss in the church? It looks like the conservative churches are abandoning our denomination and young people just aren't coming."

"I think whatever's going on is much bigger than any of us or any one church—even bigger than our Presbyterian denomination. I don't think there's much we really can do," I added, emphasizing the final word. I was still mulling over the images of the burned Yellowstone forest and the sagging homesteads that were still fresh in my mind.

"What do you mean, there isn't much we can do? We have to do something!" he said, with just a little frustration.

"I think we're going to have to let go. Because we're about to go on an epic theological roller-coaster ride!" I said.

He had hoped for a different answer. And he expected more from me, an ambitious, out-of-the-box thinker who had always been their third son.

I was trying to be clever, sure, but I gave him the only answer I had. It was honest—and insensitive. I should have known better. He wasn't looking for an answer; he was expressing his grief and I had dismissed it. Talking with Christine on the second day of the pilgrimage, I knew I was using her to tell the story of what was happening in the Church, but she was a willing victim. I was using Dave's dad too, but he didn't know it. I saw the jarred look on his face and I felt bad.

I went to bed that night wondering if my mom was going to call. She still had 24 hours. I didn't know which I feared more—her calling or not calling.

DAY 33
Loveland, CO
Rest Day, 0 miles

I WAS READY TO DIVE IN HEART FIRST as soon as my eyes opened. I would still be waiting for my phone to ring and, if it did, was ready to change plans in order to see my mother. Meanwhile, I was returning to the church that had played a big role in shaping my passions, interests and commitments. And I would spend time with some of the step-family I'd inherited when my dad remarried in 1983, to his third wife, Alice.

Until the church opened, I sat at a coffee house drinking a dark roast, doing some journaling, and letting my emotions catch up to me. If I ever returned to Loveland, this would be the kind of joint I would frequent—the aroma of freshly ground coffee beans, the loud whine of the steamer intruding into the air, and the energetic buzz of friends talking, mothers sharing parenting clues and woes, and business people tapping away on computers and making deals on the phone.

By ten o'clock my mom still hadn't called, so I headed to the church, and drove around the site. Much of it was the same, except spruced up. A new parking lot had been added, but the lot was basically the same. The building, from the outside, was virtually unchanged. A new family center had been built, indicating the congregation had fared well in recent years.

I walked through the double glass doors into a lobby that was completely new; I recognized almost nothing. The staff was new too, though that didn't surprise me. I went to the reception window.

"Hello, can I help you?" the receptionist said, predictably. Two other office staff were seated within earshot.

"Hi, my name is Brian Heron," I said. "I grew up in this church. I'm a Presbyterian minister myself now." I explained about the pilgrimage. "I was hoping I might walk through the building?"

She was very polite. "Feel free to take a look around. The sanctuary is being remodeled right now, but let us know if you have any questions."

The same reception any person might have gotten. "Thanks, I appreciate it," I said. But subconsciously I was disappointed. Had I expected to be welcomed home like the prodigal son, with open arms? And recognition: "Oh, Brian Heron. We've heard about you! Let me get our current minister, I'm sure he'd like to meet you." Didn't they realize I'd cycled nearly 2,000 miles to get here? Did they not realize the significance of that?

It thought it ironic that I happened to show up while they were in the middle of a remodel; my pilgrimage was also a way of remodeling my own life. I walked into the sanctuary. The shape was still as I remembered, but the space was almost entirely covered in clear plastic sheets.

I stood in the back, remembering the night I broke into the church. I was eighteen, just a few weeks shy of graduating from high school, and feeling sort of lost and directionless. That particular night, I was wandering the streets with no specific purpose, and my feet took me to the church without any real intention. I circled the building looking for a possible way in, and finally found a door that hadn't been locked properly. With one good hard yank, I dislodged the remaining lock to gain entry. Thank God this was before churches began alarming their buildings.

Today (especially after a stint as a probation officer), I realize this is technically breaking and entering. But back then it didn't feel that way at all—I was just looking for home. I went to the one place where I felt accepted and as if I belonged. I didn't steal video equipment or look for loose cash, I just wandered around the building. I did briefly venture into the kitchen looking for cookies, a habit I still haven't broken. Now, wandering through the fellowship hall, I recalled the laughter and energy around inter-generational potlucks gone by. I went downstairs, where I had enjoyed nine years of Boy Scouts, eventually becoming an Eagle Scout. A hasty dart across the hallway brought me to the choir room, where I fingered the adult chancel choir robes, robes I'd proudly worn when I was invited to sing with the adult choir. At last, I made my way up to the sanctuary, sat in the pew I'd become accustomed to, and felt the warm spirit of all those who had loved and cared for me in that church.

My lukewarm reception that day mirrored the uneasy relationship I have today with the Church in general. I appreciate the Church for its rich rhythms and caring community, but I have also, like my contemporaries, come to distrust the Church for its too narrow religious focus. Like a child going off to college, I still appreciate the Church for the roots it gave me even as I explored beyond the edges of traditional Christian community and belief. As I walked out through the front door (the same door I'd broken into thirty years prior), I felt sad that my old world had disappeared. Yet in its place was an invitation to a new world, a world that—maybe—I was supposed to have a part in creating.

I checked my phone again. My mom still hadn't called.

I spent the rest of the day reacquainting myself with people and places that had meaning for me. I sat in the old park near the lagoon where ducks and geese floated; ate lunch at a picnic table; and watched children playing on the equipment, just as I had once. I visited with good friends, Bob and Judy, who had introduced me to my first real love, their niece from Oklahoma; we drank tea out on their patio. I thought about the late nights when their niece and I would keep the couch warm with a little innocent teenage necking long after her aunt and uncle had retired to bed. Later I joined my step-family for take-out pizza, while my step-nephew splashed in the lake right off their back yard. We talked about their mother, my dad's third wife, whom we had shared for twenty-five years, and about the four-day-long, painful journey of watching her die after routine, but risky heart surgery.

By the time evening arrived, I had a Disneyland-like hangover—you know, that dizzy feeling you get when you've had too much stimulation and up-and-down rides, to the point where you can barely walk straight.

After two days of reconnecting and visiting, I felt I'd gotten what I came for. Loveland brings with it both a deep longing for home, and also the pain of feeling homeless. As I prepared to leave, I felt I'd uncovered what was real about Loveland and what was projected. I still had many good connections there despite three decades of neglect. But it was also clear that Loveland would never be home for me again. I could never go back and recover what was good or restore what was lost. Home now had more to do with being close to my two adult children; it was associated with the community of Portland and the unique role I had carved for myself as a church minister and community leader.

I went to bed feeling I was nearing the turning point of this trip. Loveland was the eastern-most stop, but it wasn't quite half-way: the real symbolic turning point lay high up in the Rockies. In two days, I would attempt to reach the highest point on the whole 4,000-mile pilgrimage as I rode up Trail Ridge Road—the highest paved highway in the world at 12,183 feet.

My mom hadn't called. It was time to move on.

PART FOUR

No Mountain Too High

August 12 – August 17

The Rocky Mountains at the summit of Trail Ridge Road—12, 183 feet.

DAY 34
Loveland to Estes Park, CO
40 miles

AUGUST 12—MY SON'S twenty-fifth birthday. It was the first birthday of either of my two children I had ever missed. I felt bad that I wasn't there to celebrate with him. Yet I also felt that somehow I was doing this haul-ass ride as much for him as for me. I'd lost something of myself over the years by pouring too much of myself into a dying marriage and a profession where the needs are always greater than one's ability to meet them. I owed it to myself and I owed it to my children to recover some of the vitality and passion that had once characterized me.

I was excited to take off again and resume my time in the saddle. I would be riding a little less than forty miles to Estes Park, which buzzes busily year-round at the entrance to Rocky Mountain National Park. The route from Loveland to Estes Park was one I had ridden dozens of times in the early eighties, as my racing partner and I trained for competition. A smile curved my lips, as I pushed my way up hills where we used to see who could outgun the other. Keith could generally outrace me on longer climbs that required a consistent, steady rhythm, suited to his wiry frame. I would usually beat him to the top of the smaller hills with my larger, more muscular frame that was well-suited to short bursts of power.

I stopped by a memorial in Big Thompson Canyon to pay my respects to those who died on the eve of the 100th anniversary of Colorado's founding in 1876. On August 1, 1976, a flash flood caused by ten inches of rain bursting from a cloud in a short, 45-minute span suddenly ripped through the canyon, taking 143 lives with it. I had slept outside that night at my home in Loveland, and I remember the ominous dark cloud above the mountains. The next morning, and for many days after that, helicopters flew overhead looking for bodies. It was years before I could hear the whirling of chopper blades without getting a sick feeling.

Moving on again, I found the ride was as glorious, in fact, even better than I remembered. During the years of training, I was more focused on my speed and how my body was responding—it was work. This time I was able to stop and enjoy wildflowers, ride slowly along the creek at Glen Haven, and even chat with travelers enjoying the mountains with their children. I stopped for an over-sized cinnamon roll at the little rustic store in Glen Haven and stuffed it into my panniers, hoping it would survive into Estes Park where I could offer it as a gift to my hosts.

I also felt nervous—a certain tension in my body and a swirling in my stomach. I knew how difficult Trail Ridge Road was going to be. I had climbed it twice in my early twenties and it was difficult then. Now, thirty years older and carrying fifty pounds of gear, I was about to tackle it again. The other sobering detail is that because Trail Ridge Road is above timberline, you don't just go as far as you can and then camp: you either get over the top or you don't. If you don't, you must coast back down at least 4,000 feet in elevation to find a safe place to camp. Afternoon thunderstorms regularly whip up into a wicked frenzy as they pass by, and you don't want to be exposed to the lightning when that happens.

Something else wasn't right. I felt I was only getting about 80–90 per cent of each breath I took; I couldn't quite expand my lungs all the way before my ribs fought back. Certainly, the elevation was high: I was ascending from 5,000 feet to just over 7,000 feet. But I'd been riding at that elevation for over two weeks, so it didn't make sense that I would be suffering from altitude sickness. After cresting the summit that overlooks Estes Park from the north, I enjoyed a swift and delightful descent into Estes Park. Once again I was greeted by Warmshowers hosts, this time Marc and Diana, a young couple dedicated to as near an organic lifestyle as they could achieve. They had a garden, used their bikes for errands, and ate only non-processed foods.

After settling into their extra bedroom and taking a shower, I rode into town to find dinner. Nothing sounded good; in fact, the thought of food made me feel sick. Feeling lethargic and slightly in a fog, I lay down in the park and fell asleep. After a short nap, I surveyed the town again for food that sounded appetizing. This was so unusual—typically, I'm ready to eat about anything and everything after a good hard ride. Finally, my eyes settled on a sushi bar. Miso soup, lots of water, a salad, and fresh salmon and tuna *nigiri*, all washed down by an extra-large Sapporo beer. It was just what I needed: it seemed my body was crying out for minerals after eating poorly in Loveland when I wasn't riding.

This was not how I wanted to feel the night before Trail Ridge Road, a challenge I anticipated would be the most severe and punishing of the whole trip.

DAY 35
Estes Park to Grand Lake, CO
48 miles

I GOT UP EARLY, enjoyed a good breakfast prepared by my hosts, and headed for town. I was praying that the sluggishness of twelve hours before hadn't lingered through the night. At the grocery store I carbo-loaded, consuming a couple of donuts, and stuffed my panniers with fruit, protein bars, and Gatorade. I took a few deep breaths, looked at the mountain pass before me, and said, "This is it. This is the top. It's homeward bound after that."

I settled into a good, easy rhythm; this day wasn't about trying to break any speed records. Survival was all the accomplishment I needed. Trail Ridge Road isn't the steepest grade I've ever faced: it certainly has many steep sections, but usually within a few hundred yards those ease off again, so a cyclist can let some of the painful lactic acid accumulation in the legs dissipate. Where Trail Ridge Road gets you is that the climb lingers on for over twenty miles, rising from 7,000 feet in Estes Park to over 12,000 feet at the summit. Moreover, five miles from the top you leave timberline, the winds begin to pick up—sometimes ferociously—and the cold air begins to take a toll on your lungs.

I spent the first part of the ride pedaling steadily and stopping at vistas to take pictures. I wanted to send proof back to family and friends that climbing Trail Ridge is serious business—as you look down over the valley, you can see the road snaking its way up the mountain, occasionally making a switchback, and your vantage point highlights the elevation gain.

At one point, a tour bus filled with senior citizens stopped to marvel at the vista. Some of the women gathered around me, stroking my ego as they chattered about how strong I must be to attempt such a feat.

One woman, clearly in her eighties (God, that's a dangerous statement!), grabbed her friend's arm, handed her the camera, and said, "Take a picture of us together." She sidled up to me. "Sit with me here on the ledge."

I laughed at her playfulness. "Looks like I don't have a choice." I decided to play along. "Here, sit as close as you can." She nestled right up to me and we put our arms around each other, as if we were girlfriend and boyfriend sending pictures back to our families.

This pilgrimage was serious business: remodeling my life and identity, wrestling with losses, and climbing impossible mountain passes. Yet I was pleased I could still be playful with a little encouragement.

The brief window of fun gave me a surge of energy as I remounted my bike. But it was not enough. Despite five weeks in the saddle, nearly

2,000 miles logged, and a deliberate intention to ride easily and steadily up the climb, with three miles to go my legs were completely shot. I stopped, stretched out my legs, and massaged the tenderest places, hoping I could keep the blood flowing long enough to reach the top. I remounted and my legs immediately began twitching, the muscles all threatening to go on strike. Five hundred yards later, I stopped again and walked around until my muscles felt looser. I remounted my bike and the twitching returned.

I groaned at the thought I might have to walk my bike up the last stretch, something I would interpret as a minor defeat and a blow to my ego. I kept my legs moving in my smallest and easiest gear. Every time a muscle would go into a spasm, I stood up on my pedals and stretched that muscle out while continuing my ascent. Truth be told, I was largely driven on by the oohs and aahs from passengers in the cars snaking past me. Not only did I want to make it to the top without walking, I now felt a responsibility to them, like a wheelchair-bound athlete needing to cross the finish line of a marathon. I had fans cheering me on. I couldn't let them down.

I neared the top and was overcome with relief and raw emotion. It is one thing to see the rugged and stunning beauty of these Rockies after driving up in a gas-propelled vehicle. But there is something about experiencing it with your body. To feel the burn in your lungs as you cycle up beyond timberline, to fight the persistent cramps telling you that you've gone one pedal stroke too far, to listen to your body as it demands more water and more food, magnifies the experience. It's as if the physical exertion the terrain requires is an invitation to be part of the terrain and the beauty. The line between observer and observed dissolves. I was no longer looking at a mountain: I was part of the mountain.

But my emotion ran deeper than just the beauty I felt I was participating in—my successful arrival at the top signified the recovery of a long-lost part of myself. While there were many places and people to reconnect with on this journey, Trail Ridge Road was one of the most important to me. I grew up in these Rocky Mountains with their invitation to participate in Nature; fishing, hiking, skiing, cycling, and camping were part of my normal activities. Somewhere in the course of marriage, ministry, and the raising of children, I think I lost contact with that part of me. My personality includes a ruggedness and an adventurous side that I had allowed to become domesticated.

Part of the reason for the pilgrimage, I believe, was that I had to find both the edges and the limits of that part of me. Truth be told, if I'd made it halfway up the mountain and discovered that at 51 I wasn't capable of what I could do at 21, it would have been disappointing, but okay. I needed to know what parts of me I could recover and what parts it was time to relinquish. I found out exactly what I needed to know: I'd been pushed to the absolute limit of my strength, but I had done it. I had crested the summit of Trail Ridge Road, the highest paved highway in the world. I was not as physically strong as I was thirty years before. But psychologically I felt Herculean.

When I reached the top I was too exhausted to even celebrate my achievement, but I gritted my teeth and took pictures as proof to others and myself that I had done it. I ate a leisurely lunch at the visitor center while my legs pretended to recover and my lungs to expand again (I was still having trouble getting full breaths). I saw a few other cyclists and we made eye contact, but I hardly had enough energy for a conversation. Those cyclists looked fresher than I felt, but they were all one-day riders who had parked at the bottom, ridden to the top, and would soon scream back down to where they'd started. I was exhausted, but I was lugging fifty pounds of gear. I felt pretty good about myself.

One woman cyclist, a little younger than me, and trim and fit as a marathon runner, pressed me. "Wow, where are you headed? You've managed quite a feat today."

"It's a long story," I said, "but I'm starting to head back to the West Coast now before returning to Portland."

"That's so cool! Is this just for fun?"

I was tired, but her interest deserved a response. "Well, it *is* fun, but it isn't just *for* fun. I'm a minister," I explained a little wearily, "studying the shift between religion and spirituality, and the decline of mainline churches."

Her final comment said it all. "Oh… denominationalism," she said, insinuating it was a notion from a bygone era, like "white-only eating establishments."

Ninety minutes later I pointed my bike downhill, and fourteen miles later limped (if one can limp on a bike) into the town of Grand Lake. Thank God I had gravity pushing me, because there was no push left in my legs. After a shower, some time to recover and massage my legs, I meandered through the resort town with other tourists. I found a restaurant and bar spilling over with energy. Compared to the early weeks of the pilgrimage, I was still tending to look for places where there were people. I had transitioned from needing solitude to needing connection—I was psychologically ready to head home.

I returned to my motel room and got out my maps. My original plan was to continue riding south through Colorado, and cross over to Utah through the Durango area. From there, I would ride through southern Utah before inching my way up to catch Highway 50 and the "Loneliest Highway in America" as it crosses the Nevada desert.

What I did next was not an impulsive decision—I'd call it an intuitive decision. I decided to stay north in Colorado and pick up Highway 50 just east of Nevada. This did two things: first, it cut about 200 miles off my total trip, thus easing concerns about returning much after the originally allotted time. (By the way, Eastminster had emailed me in Loveland to say it was important I take the time I needed, and not to worry about when I got back. Nice bunch of people they are!)

Second, and more importantly, the original route included an additional three 10,000-foot passes. After successfully conquering Trail Ridge Road I had nothing left to prove to myself or others, and I couldn't stomach the idea of having to punish myself for an additional ten days. I made the decision and didn't give it a second thought.

DAY 36
Grand Lake to Walden, CO
74 miles

IN GRAND LAKE, FOR THE FIRST TIME on the entire pilgrimage, I went to church. The place was appropriately named The Church of the Pines, which reflected the material it was made of, and the pine-covered mountains surrounding the small town. I rolled into the church lot all loaded up and wearing my cycling gear. The sanctuary was almost completely full; I chose a seat toward the back, near the door. I didn't want to make too much of a spectacle of myself in my cycling duds among the Sunday crowd, some dressed in their Sunday best, but most more casually. Up front was a full band consisting of piano, drum, saxophone, trombone and guitar, unusual for a Presbyterian Church. I reviewed the bulletin and found the explanation: it was their annual Jazz Sunday.

The pastor began the service with a few announcements, and then asked if there were any visitors. I knew the routine: I stood and introduced myself as a fellow Presbyterian minister passing through on a ten-week cycling pilgrimage. The pastor welcomed me, adding, "That's the thing about showing up at a Presbyterian church—it's like coming home."

I smiled, knowing that my pilgrimage was about wrestling with the truth of that, and if it were true, in what way was it true? I was reminded of the gift of community as the jazz sextet—all participants in the congregation, no hired hands—played. The church had a wonderful energy. People clapped and laughed; the prayers reflected a close-knit community, where people knew each other intimately and truly cared for each other.

Yet it was like most other mainline churches: the heads in front of me were almost all either white or bald. And despite my familiarity with the liturgy, I could understand why most people would rather be cycling, fishing, or hiking on a Sunday morning than praying, reading scripture, and listening to a polished preacher deliver a well-thought-out sermon.

The bulletin did leave me with a parting gift—a "Thought for the Day" in which a familiar Presbyterian author was quoted: "The place where God calls you is the place where your deep gladness and the world's deep hunger meet." Exactly what I was wrestling with on this pilgrimage: discovering where my passion (deep gladness) and the world's hunger met. I was not convinced it was in the church as a pastor. I left The Church of the Pines feeling neither more hopeful nor more discouraged, just confirmed in my belief that what we know as church is passing away. It was a nice morning, but this one uplifting Jazz Sunday wasn't going to turn back the tide of change that I could feel, but could not quite name.

The afternoon was crisp and cool. I rode to the town of Granby, just a few miles down the road from Grand Lake, where I left the main highway and immediately began another serious climb. But after the strenuous effort of the day before, this climb was not nearly as taxing and never got above timberline, which has a climate of its own. A light rain started halfway up the climb, but was never enough to drench me, acting more like a mist machine that kept me cool as my body continued to heat up from exertion. As I reached Walden a large rainbow nicely framed the town.

I was struck again, as in Oregon, that even as my soul grieved for my life, my profession, and my church, signs of goodness had a way of breaking through.

DAY 37
Walden to Steamboat Springs, CO
58 miles

I WOKE UP LOOKING FORWARD to riding to Steamboat Springs. When I was a child, our family traditionally took a few days in Steamboat every summer, camping in the same spot and swimming in the large, cold swimming hole created by a bend in the stream, where a massive boulder served as a diving board. I will never forget how my parents tried to hide my sister and me from a group of young skinny-dippers who had discovered our sacred swimming hole. Often we camped with another family, and three of us men (I was actually a boy, but I liked thinking I was going with the men) would hike three miles upstream and fish down all day, catching dozens of trout, mostly brookies with an occasional rainbow trout hooked.

I suppose it's safe to say now that we brought in dozens of fish over our limit. I remember one trip when we came back with nearly a hundred fish—probably five or six dozen above the legal limit. My dad, probably concerned about leaving me with the lesson that it was okay to break the law, said we were actually doing the fish a service. We had come upon a stream that was difficult to reach without scrambling down steep embankments. With so few fishermen, there were too many fish for the food supply in that three-mile stretch, and most of the fish we caught had heads much too large for their bodies. We were thinning out the fish population so that those who did survive would be larger and healthier. "We are following a higher law" seemed to be my dad's explanation. That was good enough for me back then; I just loved catching fish.

The last time we went to Steamboat to fish it was just my dad and me. I was nineteen and only weeks away from heading off to college in Idaho. Although I didn't know it at the time, my dad's marriage (to my second mom, the one who hadn't called back in Loveland) was in trouble. It was the first time I had felt I had rights to his personal life, and he and I talked about living in our household, and how much we had both yearned for a home with more love, kindness, and joy. To this day, I cherish the image and memory of sitting around a campfire staring into the dancing flames, and pouring our hearts out—as much as two men who had practiced a lifetime of emotional repression could. I always felt my dad had a kind heart. The honesty and intimacy of that final father/son fishing trip before college confirmed what I'd often felt, but rarely seen.

As I was preparing to ride back into the memory of those cherished childhood years, my mother called me. (Before you get too excited, this was my birth mother. Remember, way back in Bozeman? I know. It's confusing, believe me!) She now lived in Wisconsin within walking distance of my sister, her second child.

"Hi Mom," I said. "I'm surprised to hear from you."

"I thought I'd call and wish you good blessings for the rest of your journey," she said. "I've been following your blog. Where are you now?"

"I'm just loading up to leave Walden, Colorado. In the northwestern part of Colorado. I should be in Steamboat Springs tonight."

"Well, I am just so proud of you, son. God has given you special strength."

"Thanks, Mom. I'm having a great time. By the way, I did get to see Uncle Max and Aunt Shirley in Bozeman. Thanks for putting me in contact with them."

"Oh, I am glad. Listen, son, I won't hold you up any more. I just wanted to let you know I love you," she said.

"Thanks, Mom. I love you too."

This had always been our pattern. Her divorce and her decision to leave my sister and me completely in my dad's care had severed the normal emotional intimacy that develops between a young child and a mother. We had no contact with her until my father arranged a one-hour meeting with her while on a trip to California when I was sixteen. After that, with the exception of a handful of letters, I had no contact with my birth mother for another sixteen years. Then, out of the blue, she showed up on my doorstep in Wisconsin when I was thirty-two, in my first pastorate, and raising two children—who were a bit bewildered to discover they had a previously unknown grandmother.

She and I spent three days catching up, taking long car drives, and trying to figure out what had happened thirty years prior. Some spark was reignited in me—I wanted to get to know this woman who had brought me into the world.

For years we tried to rekindle some form of a mother/son relationship, but it was awkward and forced. I remember the freeing conversation we had when we both admitted we were trying to impose something on our relationship that wasn't there. We decided that, despite being mother and son, we would admit our lack of connection. Our relationship would be built on what was real, rather than trying to recreate what should have been.

There was little emotional connection between us, but we had committed to being present to each other. A few times a year, at random, I called her; this was the day she chose to connect.

In the space of four days, I'd attempted to contact the mother who had primarily raised me; had dinner with my step-siblings from my dad's third wife; and had a surprise call from my birth mother. If my dad's fourth wife (whom he'd married the year before) called now, the circle would be complete.

I rechecked my gear, and steeled myself for the ascent up Rabbit Ears Pass, a favorite landmark I would look for as we neared Steamboat

Springs on our annual family trips. The first miles were casual. I felt like a tourist, taking my time to admire the plush meadows, the steep mountains off in the distance, and the small streamlets that ran alongside the road.

I stopped to take a picture of a herd of cows. As I fiddled with my camera, the cows trotted over as if I'd rung a dinner bell. I stared at them; they stared back at me. "You are my friends," I declaimed. "I like you." It was refreshing that someone was interested in me. Even if it was just a herd of cows.

I had only traveled a few minutes when a scene to the left of the road caught my eye. In a serene and lush wild pasture stood seven normal-sized horses, circled up, their heads turned inward much like a football huddle. Thirty feet from the cliquish clan, a Shetland pony, one-tenth the size of his equine cousins, turned his back to them. They were perfectly posed for a shot with the caption, "Ever felt you didn't fit in?!"

I didn't immediately fall into a woe-is-me frame of mind, but the picture seemed to mirror my complicated family history and the underlying reasons for this pilgrimage. I have spent a lifetime wondering where I belong. In the early sixties, I was the only child of divorce among my classmates, and my dad was unusual in gaining custody of his children. Now that story was playing itself out again: I was serving in an institution more suited to a generation that would soon pass away than with my friends and peers.

As I remounted my bike, an old Peter, Paul and Mary song surfaced. I used to love to sing it in Racine, Wisconsin, when life became excruciatingly lonely for this West Coast, earring-wearing pastor trying to find his way in the buttoned-up, proper Midwest. "Sometimes it takes a winding road to lead us home," I sang, "while you're windin' round, my friend, just don't go windin' round alone." The challenge, the winding roads, fighting the fight. And a lonely Shetland pony. No wonder at that moment it was my theme song.

Rabbit Ears Pass was deceptively hard. I rode at a consistent pace up the bulk of the pass, believing that the top I could see was the actual summit. Three times I got it wrong. I would hit a crest, descend for a short stretch, and be faced with another painful climb. When I reached the final summit at 9,426 feet, crossing the Continental Divide yet again, I cursed at the pass—as if it cared one whit about how I felt.

Another cyclist came huffing and puffing toward the sign. "Fuck that," he screeched, shaking his head. I'd expressed the same eloquent sentiment, except as a God-fearing pastor I'd added a "goddammit" for good measure. We caught our breaths, let our anger dissipate, and took pictures of each other. He was from Melbourne, Australia, and had no specific destination in mind. I told him I was a pastor from Portland, Oregon. I was at this point wondering if I would know when I had "arrived" either.

We howled down a tear-inducing descent of 3,000 vertical feet into Steamboat. A massive mountain served as backdrop to a valley of an almost unnatural green, reminding me of pictures of valleys in the Swiss Alps. I wanted to take pictures, but I was hitting speeds of more than 45 mph, and didn't want to do anything that would detract from the pure ecstasy, adrenaline, and joy I was experiencing. Not even for the perfect picture.

Descents like that can be dangerous: one misplaced rock or a short glance away just as a pothole races toward you, and you're in trouble. But that's why I do it. Whether cursing the gods for a punishing climb, or praising the heavens for a ridiculously exciting descent, I feel so alive. Pain or adrenaline, at least I'm feeling something—unlike the growing numbness of religious institutions that have lost their vitality, but aren't brave enough to feel their grief.

My companion, Alex, and I sped into Steamboat. Neither of us had made plans for lodging, so we soon agreed to split the cost of a motel room. We settled in, each had a shower, and then we went our separate ways for the evening. I was itching for a dinner that promised more than just large portions; I wanted an experience and I was willing to pay for it. I spotted a restaurant with an upper deck overlooking the river and the small park that serves as a community ski area in the winter. It was a perfect evening. I slowly consumed apple-glazed pork loins, a couple of pale ales, and a chocolate torte for dessert. The waitress was especially pleasant and attractive, and just a little younger than me. It felt good to share casual conservation with a woman; I'd been on the road for over five weeks and was missing that.

I returned to the motel room, spread out on my bed, and wrote my blog for the day. Alex slipped through the door a little while later.

"How was your evening?" I asked.

"Good. I made my way around a couple of pubs, and had a great banger and mash dinner."

"I decided to go the route of luxury tonight. I spent over fifty dollars on my dinner, but it was worth every penny," I said. "Plus my waitress was pretty cute."

Alex snickered. "I thought you were the good pastor type!"

The ideal opening. I shared my view on the decline of mainline congregations in America.

Right away he latched onto the subject. "I know exactly what you mean. My grandparents are real church-goers. They attend almost every Sunday, and whenever we visit they want us to go with them. My parents, of course, were raised by them and they all went to church, but I think they drifted away after high school. My parents never expected us kids to go to church."

I nodded. "I'm probably about your parents' age. Our generation largely left the church when we reached adulthood."

"To tell you the truth, my friends and I are all in our twenties, and church just isn't on our radar. It's not that we have anything against it, it's just irrelevant to our lives," he said.

I knew the story; I had heard it for years. Christine and Michelle confirmed it on my second day in Oregon, and my children felt the same. Despite living on a different continent, Alex was very much like my own twenty-something children.

I went to bed and the Peter, Paul and Mary song came back to me. But now I sang a different verse:

Yes, there are hands here to comfort you;
And if you need, there are tears to cry with you too;
And there are hearts that will sing with you;
And voices to cheer when you've finally made it through.

DAY 38
Steamboat Springs to Craig, CO
47 miles

MY BIKE COMPUTER REGISTERED 2,000 miles this morning. In truth, it was probably more like 2,075 miles, as my computer had lost a few miles in the two rainstorms I'd encountered. Whether coincidentally or because I had reached the 2,000-mile mark, I felt myself riding into an empty psychological space.

I was riding beside the cold, fresh water of the Yampa River running about fifty feet below me as I glided easily along the two-lane highway taking me closer to the Colorado/Utah border. I had a fun flirtation with a hay baler, which was traveling much slower than the cars and only slightly slower than me. As traffic lined up behind the tractor, I passed it on the right. The woman driver and I smiled at each other, as if we both knew we'd be dancing together on the road for a while. A straight stretch allowed the cars to dart around her, passing me just as quickly. A short, steep hill faced me, and the tractor chugged up, passed me, the driver and I exchanging another smile. We repeated this two more times until the road flattened out. I overtook the tractor and slowly put it far into the distance, never to see it again.

After playing a little leapfrog with the hay baler, I entered a new space. During the first week, the campus of the College of Idaho had drawn me forward. Then Bozeman became the motivator, as I battled with the Sawtooths and the Continental Divide into Montana. I was greeted by the prospect of wide-open spaces as I began trekking across Wyoming, but I had Yellowstone Park to inspire me, as well as the lazy little town of Thermopolis, where I'd lived with relatives—Loveland and the Rocky Mountains were the real interim destination points. Steamboat Springs was the final point where I had story until reaching the West coast. The next location that held some of my past was Sacramento, California, and the Bay Area. There I would reconnect with places associated with my now-defunct marriage, the seminary I graduated from, and Lake County, where a ministry that had great promise ended badly. As I put Steamboat behind me, I became unexpectedly overwhelmed by the vastness of this next leg: a full 1,200 miles that included the imposing and dangerous Nevada desert.

I was at the border of a genuine wilderness. I knew well enough that the only way through was to take it one day, one mile, and one pedal-stroke at a time.

As I rode, I began wondering what purpose I still had to be riding. Although I'd faced a few moments when I questioned what the hell I was doing, I had felt propelled by some inner purpose to do with my past. I had also desperately needed solitude in those first few weeks. But since Casper, Wyoming, I had begun to feel the need to re-connect with people and re-enter the community in some way. What would keep me going while I crossed the large western expanse that included the rest of western Colorado, the width of Utah, the desert of Nevada, and the Sierras? To sustain my current average pace of 65 miles per day until I coasted down into California in three weeks, I would need to find some inner purpose.

Not having produced an answer, I rode as far as Craig and decided to stop. The next town with any significant services was Dinosaur, 90 miles away, and I didn't want to get caught between the two towns. I located a very cheap motel (costing less than I'd paid for dinner in Steamboat) in downtown Craig. The motel room was so inviting (though so small I had to lock my bike outside) that I decided this would be a good place to take an extra day. I needed to rest my body after four days of crossing the Rockies, and I desperately needed a massage. Something was not right in my ribs: I couldn't take a full breath without a gnawing, sharp pain.

I went to a local diner for a steak-and-potato dinner, followed by a large piece of homemade cherry pie with a heaped scoop of French vanilla ice cream slowly melting on top. I was ready for another book after finishing *The Age of Faith* by Harvey Cox. Recognizing my terrible habit of reading only books that have a direct correlation to my work in ministry, I made a commitment to pick something just for fun. As I strolled to a used book store, I pondered the first question of the Shorter Catechism of the Presbyterian Church: What is the chief end of man? The correct answer every confirmand learns is: The chief end of man is to glorify God and enjoy Him forever. Once you get past the patriarchal language, it makes a pretty good point—we are supposed to both do good for God and enjoy God. I had worked at the first and often failed miserably at the second.

I scanned the used books in the fiction section. One book immediately caught my eye—Steven Galloway's *The Cellist of Sarajevo*. The back cover summary confirmed my choice: "In a city under siege, four people whose lives have been upended are ultimately reminded of what it is to be human." I couldn't wait to dive into this "just for fun" story.

DAY 39
Craig, CO
Rest Day, 0 miles

HAVING STARTED MY STAY IN CRAIG with a little luxury the night before, I was ready to keep this theme running. I wheeled my way to a Village Inn restaurant on the far side of town. There I dove into the novel, *The Cellist of Sarajevo*, while enjoying a rich waffle layered with bananas and pecan sauce. Two hours and many cups of coffee later, I searched the yellow pages hoping to find a masseuse who could see me that day. I was lucky; a local massage studio had an opening later that afternoon. I retreated to my motel room to work on an essay on postmodernism and the Church, which had been circulating in my mind during the last hundred miles or so.

As the time of my appointment neared, I cycled the two-mile jaunt to the massage studio.

"I hear you're badly in need of a massage," my therapist said, leading me to a treatment room.

"Yes. After five weeks of cycling, my body is pretty bound up. I had my last massage in Bozeman, Montana, three weeks ago."

Once I'd stripped and lay face down, relaxed, on the massage table, she began working. I should have kept quiet and concentrated solely on getting the kinks worked out of my body—but I often don't know when to stop, and told her the reason behind my pilgrimage. Soon she was telling me about her Christian walk and how churches were abandoning God.

I listened politely until the conversation ran out of energy, and then brought up the subject of the pain in my ribs. "It's weird. I can feel it both in front and in my back. It keeps me from getting a full breath," I said. "I have to constantly reposition myself to stop it hurting too much."

After some investigation, she said, "Brian, you have a rib that's slipped out of position."

"What does that mean?"

"Well, it means you're probably pretty uncomfortable," she teased. "I can release some of the tension around the rib, but I doubt it will slip back into place until you resume normal activities—like not being bent over on a bike all day."

I groaned. "You mean I'll have to grit my teeth through it for another five weeks?"

"I'm afraid so."

I wasn't thrilled with the news, but I would survive. It wasn't altering my riding technique or even the number of miles I was committing to—it just hurt. All the time.

I still had half the afternoon and the whole evening to do whatever I wanted. I ate a late lunch/early dinner—a better pizza than I'd eaten for a long time—along with two buzz-inducing beers that left me in a completely relaxed state. Back to my cozy little motel room for a nap. When I rose, ready for more luxury, I went to a movie for the first time on the trip. All the towns for the last 500 miles that were large enough to boast a theater had been playing the same two movies: *The Rise of the Planet of the Apes,* and *Cowboys and Aliens.* In the well-preserved old-fashioned theater, where lamps and couches still graced the lobby, I ordered a large popcorn, soda and Red Vines, and gorged on the tasty and visual delights as apes and humans battled for supremacy.

But I still hadn't spoiled myself enough. On the way back from the movie theatre, I stopped at a convenience store to buy a pint of milk and a family-sized bag of Little Debbie chocolate donuts. I sat on my bed with my computer and my snacks, and finished writing about postmodernism, the decline of the mainline Protestant Church, and the rise of the globally connected, religiously pluralistic, and multicultural world in which we now live. In the back of my mind, a question arose: was I desperately trying to keep my identity as a minister, maybe even craft a new identity as a minister with expertise on the current cultural/religious shift? I might be riding my bike around the western United States, but my mind was working hard to understand and hold onto my place in the world. The Church may be in decline, but it seemed I wasn't going to give up my profession as a religious leader easily.

Completely sated with beer, pizza, popcorn and snacks, I looked forward to a full night of deep sleep in preparation for a long stretch of 90 miles to Dinosaur, on what was predicted to be a hot August day in the expanse of northwestern Colorado. The masseuse had also warned me to watch out for rattlesnakes. They love to get out on the hot pavement and sun themselves, she had reminded me.

I wasn't scared of the rattlesnakes. But any place where rattlesnakes enjoy themselves is a place where survival is more important than scenery. It would be a challenging ride.

PART FIVE

Into The Belly Of The Whale

August 18 – August 22

Entering Utah and new territory.

DAY 40
Craig to Dinosaur, CO
88 miles

THE VILLAGE INN WAFFLE the day before had been so rich and sumptuous that I darted right back there next morning to properly initiate this monumental day. Once again I settled into a booth with my book, an appetite, and growing adrenaline as I steeled myself for a long, hot day in the saddle. But I didn't linger; I wasn't about to get stranded between towns in rattlesnake-sunning country.

I anticipated a long ride, but across fairly flat terrain. My internet search revealed no mountain passes to cross, and an elevation drop of 200 feet from Craig to Dinosaur—an average of two feet every mile, meaning basically flat. My body is tailor-made for such terrain—heavy and strong like a train. I can pick up speed on the flats, but the hills force my big frame to slow to a crawl almost immediately.

I had ridden for about an hour when I entered Maybell, the only town to stock up on snacks and drinks before tackling the remaining 70 miles to Dinosaur. I picked up a few items, refilled water bottles and tied an extra two-liter bottle of water and some Gatorade to my back panniers. I had barely got the pedals moving when the sign in front of a Baptist Church stopped me: "Will the road you're on get you to my place? God." I smiled at my own personal irony—I had ridden away from the god of church five weeks before in order to encounter the god of the road and the wilderness. I wasn't sure this road would lead me back to church, but I was certain that God was traveling the road with me.

Immediately after the church, the road rose a hundred feet or so. It wasn't a major climb, but was not what I expected from my research. At the top of the small incline, my eyes settled on a series of what we cyclists call rollers. For as far as I could see, the road went up and then it went down, up and down, in a series of 100-, 200-, and 300-foot climbs and descents. I kept calm and rode on, took big gulps of water every few minutes, and reminded myself to keep an easy, graceful pace up each incline.

Suddenly I saw a strange sight. After cresting one of the hills, I saw a lone figure coming toward me on my side of the road. *What the hell? This man is running and I'm easily fifteen miles out of town already.* I knew it would take a good runner two hours to cover that distance, but the bigger question was where he'd started from. There was no sign of a vehicle anywhere; no buildings; in fact, no sign of humans anywhere in this abandoned and inhospitable landscape.

I pedaled toward him and he continued to pace toward me. As he neared, I pulled up my bike hoping he would stop. He did.

"Hey there," the young man said. "Looks like you're out for a little ride."

"I am, but I'm more curious about you. Are you just out for a training run?"

"No, my dad, my brother and I are running across the U.S. raising awareness about holistic health." He said it as innocently as anyone else would say, "I'm heading to the store."

"No kidding?" I said. "I'm on a similar trek. Riding in a big 4,000-mile circle, listening for the shift taking place between religion and spirituality. I'm Brian."

"Jeremiah," he said. "I bet my dad would love to meet you. He used to teach religion. Our team is just down the road in the RV. Stop by and say hello."

With that, Jeremiah took off again. I understood. Once you get the legs moving it's hard to stop and start. He wanted to start running again before his muscles enjoyed the break too much. I continued west on Highway 318. Sure enough, an RV was parked a couple of miles farther down the road. Jeremiah's crew, comprised of two men and a woman, stepped out of the RV as I pulled up.

A tall, lean man with a little gray in his hair approached me. "Did you see a runner just ahead of us a ways?" He waved a hand towards the RV. "We've had a little vehicle trouble."

"Yeah, Jeremiah is just a couple more miles down the road," I answered. "He told me to make sure I connected with you," I added, guessing this must be Jeremiah's father. "Apparently we both have a thing for religion."

"I did teach religion for a few years in a Catholic high school," he agreed, "but now I'm more focused on the connection between spirituality and our health."

I nearly laughed. Here we were, out in the middle of nowhere (I can safely say that, because literally no one lives close enough to be offended by that description). While I was listening for the shift from religion to spirituality, this man was describing his own shift. We talked for a while. It turned out he had been in El Salvador, working on peace and justice issues, at the same time my sister was a missionary in that country.

We vowed to share our websites and follow each other. We were about to head in opposite directions—me to the West Coast and they to New York—when our heads swung back as one to the road.

A lone cyclist, fit, strong and fast, coasted up to us. "Hello," he said in an Italian accent.

Stranger and stranger! Jeremiah's dad and I said together, "Where the heck are you going?"

Before the cyclist had a chance to answer, another vehicle pulled up. It was clearly his support car, as the back seat was full of water, other drinks, luggage, and various pieces of biking clothing. He didn't know much English, but we were able to ascertain that Sandro was alternating between cycling and running across the United States, expected to finish in San Francisco, was raising money for cancer research in Italy, and that he thought it was very hot! We took lots of pictures capturing this happenstance meeting of cross-country athletes, all of whom were doing the near-impossible for some cause important to them.

Sandro and I both expected to finish the day in Dinosaur. At his invitation, we rode together. On the first roller he easily danced his way up while I labored under the weight of my gear. He pointed to my packs and then his support vehicle, asking without words if I wanted the car to carry them. I shook my head. I thought, no, I've ridden the first 2,000 miles with the fifty pounds of weight. I don't need the help.

Sandro was at least fifteen years younger than me, more fit (like a racer), and carried no gear on his bike. Not surprisingly, a pattern quickly developed: he glided easily up the hills, and waited for me at the top; I did my best to keep up with him on the flats. It wasn't long before I realized that my stubbornness over carrying my own gear was slowing him down. He was very kind to stay with me.

At the top of the next hill we stopped, and Sandro's support vehicle pulled up behind us. The woman crew member spoke more English. "You want some chilled water? I have a cooler here," she offered.

"Oh my gosh, yes! This 150-degree slush I'm drinking is awful," I said.

As I enjoyed the chilled water I thought about my rebuff of Kathy back in Wyoming, when she had traveled 150 miles to make sure I had water. I had rebuffed Sandro and his crew as well. Not only was I slowing Sandro down, but I was starting to hurt as well. I telegraphed a quick mental apology to Kathy, kicked away my pride and begged, "Hey, any chance your offer to carry my gear is still good?"

"Of course. You've been carrying that your whole trip, huh?" the woman said. "I can't believe how strong you are."

The comment made me feel good, naturally—but I was thankful for the chance to lay my gear aside for the last thirty miles. The constant rollers and the near 100-degree heat were taking their toll on me.

Sandro and I took off again. Without the burden, my bike and my spirit became lighter. Sandro and I acted playful for the camera; his crew was documenting this journey. He still beat me to the top of each roller, but I felt less guilty as I came up behind him seconds later instead of minutes.

If Sandro's team hadn't come along, I'm sure I would have found a way to survive the day. But I also felt it was a lucky break. I had gone through my water faster than expected, and while I wasn't climbing a mountain pass, the persistent rollers produced a day just as physically challenging as Chief Joseph Pass or Trail Ridge Road. I was doing just as much climbing, but traveling 90 miles rather than the shorter 50- and 60-mile days when I had to ride over a major mountain pass.

I was not prepared for the difficulty of the day. With fifteen miles to go I was really hurting, and my legs developed the tingling sensation that I recognize just before my muscles rebel and cry, "No more! No more!" I was in a Catch 22. My body wanted to go slower, but Sandro's wheel provided a draft effect that saved me energy. I chose the latter, but I could feel my jaw clenching and my eyes sinking into their sockets as I rode through the pain.

The large billboard sign heralding our arrival in Dinosaur pulled me along the last mile. I was completely spent, but Sandro and I stood arm-in-arm below the sign while his support crew took pictures. He and his team went to find the motel they had reserved days earlier, while I camped in the small public park that offered public showers. I set up my tent, took a shower and walked across the highway to the convenience store. I couldn't even think about mustering the energy for dinner. I returned to the park and sat at the picnic table eating butter toffee peanuts, drinking hot chocolate cappuccino and watching a most spectacular, deep red sunset overtake the Utah hills to the west.

That night I reflected once more on my unwillingness to accept help. If the pilgrimage was about proving I could conquer the West on my own, I had blown that storyline. If it was to prove to those involved (like family and church members) that I could do it without them, I had written a little footnote—maybe I could, but I couldn't do it on my own.

I fell into an exhausted and blissfully deep sleep. Before dawn, too early to get up, I shot straight up. Dozens of ants had found a small hole at the end of the zipper and were crawling on my chest, neck and face. I swept as many out as I could, but I would get no more sleep that night.

DAY 41
Dinosaur, CO to Roosevelt, UT
64 miles

THE COLORADO/UTAH BORDER is just a handful of miles west of Dinosaur. After my usual biker's breakfast of pancakes, eggs and bacon, I locked my feet into my pedals and continued westward. The terrain almost immediately shifted as I neared the border. I'd been struck by how rich and beautiful each state had been, but entirely different from each other. Now I rode through a dry, arid and rugged landscape with painted hills that guided me through the valleys. There were very few trees to soften the harsh angularity of the rock surfaces. I loved it. I stopped at the first lookout, and read the panels that described the rock formations and the native vegetation and animals. This was a land of coyotes, deer, foxes, hawks, and of course—rattlesnakes.

I settled into a relaxed pace, enjoying the emptiness, the colors of the rocks, and the sobering effect it all had on me. I was searching for a calm inner place that would allow me to address the crossroad I felt looming. I imagined getting to the Nevada border and putting my thumb out as a large four-wheel-drive pick-up truck lumbered by. What would take me about a week, a vehicle could cover in one full day. I could completely bypass the slightly terrifying prospect of soloing across the desert. I wondered if it was time to survey which towns had Greyhound depots, and plan my route based on where I could pick up the luxury of a bus. Granted, Greyhounds aren't the first thing I think of when I say luxury, but even a bus seat can feel like heaven compared to a thin, saddle sore-producing bike seat and the hard ground at night.

More than anything, I sought a purpose to ride through the desert. I'd seen hints of this approaching dilemma as I departed from Steamboat Springs, knowing that 1,200 miles separated that favorite family destination from the Bay Area, where I would pick up my story again. If this pilgrimage was about reconnecting with that story, could I not just hop right over the dry wilderness of Nevada? Besides, I was itching for more enjoyment—leisurely rides where I could look at the scenery, detour occasionally, and not be faced with gut-busting climbs and crippling heat.

I kept asking, what purpose will there be to doing this? Am I just punishing myself, like some spiritual masochist?

I made my way through Vernal, Utah, where I was greeted by a 30-foot-tall pink dinosaur sporting a sign saying, "Vernal City Welcomes You." I stopped for lunch at a briskly paced hamburger diner that never seemed to have an empty table. Despite the isolation of this town it was clear this was a community gathering spot, as friends said hello to friends, parents with small children drank chocolate malts together, and youth and elders celebrated each other as if they were family.

I rode as far as Roosevelt, a small town that seemed to be completely under construction. Almost the entire road leading into town had been torn out, and vehicles lumbered through potholes, over gravel and around orange cones. I was forced to choose a varied path, sharing the road for short sections, lifting my bike up over torn-out curbs, and riding through the occasional parking lot.

I found a reasonably priced motel before setting out to find dinner. I chose an Arby's as it brought back childhood memories of the family's monthly trip to Fort Collins for grocery shopping—Arby's was the ritual treat. I quickly regretted it. My palate had become more sophisticated over the years, it seemed; my stomach was full, but agitated. My mind, however, was thinking about the future. The more populated Happy Valley was just two days away; after that came the desert. I would face that decision very soon.

DAY 42
Roosevelt to Helper, UT
76 miles

IT WAS GETTING HARDER to push myself in the morning, and I rode out of Roosevelt late. I took my book, *The Cellist of Sarajevo*, with me to breakfast and polished off another chapter of that captivating story. Back in my motel room, I discovered my rear tire was flat. Damn! It would put my departure that much later into the morning. I didn't leave until the exact minute of the eleven o'clock check-out time.

I rode away, not completely sure of my route for the day. I would need to make a choice in Duchesne, thirty miles west of Roosevelt, where I had a choice of two routes to Spanish Fork, just south of Provo. My new Italian friend, Sandro, was planning to go north; I was undecided. According to two local residents I consulted in the Duchesne grocery store, the southern route was 23 miles shorter, but had a significant and difficult pass; the northern route also had some pretty difficult climbs, but they were spread out over a longer stretch. They added that the southern route was, by far, the more scenic. My decision seemed easy: if I was going to have to climb yet again, I might as well choose the shorter, more scenic route. I would ride over the pass to the town of Helper, before heading north again into Spanish Fork and Happy Valley. Unlike past days, this time I called ahead for a motel reservation since by now it was early afternoon. I knew I had a tough stretch ahead and I didn't know when I might arrive. I didn't want to dribble into town after dark and take the chance that every motel advertised "No Vacancy."

The description of the route was correct—the ride to Helper was spectacular. It was spectacularly beautiful, spectacularly brutal, and spectacularly exciting. The first 28 miles went up and up between tree-lined canyon walls, old abandoned homesteads, a small stream, meadows and an occasional cow pasture. It was long and just steep enough to make me hurt, but it didn't rise to the level of punishing. Had the climb continued in that fashion I would have been fine, but suddenly, about three miles from the summit, the grade increased dramatically. It was so steep I had to carve "S" patterns across both lanes of the road to keep the bike moving.

After Trail Ridge Road, I simply had no desire to keep climbing passes like this. The summit was at 9,114 feet and included the steepest section of the whole trip. When I reached the top I was completely humbled; though I would have avoided it if I could, I realized that six weeks before I would not have had strength to grunt and grind my way over a pass like this. I shook my head and marveled at how strong my body had become. I wondered out loud, where had that kind of grit and determination come from?

I caught my breath and looked out over the large expanse of rugged mountains that lay before me. That last stretch had almost defeated me, but I was at the top, victorious. I had conquered the mountain. I dropped my cycling shorts, pulled out my proud member, let out a sigh, and marked my territory with an arcing stream of yellow, steamy urine. It felt so good and so primitive. *Let every sniffing creature know—this mountain belongs to me! I own it!*

I mounted my bike yet again and discovered that the descent was as steep as the ascent. I did my best Franz Klammer impersonation as I sliced around the curves, picked up speed on the straightaways, and sped down the mountain as if it were a giant slalom course. I passed vehicles with a surge of pride and felt my ego begging for admiration from the drivers—who must have thought I'd eaten stupid for breakfast.

I reached the town of Helper through a narrow rock canyon that deserved more pictures, but I wasn't about to interrupt that wicked, adrenaline-producing descent. I had good feelings about this town. Even the name, Helper, made me feel at ease, imagining a quaint, friendly community where the residents had nothing better to do than sit around the local diner, shoot the bull, and help out the occasional tourist passing through.

I entered the dark, ramshackle motel office where a smoking clerk was barely visible in the corner.

"Hi, I'm the guy on the bike that called earlier from Duchesne—Brian Heron," I said.

"Oh yeah. Guess what?" he said, lifting the cigarette just clear of his lips. "We had another room open up if you want it. Save you five dollars."

That took it from $25 down to $20. "Sure, I won't turn down saving a few dollars."

"We cleaned it up pretty good. It should be all set for you," he said, proffering a scrap of paper. "Here's the password for the internet if you need it."

"Thanks." I was desperately in need of a good bed to crash on, a hot shower, and a restaurant that didn't know the meaning of portion control.

He gave me the key and I wheeled my bike over to the room. I should have seen the signs of things to come before I walked into my "special rate" motel room. Outside, guests stood before Weber grills heating up. Rusty tricycles and broken-down bikes were strewn around the parking lot, and the guests seemed more neighborly than the casual acquaintance one forms just passing through town. I opened the door to an over-crowded, haphazardly thrown together room. Disappointed by the quality of the room, I stepped into the bathroom to do my business.

"Goddammit!" I muttered. There in the toilet bowl was someone's left-over shit dissolving away into a blended soup-like mixture. I flushed the toilet. "What the hell?" I yelled this time. A tilt of the handle only left the sickening mass swirling around as if to taunt me into a further fit of anger. But I was desperate. I used the toilet, pretending it wasn't any worse than an un-emptied Porta-Potty on a hot August day.

Anxious to feel somewhat like a human again, I stripped my sweaty cycling clothes from my body and let out a sigh as I stepped into the shower to cleanse myself of the day and the toilet cooties. I reached for the shower knob. "What the fuck?" I muttered. The knob had come off in my hand. I replaced it and gingerly took my shower, trying not to knock the knob off repeatedly. After drying off and putting my civilian clothes back on, I retrieved my computer to search the town for restaurants. The password I was given didn't work. "Of course, why should I expect anything else?" I seethed. I walked out, turned right and headed toward what seemed like the main drag.

Luckily, the night improved from there. A large sign advertised a brewery just a couple of blocks away, where I consumed a large steak and potato dinner alongside an extra-tall mug of local ale. Just outside the doors on Main Street, the town was holding its annual Arts and Crafts festival. I meandered through the booths, grabbed some Indian fry bread slathered and dripping with honey, and lay down on the green park lawn as bands played for the few hundred folks gathered there to party. The evening was as good as my arrival had been bad.

But what had triggered such a violent eruption of frustration and anger at the lack of sanitary conditions and the disregard for the most minimal standards of a wayside inn? For that I had to dig deeper. That "goddammit" hadn't just been directed at the motel management, although they certainly deserved it! No, that choice word was directed at life and meant to give God an earful for not playing by the rules.

Somewhere along the way, I had made a pact with life. I had agreed—with no one in particular—that I would ride over mountain passes and cross hot deserts in order to change the world. I'd committed to doing everything and anything it took to ensure my children wouldn't grow up in a broken home as I did. I had made a pact with the members of my church that I would sit with their sick children, I would sing at the bedside of their dying parents, and I would stay up all hours of the night to make sure that when I preach and teach, they experience just a hint of the taste of God.

A pact with life; a pact with God. I'd promised to put my heart and soul into ministry, family and life. I promised not to hold anything back. I'd ride my bike 4,000 miles if needed. All I asked was that God hold down his side of the bargain. All I asked was that if I was going to sacrifice myself for others, the least I could expect was to be taken care of. All I asked was that if I was going to bust my butt for God, at the end of the day I could at least expect a working toilet, a hot shower, and a safe place to lay my head. With tears of frustration I pleaded, "Goddammit, God, really, is that too much to ask?"

I was not in a good place. I went to bed, first checking for used heroin needles and wondering what kind of critters might be crawling around in my sheets. I wanted to be taken care of. Where was Kathy now with her ginger snaps and cold Coke? I didn't want to be out here anymore. I was lonely, angry and resentful.

DAY 43
Helper to Spanish Fork, UT
63 miles

FROM THE MOMENT I WOKE UP, I had a bad feeling. I already felt sick to my stomach from the night spent in what felt like a room that had served as a last-ditch option for desperate one-night-stands or quick drug deals. I was shaken by the experience. I wanted to restore some normalcy and went in search of my usual biker's breakfast. I didn't find a single diner and had to settle on throwing a breakfast together from the convenience store a few blocks from the motel. I got the calories I needed from juice, coffee, and a microwaveable breakfast burrito, but it wasn't what I was hoping for. I wanted someone to take care of me—a waitress serving me, refilling my coffee as needed, and checking I was enjoying my breakfast. I was working too hard not to have someone pamper me a little.

I thought about the day ahead and the feeling of foreboding grew. I knew I was going to ride forward—the feeling wasn't going to deter me. Yet I wondered, "Is something going to happen to me today? Am I going to crack up on the side of the road as I push myself into a mental meltdown? Am I showing signs of psychic fracturing and will today provide the unwanted answer?"

Such thoughts should have scared me more. But I didn't have enough energy to feel scared—I was sad and numb. I would ride right into the face of whatever this foreboding was telling me. But it wasn't courage—simply resignation, like a criminal standing before a judge waiting to be sentenced. I was getting ready to ride over a psychological cliff.

I started up the road beneath the towering rock chimneys characteristic of this part of Utah north of Arches National Park. I knew I had another 25-mile climb to work my way over, but the map convinced me that the altitude gain was much less severe than the day before. My bigger concern was that the temperature was already up into the eighties, which meant later in the day I would likely be riding in near 100-degree temperatures again.

Ten miles into the ride, my premonition became reality. Suddenly I heard a clack-clack-clack sound—something was catching in my front spokes. I pulled off on the side of the road on the embankment leading down to the river and investigated. A bolt that secured my right pannier to my right front fork was severed; I had hit one too many orange cones in construction zones. Now the pannier hung loose.

A funny thing happened at that moment: I suddenly felt very grounded and secure. This minor crisis seemed to pierce all my projected worries and force me to focus on what was right in front of me. The severed bolt and the loss of one pannier called me back into myself. Now I had something real to deal with and my anxieties evaporated just as quickly as the crisis had hit.

I loaded the contents of the defunct pannier into the other three. This created an imbalance of weight distribution, and it took a few miles to adjust to the extra torque I needed to put into the handlebars to keep the bike from veering left. Despite the uncomfortable positioning, the landscape kept my mind engaged. The terrain was softer than the crumbling canyon walls that had loomed above me near Helper. Interrupting the rugged hills were natural stone pyramids, and the occasional cliff looking down on me. Eventually, the dry ruggedness of the area transitioned into the pine-covered forests of the Wasatch Mountains where, even on that hot day in August, a small patch of snow still lingered high up on the peaks.

The town of Spanish Fork lies at the base of the mountains, and just as I exited them, three towering, white energy-producing windmills filled the V-space between the last two hills. I rode by them, glad to arrive at my day's destination. I still had plenty of gas in the tank, but my left shoulder ached terribly from fifty miles of fighting the bike's natural inclination to go left into traffic. With this new pain, though, I noticed that the pain from my displaced rib had evaporated. Whatever the Christian masseuse did in Craig had worked, despite her prediction that I would probably have to ride with the pain until I returned to Portland.

As I rode down the final descent below the windmills, being two hundred vertical feet above the town gave me a vantage point from where I saw dozens of identical church spires, often only a few blocks from each other. It was late Sunday afternoon, and I hoped to find a bike shop that could remove and replace the severed bolt to my right pannier. Unfortunately, Spanish Fork didn't have one. The two closest towns, Provo and Payson, had bike shops, but I was told they were closed on Sundays. *Of course*, I thought, *this is Mormon territory!*

I couldn't get my bike fixed overnight, and I still needed to decide whether to tackle the Nevada desert and the "Loneliest Highway in America." It was time to take a breather, slow down, and gather myself. My bike was limping; I was recovering from two tough days on the bike, coupled with 100-degree heat each day. And I was still shaken from the grotesque and unsanitary conditions of that motel room, which had left me feeling abandoned by the world, or God, or life—or something.

Remembering the experience in Helper, I decided to spend a few extra dollars on a motel room where I could count on a clean, working toilet and wouldn't have to check the sheets for left-over drug paraphernalia. It cost me $170 for two nights, but I didn't care, I was going to treat myself well. Next door was a restaurant that specialized in barbecue. Perfect! I would refuel both my stomach and my soul with good barbecue and a beer or two. I ordered dinner and asked about the beer selections.

"Beer?" puzzled the waitress. "We don't serve beer here. We're a nice family restaurant."

My shoulders sank. I really wanted a beer. Wouldn't someone give me what I wanted?

DAY 44
Spanish Fork, UT
Rest Day, 23 errand miles

I'M NOT AN ALCOHOLIC—at least I don't think so!—but one of the first things I did in the morning was search the yellow pages for a restaurant or pub where I could look forward to getting a beer later in the evening. The pickings were very, very slim, but I finally settled on a place called Buns and Brews, imagining a cozy little pub, specializing in sandwiches and burgers served on home-baked bread, with a small selection of ales on hand.

Satisfied that I'd taken care of that, I focused on figuring out how to repair the broken bolt. Payson was nine miles south and was said to have a couple of bike shops, so I rode down there mid-morning and landed at Downhill Cyclery. A young, optimistic woman was handling the shop. She wasn't sure how to remove the bolt, but was glad to let me use the tools. I made numerous attempts to remove the severed bolt with vise grips, but it wasn't budging. She referred me to another specialty shop just two blocks away.

Utah Trikes was a mail-order shop that specialized in three-wheeled recumbent bikes (the type you can sit back on, like a recliner chair). They also offered me tools to handle my puzzling challenge. Unsuccessful, I asked if they had any more ideas. Bryce was sent up from the basement. I knew immediately that he would succeed: he had the same determined, problem-solving spirit that my engineer dad has. I could tell Bryce didn't know exactly what to do either, but that he would figure it out. A half-hour later, he'd drilled the severed bolt out of the socket, and left me another bolt and the tools to put it all back together again. They refused payment for this out-of-the-ordinary service, but I insisted that Bryce be compensated for getting me back on the road.

With a full afternoon still open and no intention to get back on the road until the next morning, I meandered back toward Spanish Fork. On the way down, I'd seen a large temple that showed more eastern influence than western. I couldn't imagine it was Mormon, with all the circular architecture and domes; I had to check it out. I rode up the graveled driveway, to where the temple stood on a short hill overlooking Happy Valley. I had arrived at the very first Krishna temple built in Utah, right there among a population completely dominated by the LDS church and Mormons. In their literature, I discovered that the Radha Krishna sect is the monotheistic arm of Hinduism, which is sometimes called the religion of 330 million gods. The experience was almost surreal, as if an alien ship had run out of fuel above Utah and landed right there between Spanish Fork and Payson!

I took off my shoes, wandered around the gift shop, and walked upstairs to their worship space. The room was almost completely empty with the exception of Hindu statues on each of the four walls. In the corners, smaller altars were placed to soften the angularity. The energy of the room was all pulled toward the center, the ceiling coming to an apex. It was a sacred space meant for meditation, reflection and worship. I took pictures, being careful that what I did honored the space. I stood for a few seconds before each statue, made sure I had internalized its effect, and then snapped a picture as a way of saying thanks.

I thought back to my childhood encounters with white-clad, shaven-headed Hare Krishna adherents at the old Stapleton International Airport in Denver. As I would approach the entrance where they were handing out flowers, I'd leave a twenty-foot gap between us—they were too foreign and weird for me then. Now I felt a little pang of grief. In my short visit, I had discovered the Hare Krishnas' beliefs resembled the values of our Christian tradition more closely than do the capitalistic, consumer-driven values of our society. I was struck by how often I'd heard them described as a cult (and therefore to be avoided), while we consider the sex-saturated advertisements of our media normal.

It was nice to have a leisurely day. Odd that it took a broken pannier to get me to slow down. I had no need to hurry, after all I had just a few miles to ride back into Spanish Fork, where I would locate Buns and Brew, and make some decisions about riding through the desert. I already felt I knew what I was going to do. Having my bike fixed and ready to go had given me a small shot of confidence, but I needed to make sure I wasn't just making an impulsive decision. I would have dinner first and then come to a final conclusion.

I took a few minutes back at the motel to replace my bike rack and make sure the repair job was going to hold. It felt like new again—sturdy and secure. With the address in my mind, I rode the few blocks to Buns and Brew.

"I can't friggin' believe this," I exclaimed as I rode up. It was closed. It was a buns and brew restaurant sure enough, but the buns were homemade buns for breakfast sandwiches and the brew was a reference to coffee.

A Mexican restaurant close by looked popular and busy. I went in, hoping they would have a beer to balance the spicy food. No such luck! I settled for refillable diet Cokes. I toyed with getting a beer for the motel room later, though it wasn't what I really wanted. I gave up on that idea too when I discovered that convenience stores in Spanish Fork sell beer, but only in six-packs. They didn't want a drunkard like me coming in to buy one beer in a paper sack! Instead, I raced over to Cold Stone Ice Cream, ordered a double sundae and called it good.

It had been six days since I'd left Steamboat Springs nagged by the feeling I was about to hit a crossroads. That day had finally come: there was no sense in riding any further toward Nevada unless I was committed to crossing the desert. I pulled out my maps and connected to the internet to familiarize myself with the 500-mile section looming large before me. First I checked the weather forecast. A heat wave was expected in the next few days, driving temperatures from the mid-nineties that I'd already been riding in, into the low hundreds. After Delta, Utah, towns were spread out between 65 and 90 miles apart. There were no services, rest stops, or watering holes between the oases listed on the map.

Logistically, it felt doable. As long as I planned well each day, I should be able to leapfrog from town to town. It would require packing about eight liters of water, as well as a full day's worth of food and snacks each day. That's about twenty extra pounds to carry, but at least as the day wore on I would be eating and drinking my way through it. I wasn't too concerned about whether I could manage to cycle across each day's little wilderness—I was more concerned about the psychic fatigue of attempting to do it day after day for a full week.

As the day wore on, however, I became convinced I had to do this. A new purpose had risen like yeast in me. I had left Portland over six weeks ago committed to playing out the theme of crossing a wilderness, as I believed it was the right metaphor for the 21st-century Church. As I neared the desert, it didn't feel right suddenly to take a slice out of this circular pilgrimage. I was leaving home and returning home, and the wilderness seemed like a piece I had to face. How could I authentically say I'd gone down into the belly of the whale on this mythic journey if I bypassed the desert? I would never feel I'd done it justice. My mind was made up; my heart was set. And my stomach was a little nervous.

I went to bed in a good place, ready for the next leg.

PART SIX

The Wilderness

August 23 – September 1

The beginning of the desert.

DAY 45
Spanish Fork to Delta, UT
88 miles

I TOOK OFF, TELLING MYSELF, *this gets to be my trial run for the Loneliest Highway stretch in the Nevada desert.* The distance between Spanish Fork and Delta was just less than ninety miles, but promised both the heat and the largely barren land that I could expect in Nevada. In that stretch, there were four places where I could fill up on water and pick up a few snacks. I would have the distance and the heat of the desert, but without the risks.

With the first pedal strokes, I knew my body felt rested. I weaved through Spanish Fork, marveling at the number of Mormon churches and steeples. I saw two Mormon churches literally across the street from each other. It didn't make sense to me until I realized that they were probably in different wards, and thus served two neighborhoods split by one street. Once I exited the town, I had a luxurious ride through farmland south of Spanish Fork in Happy Valley. For twenty miles I rode by tractors and well-groomed crops in an area I imagined required hard work, amid a lazier, less complicated lifestyle. I reached Goshen, a quiet little town that has barely grown in the last two decades. I stopped at the convenience store for my usual Gatorade, water, and snack refill.

"Hey, any idea whether the road in the distance goes up over the mountain or turns and follows the base?" I asked, directing my question to a woman casually dressed in a white t-shirt and jeans. She and the female clerk were comparing notes about common acquaintances.

"This road here?" she asked, pointing west.

"Yes, this one that seems to disappear part way up the hill."

"Yeah, it goes up over the mountain, but it's no more than a mile to the top," she said. "Where are you from?"

"Portland and heading back that way now."

"Oh, I love Portland, I've visited friends there. But I don't know if I could live in the city. The traffic is so crazy."

"The traffic can get bad," I agreed, "but I love the restaurants and theaters. Any night of the week I can take the Max light rail to a theater pub, have dinner and watch some artsy film. It's pretty fun."

We talked for a bit about Portland, and then I said, "Tell me about Goshen."

"Goshen is just Goshen," she said with a shrug.

I loved it. She'd told me nothing—and everything!

With years of racing experience behind me, I know roughly how much energy it takes to conquer a short one-mile climb. I like pushing myself and coming to the top of a rise spent, but energized. I hit the bottom of the hill and started cranking my way up. At one mile, I was still looking for a sign that I was close to the top. I pushed on. One mile became two miles, two became three, and still I kept pushing, thinking the top had to be only another hundred yards. I kept pounding on the pedals. Three miles turned into four, and it was a full five miles before I saw the crest that told me I was at the top. By then I was lightly cursing my new friend down the hill. I doubt she'd ever ridden a bicycle over that hill.

I had punished myself too early and too hard. I still had sixty miles to go, and the heat of the day to contend with. Of course, it was my own fault. My old competitive racing juices had kicked in and I couldn't resist a Superman romp to the top.

I used the rest of the day's ride as training for the desert. As I'd already over-exerted myself, I committed to pacing myself through the remaining sixty miles, practicing discipline by drinking one full water bottle every ten miles to ward off dehydration. I stopped briefly in two towns that were as close to ghost towns as I've seen: Eureka and Lynndyl were nearly empty except for a small convenience store, a burger joint, and the obligatory post office. Main street buildings stood empty and ready to conflagrate with the first errant cigarette butt. It was easy to imagine a time when miners filled the bars, and stores carried staples and supplies. But those days seemed decades past.

After Lynndyl I continued my trek to Delta, monitoring my body's response to the heat, then right at a hundred degrees. With fifteen miles to go to Delta, I was shaking my water bottle to get the last drops out. Even one bottle every ten miles was not enough, a bit of information I filed away for the next day when I would load up for my first day in the desert. I was glad of the trial run.

A cheese factory five miles from town saved me from further drying out. I ate free cheese samples, loitered in the air-conditioned lobby, and gulped a 32-ounce Gatorade. Including that bottle in my hand, I had consumed 240 ounces of liquid (equivalent to twenty cans of soda), and calculated I would need a full eight liters strapped onto my bike in the morning.

There was plenty of the afternoon still left when I rounded the wide sweeping turn into Delta. I found a motel that seemed clean and reputable, which had become more important to me since my experience in Helper. I unloaded my gear in the room, took a shower, and put on the one pair of civilian clothes I had brought with me: green shorts, black t-shirt, and Teva sandals. I left my room in search of a good dinner and hopefully a beer; it had been three days since I'd had a good beer after riding in the heat.

Walking out of the motel, I ran into Sandro and his two-person support team. Sandro knew just enough English to shake his head and say, "Too hot. Way too hot!"

"Yes, and we haven't even gotten to the desert yet," I reminded him. He walked away, still shaking his head.

DAY 46
Delta, UT to Border Inn, NV
90 miles

THIS WAS IT. I had finally reached the Loneliest Road in America—a 409-mile stretch of road even motorists are warned not to embark upon unless they are ready for the nothingness that exists. I stopped at the grocery store in downtown Delta and prepared for the first leg, a 90-mile challenge. I anticipated it would take close to nine hours. I filled my two water bottles, bought three liters of Gatorade, and another four liters of water. I stuffed four bananas, two apples, six Cliff bars, a one-pound bag of trail mix, a small jar of peanut butter, crackers, and beef sticks into my pannier and jersey pockets.

I set off, crossing the overpass above the train tracks. Seven miles west of Delta sat the small town of Hinkley, which clearly catered to the farming community with garage fronts sporting scattered tractor parts and four-wheel-drive trucks parked haphazardly. Just outside town, a sign warned: "Next Services—83 Miles."

If yesterday was a trial run, today was the initiation. This time I had to get things right. I wouldn't have the benefit of a convenience store or a well-placed cheese factory to save me if I ran out of food or water.

I was aware of riding away from civilization, just as I had been in Wyoming. But the Wyoming high desert still had a softness to it—this felt stark and empty. In Wyoming, cars breezed by me only every five to ten minutes. On other remote sections of the mountains where little traffic came by I had still enjoyed the sounds of a nearby stream, the wind lightly blowing through the trees, and birds squawking at me. Here there was nothing. The silence was overwhelming, as thick and heavy as a hot humid day in Texas. I understood what people meant by a deafening silence.

My eyes followed a semi-truck after it passed me in order to study the contours of the road ahead. I could see the faint line of the road veering off into a mountain. Did this road follow a canyon through the mountain or climb up over the ridge? I watched as the monster truck became smaller and smaller, eventually disappearing before it reached the turn in the road. I started to play a game: I would guess how far it was to some landmark like a crook in the road, a rock formation, or a change in the color of the earth from brown to alkali white. I was usually off by a factor of two: two miles was actually four and five miles was ten. Without the benefit of vehicles, trees or buildings, my brain could not accurately fathom the vastness of this empty landscape.

I had spent so much time in the days before preparing for the challenge of the desert that I hadn't even considered what gifts it might bring. I'd assumed that the vast, dry emptiness would be sobering at least, and potentially frightening. I was wrong. As I settled into the day I found myself soothed and comforted by the landscape. True, it was also unnerving to be in an environment that could suck the life out of you in the event of one ill-timed mistake. But the danger combined with its sheer magnitude brought profound comfort. It was the same feeling one gets standing on a rock ledge on one of Colorado's Fourteeners, or kayaking off Oregon's coast as a storm gives its first warning signs.

I pedaled in a consistent rhythm, determined to make it all the way to the Nevada border where the next watering hole was promised. As I got used to pedaling, I began looking ahead to the next day and the day after that. Slowly, I began to understand how being out in this desert landscape for a full week—if I were successful in my attempt— would feel. Something shifted inside. The sheer size of what I was doing and the vastness that still lay before me was sobering. I was not going to conquer the desert in the same way I'd conquered Trail Ridge Road, where I went to battle and beat it by sheer will, grit and determination. Here, I had the feeling that the desert owned me. I would have to take what the desert gave me, and bow to her superiority when her mood turned sour. If I were to cross this desert on a loaded-down bicycle, grace would play as much a part in my success as anything else.

About fifty miles into my ride, I picked up a little speck in my rear view mirror, traveling in the same direction. I watched it closely until finally I made out the outline of another cyclist closing the gap between us. As I began slowly climbing one of the day's few summits, a young man overtook me. He wore a pair of normal summer shorts and a t-shirt, and was riding an average-looking touring bike. Nothing like the decked-out cyclists I'd met in Wisdom, where we all rode up on $3,000 bicycles and gathered at the bar in our colorful jerseys.

"Fancy meeting you out here," I said teasingly as he rode alongside. "I'm Brian."

"Nice to meet you. I'm Ryan," he said.

"Looks like we're heading the same direction. Are we a little crazy or what?"

"I'm kind of liking it," he said. "It's different, but I guess that's why I'm out here."

"Yeah? Why are you out here?" I asked.

"I just needed a big challenge so I decided to ride my bike across the country," he said. "What are you doing out here?"

"Well, I don't know if I needed a big challenge," I said. "I've had plenty of that in my life. But I need to find a new life. I've had lots of losses in recent years, and now my job is going away."

"Oh, what do you do?"

"Presbyterian minister. But the church I'm at is facing closure," I said. "Ministry is getting harder every year."

"Sounds like we have something in common," he said. "I am a Seventh Day Adventist and, honestly, I felt like God wanted me to take this journey."

"No kidding," I said, trying not to swerve into him with surprise.

"Just a week ago I met up with a father and son—well, two sons—who were running across America. They were Seventh Day Adventists too. Raising awareness of the connection between spirituality and health."

"That's cool," he said. "We're a pretty tight bunch. Most of the time I've stayed in my churches or camped on their lawns along the way."

Ryan and I had plenty we could talk about, but he was quieter and more humble than me. I tried more than once to draw him out about the connection between his faith and this trip. But he was content with what he'd shared, and often quietly rode next to me as if to say, "I'm glad to ride with you, but don't mess with my desert experience."

We crested a 6,280 foot summit together. At the top, a group of four men were parked in the pull-out. Ryan and I stopped, wanting to get pictures of ourselves under the summit sign.

"How about some cold Gatorade for you two?" one of the men asked.

"Oh gawd! That would be great," I said. Both Ryan and I had brought enough water, but with the temperatures nearing 100 degrees and our plastic bottles acting like little greenhouses, our water was often just below boiling point.

"Where are you boys headed?" another man asked. I smiled, thinking that while Ryan was young enough to be their son, my gray beard suggested I wasn't that much younger than them.

Ryan said, "I'm heading for the Bay Area."

"Me too," I said. "And then I'll ride up the coast back to Portland."

"Sounds good," the first man said. "We're heading into the Great Basin for our annual week-long campout. We've been doing this pretty near thirty years now. The four of us are brothers," he said, getting chatty. "We grew up in a tight Mormon family and now we're spread out all over the States."

Here was a chance to get more evidence of the change in religious patterns. "Have you stayed in the Mormon church all these years?" I asked.

One of the brothers, with a thick gut and thinning hair, said, "No, none of us stayed with the Church. In fact, we pretty much don't do church at all."

"That's not completely true." A tall man with a good mop of hair spoke up. "My wife and I go to a Unitarian Church."

"Like I said, none of us have much to do with church," his brother replied, teasing.

I laughed at the ironic suggestion that Unitarianism wasn't a religion. "Actually I helped found a Unitarian Universalist Church in California about ten years ago. You're my kind of guy," I told the tall man, and raised my bottle of Gatorade in salute.

Ryan and I expressed our gratitude, remounted, and rode together quietly for another two hours until we reached the "Welcome to Nevada" sign and a little oasis called the Border Inn.

"I'm stopping here for the night," I said. "I hope they'll have a room." I was certain they would; only a couple of vehicles were parked on the property.

Ryan stopped too, but when he got off his bike he looked a little lightheaded. "I'll get a picture of you here at the sign," he offered, "but then I'll head up to that turn-off about two miles away. There's supposed to be a campsite not far from there."

"Don't be surprised if that's actually five miles," I said. "Don't push it too hard." I was adjusting my guesstimates to better reflect reality. My map told me the campsite was three miles from the turn-off he mentioned, and that was farther away than he thought, in my mind. Ryan didn't look like he had close to ten more miles in him. Feeling paternal, I wanted to protect him from what seemed like an over-confident, youthful decision.

I took his picture underneath the "Welcome to Nevada" sign. He left. I stayed.

I devoured a rich, fatty chicken fried steak that night at the restaurant. I sat down with my book, *The Cellist of Sarajevo*, and shut the desert and the ride from my mind. I drank a couple of Miller beers, and when my dinner was finished and I was nearing the end of the book, I ordered apple pie a la mode and coffee.

I was tired from the day's effort, sad and satisfied all at the same time. The desert was cleansing me from the inside out: here, I couldn't run from anything—there was no place to turn except to more desert and emptiness. I finally had permission to face all my losses—divorce, deaths, and a dying profession.

I turned the final page of the book, unaware the author would land one last hard, beautiful punch, a line about radical self-acceptance. I read it and burst into tears.

Two days before, I'd considered taking a Greyhound across the desert; I'm glad I didn't. The desert scared me and yet I trusted it. I was exactly where I needed to be.

DAY 47
Border Inn to Ely, NV
65 miles

I HAD NO IDEA HOW TRUE that statement would become. Just thirteen miles into the first climb of the following day, I looked up and saw an out-of-control car slip onto the soft shoulder in the opposite lane, over-correct, and slam into the embankment on my side of the road. From there it bounced over basketball-sized rocks until a much larger boulder brought the vehicle to an abrupt stop thirty yards in front of me, engulfing me in a cloud of dust and flying particles.

The rocky dust storm quickly passed. I ran over to the car. The driver, a slight, very thin woman with shoulder-length blond hair, sat dazed, confused and shaking. She and I worked together to open the driver's door. I talked to her, all the time watching for signs of shock. I didn't detect any major injuries and she wasn't complaining of any specific pain. She had scrapes, cuts and scratches on her face, arms, torso and legs, and I was sure the next day would reveal some pretty nasty bruises.

She got out of the car. Seeing the crumpled front end, she cried out, "Oh my God! My parents just bought this for me last month. They're going to die!"

"Look," I said reassuringly, "right now we just need to get you some help."

"Oh God, I just got out of drug treatment and this was their gift to me. Oh God, no, God no, God no," she moaned.

"You'll be all right," I said. "Why don't you sit down and I'll get you some water."

"I was just trying to get my cigarette. I dropped it on the floor and I just leaned over to pick it up and suddenly I was skidding all over the road." Her voice wavered halfway between wailing and crying.

I got her seated on the side of the road and offered her a liter of water. Every few minutes a vehicle came by, most of them stopping to offer assistance. There was no cell phone coverage and Ely was 50 miles away, so I asked each driver to call 911 as soon as they could. Between vehicles, the woman told me more about her efforts to recover from drug addiction.

Ten minutes later, Ryan rode up. I was glad to have a little extra help in case the woman fell into shock. We stood and chatted, waiting for help to arrive.

"Guess what?" Ryan said. "I stayed at the Border Inn last night too. It was a lot further to that turn-off than I expected. I finally turned around and came back."

I wanted to say "told you so"—but who could expect a young adventurer to listen to this white-bearded old man?!

Within an hour, a BLM truck came upon the crash site. Since the vehicle had the communications equipment others lacked, the driver immediately radioed for police and other help. A half-hour later the sheriff arrived, and I was able to let him take over.

Motorists were warned not to take the lack of services lightly. Had the woman been severely injured, the results could have been tragic. It was nearly an hour and a half before police arrived and had she needed hospitalization, the ride to Ely would have been nearly another hour. I felt fortunate that my role was limited to keeping her calm, watching for signs of shock, and keeping her hydrated. After a few questions from the police about what I'd seen and done, I was free to go.

The woman gave me a hug. "Thank you," she said. "You saved my life."

I felt that was a bit of an exaggeration. "I was glad to sit with you until help arrived."

She frowned. Grabbing my arm, she tried again to get her point across. "No, I really believe you saved my life. If you hadn't been here with your connection"—here she pointed to the heavens—"I don't think I'd be alive."

I simply smiled, and gave her another hug. "You're welcome. Take care."

I don't consider my ordained status to be a sign of privileged status with God—anyone who knows me understands that. But this was not the moment to correct her perception. She needed to express her gratitude for surviving what must have been a terrifying few seconds as her car caromed off rocks like a pinball. Her perception was not about me, but about how lucky and fortunate she felt.

I left the accident scene a little shaken. Was I in the right place at the right time or was I nearly in the wrong place at the wrong time? The woman believed that because I was there, she was still alive. I believed that because of a well-placed boulder, I was still alive. She seemed to believe in me; I believed in a rock. She believed I had a special connection to God; I was pretty sure God didn't play favorites.

The rest of the day was plain tough. Ryan and I rode within sight of each other most of the way, but we hit a vicious headwind just before making a ten-mile climb. It was busting both of our asses. We had become agitated by the time we spotted a bar—a surprise exception to the "No Services—65 miles" warnings at the border. We stopped for Cokes (actually Ryan had a Sprite as he didn't drink caffeine—such a good Seventh Day Adventist boy) and water, and endured the stares of the local beer-drinking patrons who couldn't fathom why two men would ride their bikes across this forsaken desert.

Half-way up the climb, Ryan had a flat tire. Convincing me that he had it under control, he waved me on. I didn't want to abandon him, but I also didn't want to linger on the hill, in the heat, fighting that hellish wind. The crash had taken two hours out of my morning, worried me by reducing my water supply, put me later into the heat of the day, and sapped some of the resolve I'd begun the day with. I really wanted to get into town.

It was 5:30 in the afternoon when I coasted the final mile into Ely. I was spent from the unexpected events of the day, still slightly shaken from the crash, and feeling sobered and overwhelmed by how difficult it was to cross the desert. Before I had even checked into the Motel 6, I'd made up my mind to take another rest day. It had only been three days since my last, but this three-day, 245-mile, near-100-degree trek had taken its toll. I was certain that if I attempted the next 80-mile stretch to Eureka without more rest, the desert would break me.

I gorged myself on Chinese food and Asian beer, after which I sat in the motel room eating donuts, butter toffee peanuts, and ice cream. Scenes of the woman's out-of-control car careening toward me continued to plague me. Thirty more yards and I would have been dead. I was both sad about what had suddenly unfolded, and thankful at the same time. Did I nearly lose my life? Or did I save hers? Was this a message from heaven that once a minister, always a minister? Was the desert reminding me of who I was?

DAY 48
Ely, NV
Rest Day, 0 miles

THIS WAS TO BE A TRUE REST DAY. I wanted to empty my mind, rest my legs, and shake off the lingering effects of the accident and the devilish wind. The best start would be a family diner serving pancakes, eggs and bacon. I hopped on my bike and rolled down the hill into town. Just around the corner where two highways meet stood the Silver State Restaurant. It had just the look I sought—large, roomy booths, enough patrons to make it feel desirable, but not so crowded that I would feel pressed to eat and run. I bought a USA Today, something I hadn't done on the whole trip. I would read about what was happening in the world beyond my two-wheeled reality, and work my way through a crossword puzzle, one of my favorite leisure activities. At home, I rarely went to bed without completing a crossword.

I finished my biker's breakfast, dove into the paper, and allowed myself to forget the challenges the desert had presented thus far. I had worked really hard to get to Ely. Truthfully, after Trail Ridge Road and the Rocky Mountains I was yearning to settle into a more relaxed, enjoyable pace. But between the remaining mountains in Colorado and Utah, and the long, arid stretches between passes, I was still having to dig deep just to survive each day. I knew I could survive this "loneliest road" as long as I steeled my nerves, gritted my teeth, and honored my limits. But I didn't want to just survive the desert—I wanted to enjoy it.

My mind wandered away from the newspaper. I wondered whether it were possible to get all the way to Portland without using my camping equipment. The last time I'd had to use it was in Dinosaur, Colorado, a full week ago. I closed the paper, paid my bill, and shot back to the Motel 6. I pulled out my maps and laptop, and studied the route. I was already planning to share the experience of my pilgrimage in churches once I crossed over the Sierras into California. It felt appropriate, as I shifted from the "leaving home" phase of the journey to the "coming home" phase. I counted a total of 65 Presbyterian churches still on my route, most of those in the Bay Area. Next, I studied the Warmshowers map and found hosts dotted all along my route from Gardnerville, Nevada (350 miles away), to the Oregon border.

I still had about 25 days on the road. Once I reached the Sierras, I guessed I could depend on Presbyterian hosts and Warmshower homes for most of the stretch back to Portland. On those occasions when neither was available, a motel should be within reach—as had been the case thus far. The only real concern was getting through the desert. I needed to reach each evening's scheduled destination and pray there would be a room open in a motel when I arrived. There was some risk involved, but the advantage was I could lighten my load considerably by sending home a sleeping bag, tent, pad, and cooking gear. I needed something to lift my spirits and shift the ride from an exercise in punishment to an invitation to grace and enjoyment.

I made my decision. With a touch of nervousness mixed with relief, I scoured the local businesses for a large cardboard box. I laid all my gear out on the floor and split it into two piles: what would go back into my panniers, and what would get stuffed into the box headed home. I packed the box, took it to the postal annex, and sent off a full twenty pounds. I had just lightened my fifty-pound load by 40 percent. I wasn't sure this was the wisest decision, but I felt a surge of energy I hadn't felt for weeks. I might find myself stuck between towns with no tent or sleeping gear, but the relief seemed to outweigh the risks.

It wasn't until later that evening that I realized the significance of my decision. I had just physically let go a good deal of my load, lightening considerably the burden I was carrying. Neither had it occurred to me until then that this day would have been the 30th anniversary of my marriage that had ended almost exactly five years before. The five-year mark seemed significant, inviting me to cross a threshold into a new life. I had spent those years overcoming and surviving the effects of the divorce, financially and emotionally—that was all good and necessary. But I had also begun to identify myself more as a survivor of divorce than as a person with life ahead.

I had heard it from friends and family many times: that it was time for me to lighten up a bit, learn to trust, enjoy and depend on others. Was I now being asked to let go of the baggage I'd been carrying—grief and anger over childhood abandonment; divorce; the recent deaths of a mother-in-law and stepmother? Was this pilgrimage an invitation to enjoy the winding, unpredictable road of life?

DAY 49
Ely to Eureka, NV
78 miles

"HERE WE GO AGAIN," I muttered, mounting my bike. I had three passes to climb, and with the predicted heat it was important to pace myself well. I started off a little slowly, as if I'd been drugged the night before; Tour de France racers also experience this the first day of riding after a rest day. Then something clicked. My mind went from calculating miles to enjoying what was right before me. I had a very pleasant climb to the top of the first pass; a gentle tailwind nudged me along, and my bike was much more responsive with twenty fewer pounds to lug.

After coming down the side of the first pass, I entered a long, broad, expansive valley. To the left, a dark sheet of rain descended out of a cloud about six to eight miles off. To the right, lightning and thunder were gearing up less than two miles away—or so I judged, using the

"1100 feet times the number of seconds between lightning and thunder" rule. I rode between these two thunderstorms, watching very carefully which way the wind was taking them. I was a little nervous about being in a landscape with no trees while lightning was striking; I was the tallest object out there. In the back of my mind, I stored the thought that there would be no shame in throwing my bike in the back of a pickup truck if conditions got too scary.

I slipped between these two storms, climbed the second pass successfully, and entered the next long valley before the final pass. The storms continued and multiplied. Finally, on all four sides, fast-moving, threatening storms surrounded me. I was riding right at the edge of one, hoping I would roll the dice right one more time. I didn't. The sky opened and driving rain hit me like little missiles. The pauses between lightning and thunder became almost non-existent, telling me that the lightning was right above me. It boomed and cracked all around, as if I had crawled into an amplifier at a rock concert.

I carried my bike a few yards off the road into a small grove of stunted juniper trees. Once I'd found a spot where only a limited amount of rain was hitting me, I peered out of the branches. For the next half hour, I sat in that overgrown bush while the storm let loose. It was like sitting in a high tech theater! I delighted in the dancing lightning and the booming percussion of the thunder. I felt like a nut, but who cared? I was having the time of my life. If I had a choice between sitting in a church service singing "For the Beauty of the Earth" or hiding in a juniper bush in the middle of a crackling, firework-displaying lightning storm, I would choose the latter.

The storm passed almost as quickly as it had come. When the sky offered another break, I rode on, the rest of the ride becoming an engaging game of trying to outwit the storms. I strategized when to leap forward, when to stall, when to seek shelter, and when to raise the white flag and wave down a passing sympathetic driver.

I came upon only one structure all day: an old, boarded-up house with three trees out front. It was the only shelter I'd seen for miles and the terrain ahead appeared barren of anything but sagebrush. One of those draping curtains of rain hung to the left of the road, but the rest of the sky looked reasonably clear. I pushed forward, unsure whether I was riding into another cloudburst. Ten minutes later I looked behind me, and the house and trees were enveloped in a violent downpour. This was not like Oregon rain that settles in and drizzles annoyingly all day; these storms only lasted a few minutes, but they were like bulldozers coming through, winds whipped up, lightning and thunder surrounding me, and the rain painfully piercing, as if each individual drop had been shot from a BB gun.

Toward the end of the day's ride, I realized how vividly alive I felt. The elements of nature had tested me, engaged me, and challenged me. I had fun playing and weaving my way through the storms, Nature and I trying to outwit each other in a game of cat and mouse. It reminded me of how I'd felt at Lower Yellowstone Falls, when I wanted to lean into the experience of the violent, beautiful water cascading over the cliffs. I felt that God had come out to play, and we had teased and wrestled each other until both of us went away satisfied and spent.

A sign advertising the town of Eureka welcomed me. I felt a little "eureka" in my soul. I had lightened my bike load—and maybe my emotional load—the day before. Eureka was a small, three-block town with a handful of empty buildings. A grocery store, a restaurant and two motels were still operating, and the first motel I tried had a room available; I had arrived successfully at my first destination without camping equipment. Eureka indeed! Only three more leaps of 70, 65, and 60 miles before returning to civilization.

DAY 50
Eureka to Austin, NV
70 miles

IT WAS WORTH ALL THE CYCLING just to work up the appetite to eat as much as I wanted. I had another wonderful plateful at the Owl Café across from the motel in Eureka—thick, dark brown pancakes with molten butter running over the sides of the plate, greasy over-medium eggs and a slab of ham (rather than the wispier bacon I usually ordered). The coffee was not great (no coffee roasters nearby!), but it was hot, and the young man waiting on me refilled it often.

I was more confident about getting through the desert without feeling completely shattered. I had unloaded nearly half my gear and now the length of the rides between these little oases called towns was getting shorter. Plus I was still buzzing from the spirited sparring match with the storms and the gods the day before. Today I would cover just 70 miles, and my Adventure Cycling map revealed that the first forty miles would be reasonably flat. I would need to keep a consistent pace throughout, however, because there was a steep 1600-foot climb, flattening at a false summit before another 500-foot grind to the top. From there I would plunge back down into the town of Austin.

I rolled easily through a long, flat, sagebrush-decorated landscape, broken only by the occasional rocky bluff far off in the distance. My mind went blank. I wasn't pondering anything or working through any nagging issue. I felt very Zen-like—present only to the 90-rpm rhythm of my legs, the heat blowing through me and by me, neither checking off the miles behind me nor anticipating the miles ahead. It was a delicious feeling to allow myself to be present to the pavement below, the dry terrain around me, and the persistent strain and reward my legs were feeding my brain.

By the time I reached the climb I was still feeling pretty strong, having ridden at a pace that left plenty of reserves for the last challenging stretch. For a few miles the road climbed gradually, and I easily found a rhythm that kept me riding up in elevation without putting my lungs into oxygen deprivation. Suddenly, I was at the top of a small bluff dropping to a valley floor that obviously was prone to flash floods when rain occasionally soaked the area. There was no water present, but deep gulleys had been carved out on both sides of the bridge that propelled me from the descent to the ascent.

The ascent was like drawing open curtains to discover a wall. It was too steep to find a rhythm, so I had to shift to my lowest gear and push my way up, pedal stroke by pedal stroke. Missing even one revolution would have been enough to topple me. My Zen mind from earlier came in handy: if I'd projected how far I still had to go to the top I would have been tempted to give up and walk my bike, but I broke it down into small pieces.

I think I can do twenty more revolutions. When I reached that minor milestone I assessed my remaining grit. *I've got at least fifteen more in me.* By the end I was only committing to an endless series of one revolution at a time. My head was bent, my eyes focused on the pavement three feet ahead of my front tire, as I bullied my way up the pass like a buffalo pushing a Volkswagen out of the way. I remembered the false summit, and let my legs recover as much as I could when I reached it, but my stomach was complaining and my eyes felt like they were getting that dead look. I numbed out as much as I could, knowing my work was not done yet. I felt like a child getting ready for a spanking: afraid, yet resigned to the pain about to be inflicted.

While the climbing at the end of the ride was spread out over a fifteen-mile stretch, most of it took place in the last four miles. The pass rose more than 2,000 feet in that span and required me to shift from aerobic exercise to anaerobic. Aerobic exercise relies on oxygen for energy and can be utilized for hours on end; anaerobic exercise uses the body's reserves and can only be relied on for short bursts of activity of a few seconds up to two minutes. Anaerobic exercise produces lactic acid in the body, which quickly causes the muscles to shut down. Plus it is very painful! I played a tortuous game of shifting between the two during the last forty-five minutes of riding. By the end my stomach was screaming at me, the same feeling a mile runner has after completing a race—sometimes vomiting.

As my map indicated, the road plunged down from there. I wished I could enjoy it more, but my body was rebelling and the grade was so steep I couldn't just let my bike go free and let gravity do the work. I had to keep good control of it to negotiate a number of switchbacks into town. The descent was almost as difficult as the ascent merely because I was expecting more ease and didn't get it. "Let up already!" I called out in surrender.

Safely arrived in town, I found a small motel room that could have been used as a mental health safety room. The bed was overly soft and sported six large throw pillows. Full curtains and fluffy upholstery added to the almost claustrophobic atmosphere, even as I enjoyed sinking into the bed. I did nothing for two hours but massage my legs and let my stomach catch up to me again.

By mid-evening I was ready to resume normal activities. I walked one block up to The International Café—an odd name for a restaurant in Austin, Nevada, where the International House of Pancakes (fondly referred to as IHOP) in Reno, 175 miles west, was the closest thing to anywhere international.

I consumed a small pizza loaded with vegetables and added to my mineral intake with a large beer.

While I didn't encounter an international crowd, I did find myself engaged in a number of interesting conversations.

They began with my waitress asking, "What brings you through Austin this time of year?"

"I'm cycling in a big circle through the West. Right now I'm on my way to the Bay Area after cycling for seven weeks," I said, waiting for the—by now expected—"wow" response.

I got it. But she went on, "Are you doing the Loneliest Highway route and getting your card stamped?"

"What card? I'm on the route, but I wasn't aware there was a card."

"Oh yeah," she said, "we get a few cyclists through here who are just doing this route and have cards they get stamped. To prove they did it, you know."

"I guess I missed that," I said. "But I'll have lots of pictures to show off."

"I'd love to do something like that," she said, a touch wistfully. "But I don't know how I would ever take that much time off."

"I'm pretty lucky," I admitted. "The church where I am pastor is giving me the time off and paying for the trip. I'm writing about the shift taking place between religion and spirituality."

"That's cool," she said, her face lighting up. "One of my best friends is a minister. Personally I consider myself an agnostic, but I have better conversations with my minister friend than I do with my best friends. It doesn't bother him at all that I'm agnostic."

I laughed. "To tell you the truth, if you went to my Facebook profile you'd see I call myself an agnostic Christian mystic." That was all the spark our conversation needed. Before she was called to serve other tables, we had flirted with the subjects of the Dead Sea Scrolls, Gnosticism, and absolute truth.

I was starting to think there might be more to the café's name than I'd first thought. Within seconds, my waitress's place was taken by a thin, 20-something fellow with a thick mop of uncombed brown hair. Having overheard my earlier conversation, he explained that he was on his way to the Burning Man festival, and immediately initiated a conversation about rituals and people's need for them.

Bill paid, heading back to my pillowy room, I exited the restaurant through the front screen doors. On the porch, two men were engaged in a lively conversation. It sounded interesting and I hesitated for a moment. That's all it took; they invited me to sit with them. To my right was Kent, a small-framed man who looked like he might have run a marathon or two. He was an emergency room doctor in Boulder, Colorado, and taught science of the mind and philosophy at the university there. To my left sat Eric, in loose-fitting, almost sloppy clothing, the kind that says you fit just fine in Portland. He owned a lucrative dog-walking business in San Francisco, but lived in Austin, Texas. It was as if the café had an exclusive membership. I'd gone from talking about agnosticism and the Dead Sea Scrolls to the place of rituals, and right into energetic conversations about institutional Christianity, new paradigms and worldviews with Kent and Eric.

Finally walking back to my motel room, I mused, *I just spent the evening at The International Café in the middle of sagebrush country.* I hadn't met people from all over the world there, but the people I did meet had their fingers on the pulse of a world much bigger than Austin, much broader than Nevada, and they were more perceptive than any traditional community I had ridden through thus far. It was as if I'd been dropped back in liberal Portland for the evening.

DAY 51
Austin to Middlegate Station, NV
64 miles

PANCAKES, EGGS AND BACON, and an endless cup of coffee—that had become as routine a start to the day as brushing my teeth. After an unusually deep sleep, I walked back to The International Café. My waitress was not on duty; the other characters I'd met had not returned.

But the character of the place hadn't changed a bit. I had just settled onto my stool at the bar when I heard, "A fellow cyclist! How ya doing?"

"Morning," I said, still trying to wake up my body and brain.

"Looks like you're on a long tour. I'm Peter," he said. Peter was lean, kindly and professorial, with a Mister Rogers look and manner to him.

"Oh hey, I'm Brian. Yeah, a pretty long tour. Should be about ten weeks when I get done."

"I'm just passing through Austin this time, but a couple years ago I did this same route through the desert," he said. "I loved it."

"I *think* I'm loving it too. It's hard, but I've never experienced anything quite like it," I said. "This is a sort of spiritual pilgrimage and the desert has been an important part of it."

"A spiritual pilgrimage? Have you heard of the Camino? I walked that a few years ago."

"In Spain? Yeah, I know all about that," I said. "One of my hosts on this trip did the Camino on bike last year, and a member of my congregation in Portland made an attempt on it recently."

"It was one of the best experiences of my life. As a Catholic, it was the only big, once-in-a-lifetime thing I wanted to do," he said.

We had made a good connection. We shared our love of bike touring, pilgrimages, and religious devotion (although I think he was more dedicated to his Catholicism than I was to my Protestantism). We wished aloud that Christians would be as dedicated to religious pilgrimages as Muslims, who flock to Mecca by the millions. I liked talking with someone who spoke my language.

Just outside Austin, I had a choice of staying on Highway 50 and the loneliest road, or detouring to Highway 722, the original paved section of the Lincoln Highway—the first transcontinental highway built for automobiles in 1922. The distance was slightly shorter on the older highway, but besides offering less traffic (not that there was much as it was!), it held curvier roads, and steeper ascents and descents.

I will almost always pick the more scenic road given a choice, so I made the turn off Highway 50 and looked ahead. A road as straight as a yard stick was laid out before me, in one of those views where the actual distance was double what my brain was registering. At the end of what I guessed to be a ten-mile stretch, the road snaked up into the mountain. I smiled: I was begging for another hilly challenge by taking this route.

Other images flashed into my mind, like being transported to the Willamette Valley of Oregon for this same ride. I could ride ten miles, stop for a little pinot noir wine-tasting, ride another ten, sample a glass of crisp chardonnay, ride another ten, and repeat this cycle until either I'd finished the ride or the alcohol had finished me. It was fun to think it, even though I knew I'd never follow through. I have a nasty habit of passing things like wineries, hot springs, and so on, because I love to feel my body in motion on the bike.

But my mind was telling me something. While my legs continued to push through the miles, I was becoming mentally fatigued. The desert was hard and exhausting; the delicious emptiness effectively forced me to examine in intricate detail my own psychological land-scape. But it was punishing in the same way that sitting in a therapist's office for hours on end could be. I was ready for a break. I wanted to escape the watchful, piercing eye of the desert. I wanted to ride through green rows of vineyards, sit in the sun, and drink wine. I wanted to arrive home after a long day of work or riding, sit in my recliner, read the paper, work my way through a crossword, and watch my favorite Blazers play. I even yearned for the cool, foggy coast of Oregon—an aspect of northwest living that I've complained about from the day I arrived in 2002.

The climb turned out to be more refreshing than challenging. At the base of the mountains, the road rose through a canyon with a small stream running off to the left, and a few pine trees sparsely populating the steep hillsides. The road wound around rock outcroppings, up over dry meadows, and above the canyon beginning to fade into the distance. My eyes hadn't feasted on that many visual delights since entering Nevada four days earlier. It was refreshing, even if temporarily, to have a few curves in the road again, some trees to break up the terrain, and a small stream reminding me that life did exist out here.

An hour later I reached the top, crossing a large cattle guard. Below me lay an almost perfect slalom course, as the road snaked softly through a thinly forested canyon. I knew I could let gravity do the bulk of the work while I concentrated on carving my way down the road with clean lines, so as to keep my speed as high as possible. I felt I'd been given a gift—even though what had taken sixty minutes going up would disappear in less than ten as I catapulted down the mountain at close to forty-five miles per hour.

I re-connected with Highway 50 and cycled the last few miles until the outlines of a small assortment of buildings appeared on the horizon. I reached Middlegate Station 64 miles from my morning starting point, still feeling strong and fresh. I could have cycled another 25 or 30 miles, but Fallon, 60 miles farther still, was the next possible destination with services. Since deciding to ride without a tent and sleeping bag, I needed to take advantage of any place that had lodging. My body wanted to go further, but my mind intervened—I stopped.

Middlegate Station advertised a motel, but the term had been loosely interpreted. My room was better than a tent, but the walls were not much thicker. I would swear they were simply wood paneling tacked onto two-by-fours. I heard every phone conversation, every raspy breath, and every sniff and fart from my next-door neighbor.

Middlegate Station in many ways was a special treat; I don't think it had changed much since being built as a stagecoach stop in 1850. It had changed hands many times, most recently in 1984 when, with the aid of the county, it underwent restoration. As I sat on an old worn stool at the bar, I ordered a Coors beer, watched a little football on the TV screen above the whiskey bottles, and mused over how unusual I felt in there. There were mustached men wearing cowboy boots and hats, and weather-worn gents who had clearly lived and worked on this land for most, if not all their lives. It was the kind of place even the usual tourists didn't stop. Traveling by car, they may have looked at the worn-out western buildings and decided to drive the extra sixty miles to Fallon.

But as out of place as I must have looked, I felt the same way I had at the summit earlier in the day. I'd been given a gift to be able to experience this old stagecoach stop first-hand. I ordered a hamburger and fries and drank another Coors beer before retiring to my paper-thin-walled room. I snuggled into a thinly covered bed and soon realized that my neighbor's head was no more than twelve inches from my own. I went to sleep with the rhythm of his breathing matching mine.

DAY 52
Middlegate Station to Fallon, NV
59 miles

I LEFT MIDDLEGATE STATION after a greasier version of my usual breakfast and coffee that was as weak as tea but not as good. I rolled out from my dry and dusty stay-over, and soon crested a small hill just minutes west of Middlegate Station. Before me lay a starkly barren stretch. I'd become used to the scarcity of trees over the past six days—in some places even the sagebrush had difficulty growing. But as I surveyed what lay ahead I thought, *there is desert and then there is desert!* as I tried to absorb the sheer immensity of a valley made up of thousands of acres of sand, nothing but sand. Until this point, the barrenness of the desert had strangely held me, as if I were riding in the palm of God's hand. This didn't feel that way. It had death written all over it—overwhelming, suffocating heat and a landscape that seemed to scream, "I dare you."

I knew to just keep my pedals turning and my mind focused on patiently making it to the other side—the town of Fallon, my next oasis. Before I had a chance to react, an older sedan nearly side-swiped me, the passenger-side mirror barely missing my handlebars. The carful of young yahoos leaned out the window and yelled, "Fuck you. Get your ass off our road, mother-fucking biker!" They sped off laughing, proud that they had waved their metaphorical cocks in my face to prove how big and superior they were.

I flew into a rage. I pierced the air, shaking my fist with my middle finger extended, and yelled obscenities back at them. They were long gone, but I continued in full rage mode for ten minutes until I had no anger left in my tank.

I'd had a number of close calls during the trip and over my three decades of serious cycling. But most of the time near misses are the result of drivers doing their best to negotiate the space between me, traffic coming from the other direction, and the impatience of drivers behind them. I may become annoyed at drivers who aren't patient enough to wait until a safer opportunity presents itself, but I rarely get angry. But that carful of genetically stunted, lobotomized jerks really pissed me off. There was no other traffic on the road. They had two full lanes to work with, yet they purposely edged right over to the shoulder, measured the space between me and them, and swooshed by intending to produce the maximum effect of terror. It caught me by surprise and, because I was already feeling vulnerable, took me over the edge. I wasn't sure whether I hoped to catch up with them later or not. I felt capable of "accidentally" knocking off their mirror, looking at them and saying, "Oops. I didn't realize I was so fucking close! Sorry!"

A few miles of barren terrain later, I heard the high-pitched scream of military jets. Signs appeared every few hundred yards, saying in red letters: Do Not Trespass—Military Exercises. I stopped in a little pull-out and tried to follow the sounds of the jets. Finally, I spotted two of them. I watched as they swooped down from the sky and leveled out for just a moment. When they shot back up into the sky, small puffs of dust would explode from the ground below—I was riding at the edge of a bombing range. I was intrigued, but it added to my feeling of vulnerability. This was a scary place.

I wanted to keep going. A large sand dune, more like a mountain, loomed on my right. It looked to be only a few hundred yards off the road, but the size of the dune was disorienting. For five or six miles I followed signs to Sand Mountain Recreation Area, a dune of 4,795 acres, and stood at its base, marveling at the massive size of it. I wondered why I hadn't made space for more detours like this.

As I neared Fallon, this severe section of desert gave way to irrigated farmland. I rode by military compounds, an increasing number of buildings and homes and, for the first time in over a week, green grass, farmland and pastures. The only green I'd seen for days was lime-flavored Gatorade. I relaxed. I was coming to the end of the Loneliest Road in America.

It was another short day of riding and I was soon pedaling my way down the four-lane highway into the middle of Fallon. I had time to explore and handle a few small errands. I located the laundromat and took an hour or so to wash all my clothes. I found a fairly cheap motel run by Indian Hindus, who had placed a number of religious icons around the lobby. Once again I was surprised to see signs of our pluralistic, global and inter-connected world right here in the middle of Nevada. I rode around town on my bike without my gear and felt especially free. I had just crossed the desert and was feeling very relieved. And normal again. I asked about restaurants and was directed to a

Mexican restaurant close to the center of town. It was a dressed-up restaurant meant for sitting, talking and drinking, rather than the run-of-the-mill Mexican restaurants where the ambience lags behind the quality of the food. Here the food was excellent and I lingered long, enjoying more than my share of homemade tortilla chips, a couple of beers, chicken fajitas, and deep fried ice cream.

My mind finally turned to what was ahead. I had secured lodging in Gardnerville for two nights hence with a Warmshowers host, another Warmshowers host in Vallejo, California, and six churches in the Bay Area were working on arrangements to hear my story and host me. I still had a short section of the Nevada desert to cross, but the route promised at least five intersections where small convenience stores and gas stations would likely be located. I breathed a sigh of relief as I imagined that the worst was behind me. Carson City was only sixty miles away. I would be getting back to civilization.

I had done it. I'd crossed the desert—or so I thought.

DAY 53
Fallon to Gardnerville, NV
81 miles

I STARTED THE MORNING feeling both hopeful and relieved. After eight days in barren and spirit-sucking hot terrain, starting in Spanish Fork, I'd reached Fallon, the first place to sport a little green for over five hundred miles. Quietly celebrating having crossed the desert, I parked my bike in front of Jerry's Restaurant, a bustling family restaurant that looked out to the highway. I ordered my usual pile of pancakes, eggs and bacon, consumed a tall glass of orange juice, and kept the overweight waitress busy refilling my coffee cup. Seeing my bike outside, she commented that she and her husband had just purchased bikes for their family of four to get in shape. As I paid my bill, she grabbed me. "Can I get a picture with you?" she asked. "I want my husband to see this." Another waitress took the snapshot—for inspirational purposes, I guessed—and I was off again.

Well fed, I looked forward to a fairly casual day of about sixty miles to Carson City, a small town sitting at the base of the Sierras just below Lake Tahoe. There I would be able to find a bicycle shop where I could pick up another tube of chamois butter (a wonderful salve that limits the degree of painful saddle sores) and electrolyte tablets that dissolve in my water bottles. And in Gardnerville the next day, I would have nearly a full day of rest before crossing the Sierras back into California.

I was only ten miles out of town when an older man crossed the road on his bike and waved me over.

"Hey, I live just a few miles from here," he said. "You can stop for water if you want."

"Thanks," I said, "but I pretty much have what I need."

The man was on a clandestine ride. He'd been injured in Vietnam and had occasional lapses of memory and cognitive function. His wife had forbidden him to go out without her.

"The old lady's gone into town," he said, with a conspiratorial wink. "If I don't get out on my bike every so often I'd just go crazy."

"I know what you mean," I said, though I had the feeling that how he meant "crazy" was a little more clinical in nature than I meant.

I soon rode beyond the more lush irrigated land right around Fallon and re-entered a softer version of the desert. The land was still barren of trees, but light brown grasses now covered the hills, rather than sagebrush or sand. Occasionally I'd ride past an old abandoned homestead where livestock grazed. It was still the desert, but there were signs that I was edging closer to civilization again.

Where Highway 95 crosses Highway 50, I stopped at the convenience store/gas station for snacks and water. Great! For a full week (with the exception of the one surprise saloon) I'd had to carry a full day's supply of food and water, as there were no watering holes between the little oases separated by 65 to 90 miles. As I sat outside the store eating Pop Tarts and drinking water, up rode a rough-looking teenager. He couldn't wait to tell me what he was doing.

"Hey! I'm riding my bike too."

I smiled at his enthusiasm. "Great. How far you riding today?"

"This is my half-way point. It's fifteen miles here and fifteen miles home."

"That's pretty good. Those are some real miles," I said, wanting to be supportive.

"Yeah, I've been working up to this for quite a while. I quit smoking in March."

"Hey, good job," I said, really wanting to encourage this young man.

"I started smoking when I was nine," he said, "and I just decided I better quit before it gets me."

I was impressed. "Keep at it. That smoking is nasty stuff and if you have to have an addiction it's better to be addicted to exercise than nicotine."

He waved and took off. I'd now met three people who talked of how important cycling was to their physical and mental health. Coincidence? Maybe it was a sign I was returning to something close to normal life.

The road continued in a southwesterly direction pretty much in a straight line from Fallon to Carson City. But something changed. Whether it was more open terrain or a shift in air pressure, I don't know. I do know I was faced with a brutal, punishing, directly in-your-face wind. Three-foot grasses were bending as close to the ground as possible without being broken or uprooted. My speed dropped from an average of thirteen mph to a grinding eight mph. On the steepest climbs over the Rockies, I was often held to an average speed of six mph, meaning I was now creeping along barely faster than when cycling over a mountain pass.

I kept looking at my rear tire to see if it had punctured and I was riding on a flat. But my tires were fine—I had to accept I was facing a devilish wind that felt like riding through molasses. For thirty miles and almost four hours I put my head down and concentrated on each pedal stroke, knowing that even a short pause would bring me to a complete stop. I started out cursing the wind and then found myself yelling to no one in particular, "Who the hell's idea was this anyway?" Finally, I began psychically shutting down. The thing about pain is that our bodies can only endure so much and at one point I simply went numb. I refused to feel my body and my eyes no longer cared about the scenery. My world collapsed into a small rectangle that started with my front tire and ended about six feet in front of me.

I was as close to being broken by the riding as I ever had been.

And then suddenly it ended. Completely unaware of the terrain unfolding before me, I came over a rise, the road turned 90 degrees away from the wind, my bike picked up speed on its own, and I coasted the last five miles into Carson City. It was the first bit of grace I'd received all day. A few tears escaped from my eyes as I allowed myself to feel again. But I was only getting started. The tears soon turned to sobs, my whole body convulsing with pent-up emotion, anger and grief.

The sudden, unexpected relief after nearly four hours of punishing riding was the obvious catalyst for the waterworks. But I felt the tears came from a deeper place. Maybe I had finally allowed myself to feel just how difficult those last days were in the desert. I had ridden through it—but at what cost?

Was I finally allowing myself to cry out the grief of all the loss I'd experienced in recent years—divorce, deaths and near financial collapse?

Was I finally grieving for the loss of identity associated with ministry? This pilgrimage had its origins in my realization that I had happened to land in professional ministry as one world was slipping away, but before another world was born. I often felt I was straddling two worlds, not really belonging to either.

I was also grieving for long-time members of churches whose lives were tied up in seeing their tradition survive. I felt the sadness of those who had left churches, but still sought an open, welcoming spiritual community where their unique journeys would be affirmed.

I grieved for myself. I grieved for those who felt their churches were dissolving away. I grieved for those who desired an authentic spiritual community, but couldn't find one.

The unexpected day of punishing riding was like my life: just as I thought things were getting easier, a wind blew in and said, "Not so quick. I'm not done with you yet." And so I cried. Then I sobbed. I sobbed all the way down the hill into Carson City.

If the downhill was a gift and the shift away from the wind was a bit of grace, then that theme continued. Gabe, my Warmshowers host for the next night, called as I entered the city limits.

"Brian, I see that you're expected in Carson City tonight. We aren't that far down the road. If you want, you could show up here tonight and get a full day's rest tomorrow."

It didn't take long to make up my mind. I knew that another twenty miles would push me, but now I felt some hope. The wind was crossing me at a ninety-degree angle from the east and I had hosts who were ready to take care of me if I could just pedal for another hour or so.

"That would be great, Gabe. I have to pick up a couple of things at the bike shop, but I should be there before dinner," I said, nearly crying again at the prospect of comfort.

I rode the final miles emotionally spent, but relieved in body. I was riding along Highway 395, a stretch I'd driven at least a dozen times while serving as a juvenile probation officer in the late 1990's. Even back then I'd said, "This is a place I could live." The handful of towns are all nestled right at the foot of the Sierras. Lake Tahoe is just a thirty-minute drive and Reno, the largest city in the area, is less than an hour away. As a cyclist, the combination of mountains in one direction and rolling desert in the other is perfect. On any day, you can grind your way up the mountains and be rewarded with a screaming descent, or choose a long endless road and power along, much like a train in open country.

I pedaled laboriously to Gabe's home. He and his wife lived just outside Gardnerville in a newish subdivision of southwestern-style homes that complemented the desert-like surroundings. Their windows framed the Sierras perfectly to the west. The layout of the home was roomy and comfortable, with just a touch of unostentatious luxury. It had retreat written all over it. I collapsed into the evening and later into my own private bedroom.

The day had nearly crushed me and then offered me grace. Like my life.

DAY 54
Gardnerville, NV
Rest Day, 17 errand miles

BEFORE I HAD A CHANCE to fully wake up, Gabe interrupted my coffee time. "Are you interested in going up in a glider later today? We don't need to do it now, but I need to reserve a glider if you do."

I've always had a weak stomach. I remembered a small plane experience years ago that had left me blue in the face, my stomach acting like a Yellowstone steam pot. I also knew this was an opportunity I could not miss.

"I'd love to," I shot back, eyes wide with excitement and fear.

I discovered that Gabe, my host extraordinaire, was a professional glider pilot. For years, he'd commuted monthly from Missouri to Nevada to work at the outfit, Soaring Nevada, as an instructor. Finally, he convinced his wife to move to Nevada so he could more easily continue his work, and they could enjoy the spectacular terrain and mild weather of the Carson Valley.

I spent the morning taking care of personal business. My beard had become scary looking—the kind that makes parents grab their toddlers' hands and steer them away. I found a barber shop and waited my turn, while an older man finished getting his hair cut and a mother instructed the barber just how much hair her primary school-aged son should have removed to look respectable.

Looking more respectable myself, I next rode around town looking for the old office I used to visit when supervising my juvenile caseload as a probation officer. The Rites of Passage (ROP) boot camp was a little over an hour east of there in the desert—a location meant to discourage the charges from running. The office no longer existed.

I sat at a deli and took some time to write about the prior day's experiences. While cycling I tend to live on Cliff Bars, bananas, nuts, and chocolate donuts when I can find them. I felt normal sitting down and enjoying a turkey sandwich with chips and a Diet Coke.

The afternoon was reserved for my glider ride with Gabe. I was nervous even as I pretended calmly to prepare. I knew my stomach would likely protest. But eyeing the gliders, I also realized that the space reserved for the pilot was narrower than a movie theater seat and enclosed by a clear plastic cover just a couple of inches above his head. In addition to having a weak stomach, I can get claustrophobic in enclosed spaces. I'd once been shut in a folded-up trailer space by my so-called teenage friends, who locked the door and abandoned me. Ever since then, I haven't liked being enclosed in a tight space. The glider looked little better than a casket.

Gabe put me in the front seat and I began meditating, trying to keep from freaking out as he lowered the plastic shell over my head. Down it came. I closed my eyes and breathed in and out, resisting the urge to start screaming and throwing a tantrum. The tow plane hooked up the cable to the nose of the glider. We taxied down the runway and within a matter of seconds were lifted into the air. I relaxed and started looking at the squares of farmland, horse ranches, and luxury homes far below.

After the tow plane released us, Gabe spent the next 45 minutes gliding over glistening Lake Tahoe, swooping up and down above forested mountains, and tilting side to side as we surveyed Carson Valley below. Gabe allowed me to steer for a couple of minutes—I was glad when he resumed control. After a couple of playful sweeping turns, Gabe could tell that my stomach wasn't going to last much longer. We made our way down and gracefully landed on the runway as if stepping off the last rung of a ladder. Nothing to it. I spent the next few hours drinking 7UP, lying on the green grass and waiting for my stomach to find equilibrium again.

The irony of my two different days in the wind was not lost on me. I laughed at how the wind had brought me to the point of cursing it and life itself the day before. Then, in the glider, I was struck by Gabe's expertise in using the power of the wind to lift us higher in the sky, swoop playfully like a bird testing her wings, and turn the wind into a graceful friend rather than the ugly enemy I had experienced the day before. Even listening to Gabe talk about wind was an experience. He rattled off information about updrafts and downdrafts in a rapid-fire staccato, all with a gleam in his eye. He even used the word "spiritual" when referring to what the wind meant to him.

I started to feel bad that I'd taken my experience so personally the day before, as if the wind was targeting me and only me and took pleasure in punishing me. Yet further reflection made me realize that if I asked myself not to react negatively to the wind one day, I shouldn't have a positive reaction to it the next. I settled on the thought that to be engaged with each day and with life, I needed to feel whatever I felt. One day I resented the wind and life for its harsh treatment; the next I was singing its praises and full of joy at the way life sometimes tickles us with delight. I decided that life or God didn't want a white-washed version of me, but all of me—my most honest, raw, and authentic self.

It took most of the afternoon and evening for my stomach to return to my body. But the day continued to heal the wound that had opened the day before when I'd felt so crushed. I spent another night in the guest bedroom that was as good as any luxury hotel. We enjoyed a delicious lasagna and salad meal, and sat round the table drinking beer, jabbing and teasing each other as we discussed cycling (of course), religion, Catholic priest abuse, and politics. While we did not see eye-to-eye on every issue, our conversations were engaging, fun and energizing. This was how it was supposed to be—diversity and dis-agreement held softly in the context of curiosity and mutual respect.

The day was not quite over when we retired to the expansive living room facing a large screen television. I had missed nearly the whole Tour de France while on my trip. Gabe ran through his list of recorded shows and pulled up the stages of the race that had determined its winner. I sat on their soft couch letting the cushions enfold me, rel-ishing this short but wonderful respite where I had nothing to do but receive the care and hospitality of my hosts. It felt wonderful to be taken care of—exactly what I had yearned for way back in Helper in the motel from hell.

I needed the pampering. The next day I would face my fifth and last mountain range on the trip: crossing the Sierras at Kit Carson Pass with an elevation of 8,574 feet—nearly 4,000 vertical feet higher than my Gardnerville layover.

PART SEVEN

Return Of
The Prodigal Son?

September 2 – September 11

First Presbyterian Church in San Anselmo, CA.

DAY 55

Gardnerville, NV to Placerville, CA
110 miles

I WAS ALMOST SORRY TO LEAVE in the morning. Riding a bike every day for dozens of miles—sometimes in a duel with a mountain, sometimes trying to survive a desert terrain—is really hard work. I had enjoyed a day and a half of letting others pamper me a little, attending to minor details like a bank stop and a beard trim, and enjoying the luxury of time to write and reflect, all in the comfort of a home built to take full advantage of the mountain views. I could get used to it! I lingered over saying goodbye.

"Okay, Brian, let's get some good pictures," Gabe said.

I posed first in front of their home and then with the Sierras as my backdrop, leaning against my bike and smiling.

"Your turn," I said. Gabe stood arm-in-arm with his wife as I snapped some reminders of our time together.

"You have to promise me to let me know when you get to the other side tonight," Gabe said. "Okay?"

I felt he was treating me like a father concerned about the safety of his over-adventurous son. "I will," I promised. No one else had made the request, but I wanted to honor his concern for me and the connection we'd made in our short two days together.

I leaned my bike against their garage door. Gabe and I embraced, he patting me on the back. Gabe handed me off to his wife and we embraced. I tried not to linger too long in her arms: it felt really good. I had come out of the desert in more ways than one.

I had about ten miles of riding through pastoral farmland that followed the base of the mountains south before turning west on Highway 89. I felt anticipation and apprehension about the day's climb, but settled into a nice rhythm as I prepared mentally for Kit Carson Pass. The Sierras are a very different experience than the Rocky Mountains in Colorado, where it can take a number of days to successfully pass through and over them. The Rockies present a number of passes that must be conquered to negotiate from one side to the other. In contrast, the Sierras are much easier, quickly rising about 4,000 feet from the Nevada side and then dropping almost to sea level over the next 80 miles on the western side. One massive climb and one long descent and you're done.

I neared the turnoff signaling the beginning of the mountain challenge, made the turn, and began to ascend. The farmland dissolved away, the foothills serving as transition from desert to mountain. Green, irrigated farmland was replaced by the harsher grasses and sage of the foothills. It wasn't long before I entered the first rocky canyon leading to the summit. It was rugged and steep terrain, but a stream cascaded briskly to my left, and the sage was replaced by a forest of tall pine trees.

I dug deep to match the steeper grade. Then a funny thing happened: my breathing deepened and my body relaxed. I felt a sense of relief—I was coming home. Not in the sense that I was nearing the Bay Area or was one day closer to my final destination in Portland, but that I was back in the familiar terrain of the mountains. There's a ruggedness and a temperamental nature to mountains that one must respect. Although they require a deeper, gut-level determination to cycle through successfully, the terrain and the landscape reflects something deep in my soul. The air is thinner, yet I found myself breathing more deeply and freely. I had to gear up for the climb, yet my body actually relaxed.

I was surprised how easily I pedaled up to the 8,574-foot Kit Carson Pass summit. Only twice did the steepness require me to rely on gutsy reserves to power my way up. For most of the ascent, I settled into a nice climbing rhythm that I could have carried on all day.

I crossed the summit and began celebrating the fact I was rolling down toward the Central Valley of California. I'd conquered yet another pass on this gargantuan, 4,000-mile, slightly crazy journey, and had successfully ridden over five mountain ranges. As I descended, I was surprised that a subtle sadness overtook me. I had just put the last major pass behind me and already I was grieving at leaving the mountains. Already I was thinking about the next time I might pedal to the base of a mountain and anticipate working my way through miles of rugged granite canyons, looking back over the valley thousands of feet below, and breathing in the fresh, thin mountain air just below the heavens. Having recovered the feeling of coming home on the Nevada side of the Sierras, I was already grieving as if leaving home again on the west side.

I had just passed the crystal clear Silver Lake, below peaks that still held a few patches of snow on their barren tops, when I stopped for lunch. A young family took the table next to me. Before I knew it, they were offering me their home when I arrived in Placerville later that afternoon.

From there, the ride became more complicated than expected. It was already going to be the longest day of the trip so far, but a couple of wrong turns and backtracking added more than an hour and ten more miles to the trip. One last steep hill before Placerville nearly busted my butt, and I limped into Placerville feeling like a wrung-out rag.

I pulled out my phone to call the young family and let them know I'd arrived late and would be staying at a motel; they had young children and I didn't want to upset their routine—nor did I want to have to work around their routine. I opened up my phone and saw that I'd missed a call from Gabe.

"Hey, Brian," the familiar voice said. "Gabe here. I haven't heard from you. Just making sure you're okay. Thought you'd be over the mountain by now. Please give me a call when you get this."

I called him back and explained that the trip had taken longer than expected, but I was safely in Placerville. I enjoyed the subtle hint of parental concern.

I settled into a comfortable motel room, took an especially long, hot shower, and sat on the bed working the lactic acid out of my legs. When I had enough energy to move again, I coasted down the road to the first wave of restaurants.

I chose a sushi restaurant, thinking if the food was as good as the Asian decor it was going to be a treat. The waitress, a thirty-something woman with short brown hair, a roundish figure, and a friendly personality, seemed to give me extra attention. After discovering that I'd ridden 110 miles that day, she said, "Well, let me know how I can take care of you."

"Thanks," I said, "I'm really looking forward to some good sushi." Something in her tone told me there was a little flirtation going on. I liked it—but all it really did was make me yearn for that elusive thing called home. I didn't want a one-night stand, I wanted a place to be known and belong. Even if I'd wanted to take the bait, I had no energy left for playfulness. Once dinner was done the only companion I wanted in my bed was sleep.

I pedaled resentfully back up the hill to the motel, exhausted. Only after completing the last routine chore of the night—brushing my teeth—did the significance of the day sink in. I was moving into another stage of this pilgrimage. I had crossed the Nevada desert and was now in California. I'd just conquered the last mountain range.

The next day I'd be in Sacramento, where I would eat dinner with a local pastor and begin a series of stays with Presbyterians—the group I had ridden away from eight weeks before. It was time to shift gears. Time to share my story with the Presbyterian community.

DAY 56
Placerville to Sacramento, CA
64 miles

I WAS ASLEEP BEFORE ELEVEN, yet I still didn't wake up next morning until half past eight—nearly ten hours of dead-to-the-world sleep. Even awake I moved slowly. Rather than rush out to have breakfast, I made the small pot of weak coffee provided in the room. I did a little floor yoga, checked emails, and scanned the internet news for recent big stories. In other words, I procrastinated. I didn't want to move. I used every minute available until check-out, timing it almost to the second.

I needed a place that was still serving breakfast, even though it was nearing the lunch hour. I spotted a nondescript breakfast franchise a few blocks from my motel—they were sure to still be serving breakfast. I ordered a waffle, two eggs and bacon, along with coffee. The food was as forgettable as the building: the waffle had the flavor of cardboard and was only saved by a flood of high-fructose corn syrup. The worst part, however, was that the waitress seemed to forget that the room she'd put me in existed. After plopping down my plate as if feeding the hogs, she disappeared. I'd already drained my first cup of coffee. I ate, keeping a watchful eye for her. She didn't return. Finally, as she cleared my plate and handed me the bill, I got the second cup of coffee. I felt like I was back in Helper, Utah, where my motel room had not demonstrated a single shred of care. Dammit! I wanted someone to nurture me.

I remounted my bicycle and made my way through town. Cycling slowly through Old Town Placerville, I rode by a handful of quaint breakfast establishments with brick-layered patios, umbrellas, and planted flower beds serving as the boundary. I kicked myself for stopping at the first place I saw. I'd gotten needed calories at the waffle house, but it hadn't fed my soul in any way at all. I shook my head, said *shit* under my breath, and turned my mind and soul to the cycling ahead, knowing it would feel more nurturing than my morning experience.

The elevation from Placerville to Sacramento drops another 2,000 feet over a 65-mile stretch. While that doesn't paint a picture of steep descents, it does lend itself to a casual and leisurely style of riding. Gravity does at least ten percent of the work, and it feels like a stronger friend is riding alongside you with his hand on your back, giving you that little extra push. In addition to the pleasantly easy elevation loss, Sacramento has one of America's finest biking/walking trails. The American River Bike Trail follows the slowly flowing water all the way from the town of Folsom, 32 miles east, into downtown Sacramento. While I hadn't had too many difficulties with traffic, it was still nice to be on a stretch where I didn't have to worry about a car drifting into the bike lane, or taking a right turn in front of me—or encountering a carload of jerks.

I rode alongside the river and vicariously enjoyed all the river enthusiasts rafting, kayaking, swimming, and picnicking in the dozens of parks lining the river. I entered Sacramento proper and had a chance to resurrect my old time-trialing skills as a young woman sped by, clearly in training as a racer. I picked up my pace a bit, and for the next ten miles we played a game of cat and mouse; I overtook her and quickly became the mouse as she chased me down. No words were spoken, but it was clear she didn't want an old man outracing her. I enjoyed the temporary resurgence of competitive juices that had been part of my life three decades earlier.

It took a number of phone calls to locate my dinner host's home, but I finally arrived as they were putting the final touches to a dinner for five. I joined the Barnes family for dinner and was struck (maybe even overwhelmed) at being thrust abruptly back into the world of church. Around the table were Reverend Barnes and his wife, and another couple from the church who would act as my night-time hosts. Reverend Barnes was an enthusiastic, creative, and visionary pastor, with strong ideas about how to transform his aging congregation to one of the emerging, spiritually diverse, experimental congregations of younger generations. But I was troubled by the spirit of our conversation. We were battling the same issues. He knew the church was not sustainable as it stood, and was using every ounce of his energy and creativity to open up a new conversation. But our conversation was laden with a thick blanket of grief and desperation, unlike the conversations I'd had with dozens of people on the trip. They were asking new questions and weren't burdened by an institution they had abandoned years before. In those conversations, I had felt we were teasing out exciting possibilities.

Reverend Barnes and I made plans for morning worship, and he ran through the bulletin, showing me where I would take a role. His hope was that my presence would introduce his congregation to the language and world of those calling themselves "spiritual, but not religious" as they wrestled with what it meant for them and their church.

I left the Barnes' home, and put my bike in the back of the truck of my overnight hosts. They lived a few minutes away, directly across from the church where I would speak the following morning. We sat around their dining room table and talked about church some more. Linda brought me all the way back to my initial conversations in Oregon when she said, "We raised our two children in the church, but they drifted away in their late teens."

"Uh-huh," I said, having heard the same story hundreds of times.

"Yet our children are two of the most spiritual people I know," she added.

"You aren't alone," I said. "All over, I've met people who have adopted the basic values of church, but see no need to step into the building."

I went to bed that night feeling ambivalent. I was honored to be asked to speak at the church about my experiences. But I wondered if I'd held some grandiose hope that I would ride my bike for eight weeks over 3,000 miles, across five mountain ranges and one deadly desert, to be lauded heroically. That I would bring back some treasured truth that would either save the Church or establish me as the foremost expert in the death and resurrection of mainline Protestantism.

In fact, nothing had changed. I had busted my butt on this pilgrimage and the Church was still the same old Church.

DAY 57
Sacramento to Vallejo, CA
68 miles

SUNDAY MORNING. For the first time in eight weeks, I woke up ready to prepare for worship leadership, as I had hundreds of times over my professional career. In many ways, my preparation had been done on the road in the weeks beforehand: my only role in the service was to lead some of the liturgy and be available for a Q-and-A sermon about my pilgrimage.

I had been instructed by Reverend Barnes to wait until I heard the processional hymn before making my entrance. I stood with my bike on a covered patio, out of sight of people filing into the church. I heard the first few notes of the grand old hymn, *O God, Our Help in Ages Past,* and hopped on my bike. Down the center aisle I rode, in place of the usual choir entrance. It was the first time I'd ever ridden my bike into the sanctuary as an act of worship; I'm sure it was the first time the congregation had ever seen it. Only if it was Palm Sunday and we were retelling the story of Jesus entering Jerusalem draped across the back of a donkey could it have been better. I dismounted and took my seat up in the chancel area, where the pastors generally sit. I felt almost naked: rather than the white, flowing preacher's robe and colorful stole, I was clad only in tight-fitting cycling shorts, a red and black jersey, and my Jesus sandals.

I looked out over the congregation; the feeling that had overwhelmed me the night before returned. The pews were maybe twenty percent full—about twenty-five individuals were scattered around sanctuary built for 150. I saw the usual blue-rinsed and white hair, mixed in with a few decorative Sunday hats worn by some of the older women.

Reverend Barnes and I breezed through the usual liturgy of announcements, responsive readings, prayers and hymns. When we reached the sermon, he introduced me as a nationally recognized cyclist. I immediately flushed. True, thirty years before I had qualified for the National Championships twice, but now I was just a guy with an ambitious goal, fighting for my place in a religious world that was eroding. Especially after sensing how little impact my pilgrimage had on the world of church, such recognition as a national figure seemed dramatically overblown. But the pulpit wasn't the place to correct him and I let it go.

He forged ahead into the Q-and-A. "Brian, what has been the most significant thing you have learned on the pilgrimage?"

"There is a whole shift taking place," I said, "that could be fairly represented by saying we are moving from religious adherence to the exploration of spirituality. If you want evidence, just go to your local bookstore. While our churches are dissolving away, sales of books on religion and spirituality are exploding." I fleshed out my theme.

Next, the minister asked, "And what was your most challenging experience on the road?"

I recounted how, on the other side of the Sierras, the wind on the last day in the desert had nearly crushed me, leaving me sobbing as I coasted down into Carson City.

"And the most enjoyable?"

"Trail Ridge Road in Colorado," I said, almost tearing up at the memory. "It's the highest paved highway in the world. When I reached the top, even in my exhaustion, I was so elated by what I'd accomplished. I was thinking of that youthful Brian who had climbed it twice before in his twenties, and how impressed he was that this old man with a gray beard had conquered it carrying fifty pounds of gear."

The reverend continued the worship liturgy while I sat up front, patiently waiting for it to end. While he spoke, I watched a father and son ride by the church on their bikes, enjoying that sunny, warm, Labor Day Sunday morning. *Which of us is really honoring the spirit of worship?* I thought. *The father and son out for a Labor Day weekend ride? Or us in our pews, facing the cross and praying to a god we think we know?* I was doing my duty by bringing my story back to the church, but my heart was out there with that father and son.

I left the service thankful to get back on the road, where I could feel the sun on my face and the breeze tickling my skin. I was thankful for Reverend Barnes' enthusiasm and dedication to transforming one of our struggling, dying churches. But I rode away feeling that the Church does not need pastor/saviors. I had a clear vision that what many churches needed were ecclesiastical hospice chaplains. Images returned of the burned forests of Yellowstone Park, and the sagging homesteads I'd ridden by in most states. One message penetrated my thoughts: *We have to let go. We have to allow Church as we know it to die.*

As I left busy Sacramento, I rode through rolling brown hills covered with patches of oak trees. In the valleys between the hills, dozens of small vineyards and wineries piggy-backed on the success of nearby Napa County. It was familiar terrain, as I'd ridden in hills very similar to this while living in Lake County, about eighty miles northwest of there.

I rode to Vallejo on the northeastern edge of what constitutes the Bay Area. It was strange to be riding into a metropolitan area; with the exception of Sacramento, Boise was the largest city I'd ridden in and that was seven weeks earlier. Most of my riding was in the solitude of mountains, across lonely prairies, and in barren deserts. The towns I'd encountered were more the Lake Wobegon variety, where arriving felt like walking into someone's home. This was a wholly different experience: an urban wilderness as tricky as the desert to negotiate, but for different reasons.

I had contacted a Warmshowers host while in Nevada. Bruce had agreed to meet me a couple of miles from his home and chauffeur me to his place. I called him as I entered Vallejo and told him my route. As I coasted down a hill, I saw a cyclist climbing easily up. He waved and negotiated a quick u-turn to join me for the final blocks.

"I don't have a guest room, but I've set up my garage to host guests," he said; here was the real deal.

"That's fine," I said. "I'm just glad not to have to sleep on the ground. And to meet good people like you."

He opened the single-car garage door; the place was loaded with bicycles, old tires, spare parts, and a work stand. It wasn't as comfortable as a motel or luxury guest room, but it was perfect—a cot crammed in between racing bikes and extra wheels.

I treated him to an especially tasty Thai dinner at a restaurant close to his home. We talked about bikes, a little about the pilgrimage and its themes, and tours that he'd taken. Back at his house, he pulled out his own malted brew; it was dark and syrupy. I'm more of a bitter IPA kind of guy, but I wanted to honor my host and take advantage of all the rich experiences offered by my trip. I took a taste and must have shivered.

"You don't have to drink it," he said.

"No, it's fine," I lied. "Just a little darker than I usually drink." I forced it down a sip at a time, as if I were drinking eight ounces of cough syrup. I loved the experience—but not the taste.

Once I was alone on my cot in the over-packed garage I felt sad, and I didn't think it was the effect of the beer. It had something to do with being back in church. I had a full week ahead of staying in the homes of fellow Presbyterians and speaking about my pilgrimage. But if my experience from the morning was any indication, I was riding back into the church world as the bearer of bad news. Not only did I not have any revealing and hopeful answers, I wasn't sure the church even wanted to hear what I had to say. I felt very alone.

DAY 58
Vallejo to San Anselmo, CA
27 miles

IN THE MORNING it was still there—a gray cloud hanging over me that wasn't going away. It was foggy outside, but this fog was in my heart and soul. I hoped my mind could do some sort of mental or spiritual gymnastics to put a different spin on what I was feeling. But there was no way to sugarcoat this: if I were to stay in the ministry, my focus would be long-term congregational hospice work.

The Church is based on a Christian narrative of death and resurrection. Everyone loves Easter and the story of resurrection, but shies away from Good Friday and crucifixion. I felt I would be spending the rest of my career living within the themes and metaphors of Good Friday. I would walk with churches in the final stages of their ecclesiastical life. Even on good days, death, grief and letting go would be somewhere in the air or nipping at our heels.

I thought back to the very beginnings of the pilgrimage when I'd met with Christine. I had started the pilgrimage with the unconscious hope that I would somehow be able to beat back the waves of grief beating at the walls of the Church and professional ministry. I had some naive and idealistic hopes that I could outrun it, or even use it to my advantage as I conquered rugged mountain passes and emerged victorious from the mouth of a desert—like the one last contestant on *Survivor*. Now, rather than being a passing wave of anxiety, this grief seemed only to expand and deepen.

I'd been riding on open road for weeks and, despite the gray emotions, I was looking forward to a day of varied riding as I negotiated the bustling streets of San Francisco. My destination was Marin County, just north of San Francisco, and the small town of San Anselmo. A second-year student called Nick, who had been contacted by a local pastor about my trip, had offered to put me up for the night in his seminary apartment. To get there, I would cross the Bay in a ferry, travel through San Francisco, do the obligatory ride across the Golden Gate Bridge for the photo opportunity, and then make my way through Sausalito, Marin City, Mill Valley, Corte Madera, Greenbrae, Larkspur, Kentfield, and Ross—all small villages—before arriving in the equally quaint town of San Anselmo.

This was an important part of the trip: I was married in San Anselmo; both my children were born at Marin General Hospital in Greenbrae; my ex-wife, Lisa, grew up there and her parents lived there the entire time I knew them. I graduated from seminary in the area, and many of our closest family friends on Lisa's side had lived in Marin County. I had wonderful memories of Christmases and birthdays shared with those people, who were more like family than mere friends. The longing for belonging that I had carried since childhood was often met by this rare group of family friends.

Not for the first time on this trip, I needed to discover how much of home still existed for me in this place where much of my adult life, family, and career was shaped.

I drowsily rolled away from my temporary garage home. It was just a five-minute jaunt to the ferry terminal, where I bought a ticket. Fifteen minutes later, with a strong cup of coffee in my hand, I was sitting on the ferry, enjoying the cool, misty air as I sat back in one of dozens of chairs lining the windows on deck. It was almost surreal—allowing another vehicle to transport me. For eight weeks straight I'd woken up, packed my gear, mounted the bike, and waited for my body to adjust to the reality of cycling all day. This morning, with the exception of the short trek to the terminal, I sat motionless. The stark contrast with previous days made me realize suddenly how hard I had pushed myself throughout the trip. I was a little scared of getting used to letting someone else do the work; I was nearing the end of my trip, but I still had 800 miles to go, including all of Northern California and the entire coast of Oregon. I felt tired, really tired.

With all my gear around me, I was an easy target for curious travelers. Two fellow cyclists meandered my way, both about my age, looking fit and happy.

"Where are you going?" one of them asked.

"I'm heading home now—to Portland. I've been cycling for eight weeks, throughout the West," I said, trying to downplay the immensity of the trip.

"Wow, that's quite the trip," the woman said. "Just for fun?"

I described my arrangement with the church and my area of inquiry. To my surprise, she immediately brightened.

"I'm so glad someone is studying this! I'm Amy, by the way."

Amy and I talked while her buddy looked on, interested, but quiet.

"I work with young adults, Brian, and there's a whole generation who are passionate about their spirituality. I see them taking on causes for social justice, the environment, and human rights, much as our churches have done for decades."

"I know," I agreed. "The churches I work with keep asking, how do we get young people into our buildings?" Almost simultaneously, Amy and I shouted, "That's the wrong question!"

"It's not about getting them into the church," Amy said, beating me to the punch. "It's about passing the traditions of the Church to another generation."

My deep, intuitive sense that the rest of my professional life would be about helping congregations grieve, let go, and die had weighed heavily on me. That conversation with Amy didn't change the facts, but it did give me some hope. If the Church as we know it had to die, at least there was a generation—largely the Millennials—ready to accept the mantle, according to Amy. The form would be different, but the mission would be the same. I was thankful for the people of East-minster, who had embraced this process of letting go and passing their ministry to the community. Their church would close eventually, I was sure of that, but in the meantime they had partnered with the community to open a homeless shelter on their site and build a 100-plot community garden.

I disembarked from the ferry in San Francisco. It was only mid-morning, giving me a full day to cover just twenty miles. That meant I could follow whatever whim struck me. I sat for nearly an hour on a bench near the ferry terminal and snacked, as I adjusted to seeing man-made skyscrapers rather than towering rock formations. It felt almost like jet lag, this sudden immersion in a new world. Later, I meandered through the streets and came upon a Labor Day criterium bike race. A criterium is a race that is usually on a short city circuit of maybe a half-mile. The riders go round and round in a race that features a number of all-out sprints for prizes. Crashes are common as riders slip around the corners at high speeds, sometimes clipping a wheel or hitting a small crack and sliding across the pavement in a crumpled mass of metal and flesh. Although I'd won a few criteriums in my younger days, I never did get used to riding in a pack of sixty riders averaging close to thirty mph and separated by six to twelve inches.

While wandering around the course, I walked through the sidewalk tables of a corner deli. *Perfect*, I thought. *I can sit here, have lunch, and watch the race.* A luxurious hour passed quickly as I ate my turkey with cranberry croissant sandwich, while spandex-wearing, multi-colored streaks whizzed by me with the rush of wind a large pack of riders creates.

From there, I moved in slow motion through the famous Pier 39 and Fisherman's Wharf, watched street performers, and stared at the masses of people, representing every country, every language, and every style of dress imaginable. My Adventure Cycling map took me along the bay in front of the colorful Mission District, through the busy Great Meadow Park, and along the San Francisco Bay Trail before reaching the base of the Golden Gate Bridge. I cornered an Asian tourist and we made a quick pact to take each other's pictures—he with his family, me with my bike, with the bay behind us and the monstrous, famous bridge above.

I cranked up the short, winding hill to the southern end of the bridge. I was having a threshold moment: I'd had one in Loveland as I returned to my home town and made my turn west. Two days later it had happened again as I crossed the summit of Trail Ridge Road, the highest point on my trip. Now I was about to cross the Golden Gate Bridge, a national icon that people travel from all over the world to see and take the nearly two-mile walk across. Plus, my grand circular tour was now turning north: Portland was 800 miles straight up the road, and two to three weeks away.

I coasted across the bridge slowly, partly because it was unbelievably crowded, but also because I wanted to allow time for memories to surface. I remembered walking across the bridge with my infant son in a backpack on one of many day trips we took when I wasn't in class. I recalled excursions with visiting friends and family, when my ex-wife and I acted as tour guides and treated them to the not-to-be-missed Golden Gate Bridge stroll. And I thought of all the times I'd driven over the bridge, in a school bus carrying a load of YMCA youth, or in a probation sedan on my way to visit one of the charges in my care.

But as I turned north, I also felt this next leg held some important messages for me. Up to this point, the locations I'd ridden through and the people I'd seen largely represented my past. Back on the West Coast again, I was coming home, whether I liked it or not. With the exception of four years in Wisconsin, my whole adult life since the age of 26 had been spent somewhere between the Golden Gate Bridge of California and the Columbia River of Portland. This is where I would face and wrestle with my life as it currently was.

I rode slowly through the small towns between the bridge and San Anselmo. I rode by the restaurant where my ex-wife and I had shared an anniversary dinner. I looked up at the hillside in Sausalito where a close family friend on Lisa's side still lived. I pedaled by the Mexican restaurant where I'd had the pleasure of taking the Golden State Warriors to dinner after a YMCA basketball clinic. I still remembered my disappointment when one of the star players I'd looked up to got drunk on my tab. I crossed over the hill separating Mill Valley from Corte Madera, recalling the dozens of times I had ridden that same route years before.

In Larkspur, I was momentarily yanked back into the present. Nick, my host, showed up on his bike and we rode the final miles to his place, pedaling easily together through Shady Cove, a street fringed by a canopy of large eucalyptus trees, with upscale multi-million-dollar homes on both sides. I thought back to our son's first Halloween and the king-sized candy bars he received from these wealthy residents of Ross.

Nick reminded me of my younger self. He had grown up with a passion for religion, and by the time he reached seminary had already been introduced to a broad spectrum of religious traditions. He cooked a garlicky stir fry and together we ate, drank beer, and dug into the topic of religion and seminary.

"You know, Brian, I sometimes wonder if I'm a circle trying to fit into a square hole here."

"What do you mean?"

"I have all this background studying Buddhism, Islam, and the counterpoint between religion and science. I feel I have an incredible depth to offer the Church. But the curriculum has no room for my perspective," he said.

"I think that's a big part of why I'm on this pilgrimage," I said. "I was trained to teach the Presbyterian faith, but so many of us—people I've met and myself—are spiritually curious. We want to explore the big, bold world of religion."

Nick nodded. "We'll see if I last in this place. I'm not sure it's right for me. I just assumed that seminary would be the place to get trained in walking with people on their spiritual journey. But now I feel I'm getting an orientation on how to be a corporate man—except this corporation is the Church."

I raised my eyebrows. "Oooh, I haven't heard it put quite that way before, but that's right. A few weeks ago I came to the conclusion that I'd been trained as a pastor of the faith."

"A pastor of the faith," he repeated, mulling over the words.

"I think that's like you calling it a corporation. I don't want to represent just one faith anymore. I want to work with the faith and spiritual values that people come with."

Nick nodded again, more vigorously. "Yeah, yeah, I get it."

I had mixed feelings about Nick continuing his education. The Church really needed people like him, with energy and passion, and a broad exposure to more than just Presbyterian theology. I wanted Nick to join me in breaking through the cloud of grief hanging over the Church. But I also wanted to tell him to get out now. It was easy to imagine him involving himself in a local church and getting beaten up, abused, and eventually losing all faith in the Church.

DAY 59
San Anselmo to San Rafael, CA
9 miles

WHEN I WOKE UP in the bed that Nick's son usually slept in, Nick was already off to classes and I wouldn't see him again. I walked downtown, as I had hundreds of times twenty years before, and ate at a quiet, fifties-style breakfast café right next to the donut shop I'd frequented with another classmate and our two oldest children on Saturday morning—our gift to ourselves and our wives.

My next stopping point was literally over the next hill, less than five miles away; I had all day to reacquaint myself with San Anselmo and the surrounding area. I pedaled up to the seminary, situated at the top of a hill overlooking the valley as many seminaries are—something about being closer to God and looking at life from a lofty perch, I imagine. A few people—likely students, faculty, and visitors—were on campus, but I didn't recognize any of them. It had been twenty-two years since my graduation, and most of the professors who had mentored and taught me were now retired or had died. I wandered through the three-story library where I'd spent hundreds of hours studying and reading. I stood on the large patio in front of Geneva Hall, a place often used for large wedding parties who wanted the perfect backdrop of the towering Mount Tamalpais. I rode by the student family housing, where Lisa and I had lived when both our children were born. I pedaled into the driveway where our son, Phil, used to ride his tricycle with other children his age, and remembered the day he rode right into a Toyota truck tailgate that had been left open. He still bears the scar at the top of his nose where the sharp edge opened his flesh.

If you dropped a ball at the top of the seminary hill, there's a good chance it would roll right onto the property of First Presbyterian Church at the bottom. It is a sort of unofficial seminary church because of its proximity, and many professors make it their church home.

First Presbyterian held deep significance for me. Lisa and I were married there in a grand wedding with three hundred guests, from where a 1947 Packard convertible bore us to the equally lavish reception in Fairfax, a couple miles away. My in-laws were active members there. Both of our children were baptized there.

In fact, I was baptized there as an adult. Before ordination I had to present a baptismal certificate or record. I had assumed I'd been baptized, but when it came to finding the records they simply didn't exist. A call to my dad confirmed it. "I'm pretty sure you were baptized, but I don't actually remember," he'd told me. "You know, we may have overlooked it in the chaos that happened when you were young."

Because I was in the Worship and Sacraments class at seminary at the time, I convinced the professor to let me write my own baptismal service. I used some ancient liturgies and practices; an abalone shell my birth mother had given me became the ladle the minister used to pour water over my head. "I baptize you in the name of the Father"— pour—"and the Son"—pour—"and the Holy Spirit"—pour. I was drenched. I removed my rust-colored shirt, stood bare-chested before the congregation, and donned a thin, cotton baptismal gown as the ancients had.

Holding those memories, I walked into the courtyard, an airy space between the sanctuary and the fellowship hall. The church had gone through major renovations. It had lost the paint that had earned it the designation "Big Pink" and was now a softer and more attractive beige. Nicely stained wooden benches and large leafy plants had replaced much of the cement of the past.

In San Anselmo, I'd been adopted into a new and loving family. I didn't know whether on my return I would suddenly rediscover my identity and a passion for ministry. In the event, I was struck by a persistent feeling that I was simply reviewing history and revisiting my past. The area no longer felt like home, nor even warmed a place in my heart.

I was thankful for the role the seminary had played in my life, but a nagging sense told me a whole world separated my emerging identity and the identity of the seminary. I was surprised. Seven weeks earlier I had ridden across the campus of the College of Idaho and felt at home. It had left me yearning for past pleasures. Yet back at the seminary and First Presbyterian I didn't feel known. My adventurous, seeking, curious spirit was out of step with, and maybe even a threat to, the seminary. This was not home.

Almost by default, I didn't visit a single one of the family friends who still lived there. These people had adopted me into their extended family when I married Lisa: we had shared birthdays; eaten oysters on the half shell; and drunk wine on the beach at numerous Easter holidays. One was the pediatrician for our two children, and had saved my daughter Julie when she was born with meconium in her lungs. Another was a close friend who had offered her seaside rental to our family when we needed a vacation but couldn't afford much on a pastor's salary.

But I had come to know and love them as the result of my marriage to Lisa. Now, with the divorce, things seemed different. I pedaled along a frontage road near the home of one of our closest family friends, and pondered whether to make a short surprise visit. At the intersection where I would have turned left to their house, I rode straight through. I had no stomach for re-opening that chapter of my life.

And yet I had fully expected to renew those connections before my pilgrimage began. What had changed? Could it be that when I lightened my load in Ely and let go of the baggage of my divorce, that I also put these relationships behind me? Logically, the divorce didn't have to cause a split in the seams of these relationships. But I had no emotional energy for anything having to do with my divorce. I rode right on by, putting those relationships behind me—at least for the time being.

Twenty minutes later I cycled into the more average-looking neighborhood of Terra Linda, not far from the Lucasfilm studios, where I had been invited to stay in the home of fellow Presbyterians associated with Christ Presbyterian Church. Two sisters had arranged for a handful of Presbyterians to join me for dinner and engage in conversation about my pilgrimage. Most of them were from Christ Church, a church that I remembered as one of the more vital and active while I was attending seminary.

We sat at a large, round dinner table and laughed, ate lots of great food, and drank good wine—we were not far from the Wine Country of California. It was obvious that these folks had a real love for each other. They continued telling stories, shared gossip about families and friends, laughed some more and teased each other the way only close friends can get away with. It reminded me of the closeness I used to feel among those friends I'd chosen to ride by without a visit earlier in the day.

We retired to the back patio, a large space with a fire pit, a number of lounge chairs, and tropical trees. A few more bottles of wine were brought out and we continued our conversations, largely centering on the life of Christ Church. I was surprised to hear that the church membership was now only twenty percent of its former size.

"The only way we survive, Brian, is thanks to the rent we get from a large pre-school that uses our building, and a growing Buddhist congregation that worships there on Sunday evenings," one of the sisters said.

"Wow! I know there's a pattern of general decline in our churches, but I remember how spirited your group was twenty years ago when I was finishing seminary. I'm surprised."

"Our children have all moved on," the other sister said, "and there haven't been others to replace them. Families just quit coming to church."

A retired Presbyterian minister for whom I have great respect lamented, "My daughter has become the original Earth Mother. She's done with church, she says, but develops her own rituals around honoring the rhythms of nature. She even tells me that she has a bit of pagan in her."

I was about to confirm that her experience wasn't unusual, when the first sister stepped in. "Maggie, this isn't a failure on your part. It's just the times we live in. Your daughter is still following a spiritual path. I think that's something to celebrate."

I watched Maggie's reaction.

"Well, I suppose so." Her tone didn't sound convincing.

I went to bed pondering the images and events of the day. I had ridden by the homes of people with whom I had a thirty-year history. I felt a twinge of sadness, yet the choice felt right. I didn't know whether it meant I'd permanently severed those relationships or whether I just needed to set them aside until I had stepped more confidently into a new life. It didn't matter.

The dinner conversations had lightened my grief at coming back to the Church with a message of letting go. Nothing in our conversations had made me any more hopeful for the future of the church, at least as we now know it, but the burden of sharing this message—that we were living in an ecclesiastical hospice moment—was not fully on my shoulders. Others around the table were already there: my presence only served to make it safe to say what had been on their minds for a long time. I liked that role.

I liked not being the only one in the room saying it.

DAY 60
San Rafael to Petaluma, CA
36 miles

I LEFT, HEADING NORTH AGAIN to the town of Petaluma, which claims to be the chicken capital of the world. By freeway it is only twenty-five miles, so I decided to take some of the back roads that wind their way over graceful grassy hills, through dairy farms, and by my favorite cheese factory (Marin French Cheese) that nestles in the middle of a triangle, equidistant from Port Reyes, Novato, and Petaluma. I had ridden these roads dozens of times and looked forward to being on familiar territory. It was not lost on me that the seminary campus had also been familiar territory, but hadn't felt like home. As I rode up and down the hills, took deep breaths of air (pungent, courtesy of the cows), and enjoyed terrain that hadn't changed a bit in twenty years, I felt completely at home. I loved being on the bike. I loved how my body felt, cranking out a rhythm with my legs and my breath.

I was heading to the house of my next host, Martina, the current pastor for the two North Bay churches I interned at during seminary. These two churches had nurtured me along the road to becoming a pastor; I had served them as an intern for seven months during my junior year of seminary. I had entered seminary simply out of my love for religious studies, but had balked at becoming a pastor. Two weeks after starting my internship, I found myself saying, "Oh my God. This is what I'm supposed to be doing!" It had been a shock to Lisa and may have begun the long, fifteen-year slide toward divorce.

I arrived a little early at Martina's home, so I took advantage of the time and enjoyed a barbecue dinner in one of those personality-less strip malls in suburbia. Still with time to kill, I called my daughter in Portland. I hadn't talked with her since I'd left eight weeks ago.

"Hey, Julie. It's Dad. How are you?"

"Oh my God, Dad! I can't believe it's you. I've been following your blog," she said. "You're having an amazing trip."

"It's good to hear your voice," I said. "I've been away from just about everything I know for two months. I can't wait to get home now."

"We can't wait to have you back too, Dad. Where are you now?"

"Petaluma, just north of where Mimi and Papa lived," I said, referring to her grandparents. "I should be in Lake County in two more days."

"Say hi to the crew there, will you? I miss that place."

"I will," I promised. "Love you sweetie. I'll see you soon."

I closed the flip top to the phone, my hand shaking. I had been gone a long time, cut off from my Portland community with the exception of my blog. I still had a couple of places to visit, but I was ready to go home, hold my kids, see friends, and rediscover my life back in Portland.

As I pedaled back to Martina's place, I wasn't sure I was up for visiting churches and staying in the homes of Presbyterians all the way back to Portland. I'd imagined I would spend the last two weeks telling my story and maybe, in some unconscious place, thought I'd be welcomed back like a hero. Either I would have crisp, clean answers for the church, or trailing behind me through my blog would be hundreds of people ready to start something new from the seeds I had planted while traveling and writing. That hadn't happened, and I knew it wasn't going to during my first speaking opportunity in Sacramento. Which made the thought of visiting churches all the way back to Portland for the next two weeks more unnerving. I had one church host in Santa Rosa the following day, and another in Ukiah four days hence. That would be enough. I would dedicate the rest of the trip to re-entering my private world, where my only responsibility was to my own soul's yearnings.

I arrived at Martina's home, a neatly kept, middle class, three-bedroom house that revealed her need for order. Pictures of family hung on the walls and were propped up on bookcases. Signs that she was a pastor were intermingled with the décor: communion chalices, crosses, and religious art. We shared dessert while she caught me up on events at the two churches where I had interned. I shared some details of my journey—and then we hit a snag I didn't expect.

"Our problem, as you well know, Brian," she said, "is that young people just aren't coming to church."

"Interestingly enough, I met a couple two mornings ago on the ferry who had something to say about that," I said. "One works with young adults, and in her view the issue is not getting young people in the door, but passing the tradition of the church on to them."

"I beg to differ. The responsibility doesn't lie with the church to reach them," she argued. "The responsibility lies with youth to assume their role in keeping the church going. Young people have the responsibility of carrying on the traditions of their elders."

I was surprised. Hers was a common perception I'd encountered among lay members of churches, lamenting the current generation of young people and their complete disregard for the traditions and institutions that had made this country great. It was a common theme for a generation that had shaped this country by their World War II sacrifice. But I had never heard it from a pastor of my own generation.

Entering the church world after crossing the desert, I felt like a diver who has surfaced too fast and gotten the bends. I wasn't ready to get back into the fray of the conflicted, complex, and frustrating hand-wringing of the Church.

DAY 61
Petaluma to Santa Rosa, CA
22 miles

IT WAS AGAIN ONLY A SHORT HOP of fifteen miles from Petaluma into downtown Santa Rosa. I rode casually into town in the late morning. My hosts didn't expect me until dinner time, so I had a full six hours to kill.

I'd visited Santa Rosa on many occasions (almost monthly) when Lisa and I and our two children were living in Lake County, where I was headed next. Lake County is a beautiful, agricultural, rural community in a bowl of mountains with a 19-mile-long lake in the center, but it has limited services and shopping. Santa Rosa, a 90-minute drive away, became our monthly destination to see independent films, broaden our choice of restaurants, shop at the mall, and occasionally meet Lisa's parents for dinner.

I parked my bike at a small corner park, no bigger than an average house lot, adjacent to a number of restaurants. The day was warm and sunny, and I fell asleep on the green lawn despite the hum of stop-and-go traffic, lively chatter at outdoor cafés, and children running and screaming in the park. I slept for over an hour. An old Mexican restaurant that had been a favorite during our time in Lake County drew me across the street. I ordered a large bowl of fresh gazpacho soup and a beer, relishing all the minerals and fluids entering my body. Afterwards, I went back to the park and slept again, not wanting to ride, to push or to think.

I enjoyed a sweet mindlessness all day. Late in the afternoon, my host called to confirm my visit and give me directions. I rode a few more miles to the north part of town, which would give me a head start next morning; I was heading almost exclusively north for the rest of the trip. The house, on a large wooded lot with a great view and a few fruit trees, was roomy and attractive. My hosts' kids were off at college, so I was given the room of one of their daughters. I was thankful for the comfortable bed, but felt I was trespassing a little.

Chris, my host, was involved in more than just his local Presbyterian church; he served on a national committee trying to address larger church trends. We had the usual conversation about church decline, and the growing demographic of those calling themselves spiritual but not religious. But one part of our conversation about the shift in culture stuck with me.

"The one thing I think we did right at our church," he said, "was to change the name and focus of Vacation Bible School."

"Tell me about that," I said, "because VBS seems like a leftover relic of the past, as far as I'm concerned."

"We felt the same way," he said. "Every year fewer kids came. Then one of our members suggested we change tactics. He said, 'We teach the Bible and hope they learn about God's love and the peace of Christ. What if we did the opposite? What if we held a Peace Camp and connected it to stories of peace in the Bible?'"

"That's it!" I blurted. "Today's people still care about the values that come from our Biblical tradition, but they could care less about whether the values come from the Bible or Gandhi or the Dalai Lama or the Peace Pilgrim. So what happened?"

"It worked," he said simply. "We tripled attendance to nearly 75 the first year."

I loved what they had done. They got the shift I'd been hearing for years in the ministry and on my trip. People may have drifted away from the Bible and church-going, but they still care just as much for the values that the Church teaches and attempts to embody. It was one of the first bright spots regarding the future of the Church I had experienced on my travels.

I found staying at their beautiful home both refreshing and difficult. Their two children were doing well, and they themselves appeared to have a loving and enjoyable relationship. It brought up the pain of what I had lost in my divorce. It also exposed my yearning for home.

I wouldn't have long to wait. Next morning I was leaving for Lake County, a place I would probably still reside if my wife hadn't been laid off from her job there.

DAY 62
Santa Rosa to Kelseyville, CA
76 miles

I NOW WAS ABLE TO COAST down the hill I'd ridden up to get to Chris and Liz's house, but I had to ride carefully through a thick, pea-soup-like fog. Kelseyville was my destination, one of a handful of small towns on the shores of the shallow, but large, Clear Lake in Lake County. I was excited to be returning even as a momentary wave of shame shot through me. Some of my best—and most painful—pastoral work had taken place in Kelseyville. I still have close friends there and, although we don't see each other more than about once every two years, we share a closeness that distance and time cannot erase.

The fog began to burn off as I cycled north, just off Highway 101. This was going to be a particularly hot September day. I love cycling through the vineyards and numerous wineries of the Sonoma Valley; something about wine country sets me at ease. It begs one to slow down and pause, like drinking a glass of good zinfandel. Passing the famous Francis Ford Coppola winery and tasting room, I might have been tempted to stop, but wine tasting is more of a social event for me than it is about the wine itself. Plus, I didn't need alcohol in my system when the mercury was climbing quickly.

I rode through the upscale town of Healdsburg, marveling at the shops and the money that obviously flows freely there. Just as the hills presented themselves I rolled through Cloverdale, a town I used to stop in frequently when traveling to meetings in the Bay Area. It was home to my favorite burger stand—Pick's Drive In, an old-fashioned, over-priced joint. I wouldn't stop today, but just seeing the white painted building, its canopy hanging over the two screened windows where orders were taken, brought back memories of the commute. If Healdsburg draws the wine industry, Cloverdale is a strange combination of long-distance commuters and the wine industry labor force, largely Hispanic. On the outskirts of town, large 3,000-square-foot homes were being built, while in town a handful of Mexican restaurants took care of their own.

I rode with deliberate patience, feeling my energy already being sucked out of me by the heat. I had to make sure I had something left for the difficult climb over the Hopland Grade that separates Mendocino County from Lake County. The steep, winding, narrow road used to be the primary route into Lake County before a highway was built, linking Lake County with Sonoma County at the town of Calistoga. From the Hopland side, it is a 2,638-foot climb over a short nine miles. Trail Ridge Road in Colorado had twice the elevation gain, but over a much longer stretch—Hopland Grade was steep and punishing.

I reached Hopland crying out for a cold drink. Two men watched me park my bike in front of the grocery store.

"Tough day to be out riding, isn't it?" the older of the two said. They looked as though they might have been a father/son team, the older man nearing seventy.

"What do you mean? The heat?"

"Well, yeah, what else?" he said, as if the heat was the only worthwhile topic of conversation.

"Yep, it sure is hot," I said. "I left Santa Rosa this morning in fog, but things started to heat up pretty quickly after it burned off."

"One hundred six," the younger man said. "That's what it was a few minutes ago."

"Wow! I knew it was hot, but I wasn't expecting that. I'm climbing the Hopland Grade today. I better make sure I have enough water."

"I think you're crazy," the son informed me. "You wouldn't catch me out in this sun today. It's a killer."

He might be right. I already felt the effects of the heat after the first fifty miles of riding. My legs were sluggish and my lungs resisted a full inhale, as if I were sitting in a hot Finnish sauna protecting my lungs from burning. I loaded up on Gatorade and water in the store and prayed I still had enough stamina and grit to conquer this rocky fortress.

It reminded me of the first time our family drove the route, when I was interviewing for the position at the Kelseyville Presbyterian Church. We drove from Hopland up over the curvy, snaking road. After cresting the summit and looking down at the lake and valley below, we made the equally snaking descent into Lake County. However, our daughter Julie—and her stomach—didn't make it; the curves were too much for her and whatever she'd had for breakfast ended up all over her shirt and pants, the car seat and floor. We spent the next couple of hours cleaning the car and buying new clothes for her at Kmart before resuming our tour. Maybe we should have recognized the incident as a warning, but I took the position anyway.

As I left Hopland, I noticed a church sign: "Don't be such a free thinker that your brains fall out. Study the Bible." The letters of "Bible" were drooping; I smiled at the touch of irony. The sign took me back into the history, controversy, failures and successes of my time in Lake County. I had good reasons to return to the College of Idaho, Bozeman, Thermopolis, Loveland, and the Bay Area. But of all the places I revisited, Lake County seemed to hold as much significance for my future as it did my past. It held all the unresolved pain and grief around our time there. To be honest, there were still deep wounds in my soul. I needed to return to Lake County to face whatever shame still lingered.

Riding past the sign, I steeled myself for a climb just on the edge of dangerous. I was a bit nervous; there's a difference between riding out of your comfort zone in the heat and riding into the possibility of heat stroke, and I was flirting with the subtle line between the two. Thoughts of my heat stroke-induced deliriums in Yosemite the year before came back. I knew I had to be careful.

As I gutted my way up each rising wall of pavement and negotiated the switchbacks, sweat ran down my face, chest, back and legs in cascading streams. My bike frame was getting caked with salt as sweat dripped onto it continuously. Feeling the effects of the heat, I kept drinking the water that had become too hot to enjoy.

I reached the top totally spent and starting to feel sick. Thank God for the long descent: coasting gave me time to recover as much as possible. When I reached Lakeport, ten miles from my destination, I stopped at a convenience store. I'd only ridden sixteen miles, but I had to rehydrate. I couldn't drink fast enough to keep up with the evaporation from my body. I knew it would be many hours before my body totally recovered from the over-exertion and heat, but I needed just enough resurgence to ride the last few miles to my friends' home, where I planned to stay the next two nights.

I straggled into Kelseyville trying to squeeze a few more miles out of my body. Just a few minutes of riding from my friends' home, I said out loud, "This is still home." I should have known. When we moved from Lake County to Portland in 2002 for economic reasons, I was aware of leaving a piece of my heart behind. I'd made personal connections and had a voice in the community, and it was hard to part with such a unique place.

I arrived at Peter and Kathy's house that sits on a lovely piece of land, incorporating vineyards, pasture for a couple of horses, and Kelsey Creek that runs at the back edge of their property. It took most of the evening to recover from the potentially risky situation I had put myself in during the ride in the heat. A good shower, self-massage on my legs, and lots of water to drink slowly made me feel human again—physically. Emotionally... I had a lot of questions that needed answering.

In 1997, I was forced to resign from my position as pastor of Kelseyville Presbyterian Church. But unlike most churches where the forced resignation of a pastor comes on the heels of misconduct or incompetence, mine was the result of a rapidly growing new program the church had started under my leadership. A few new people had joined the church shortly after my arrival, but had never completely integrated into the life of the church. They'd joined because of articles I had published in my column in the paper; I wrote about the Christian faith through the lens of Joseph Campbell's mythology. But the church was not ready for such language. Sunday mornings saw traditional Presbyterians mixed in with spiritual seekers—it never quite gelled. In an attempt to meet the new arrivals' needs while allowing Sunday morning worship to remain traditional, a new Sunday evening, once-a-month gathering was initiated, called the "Quester Community."

Immediately it took off. Within six months ninety people were associated with it—half the size of the church and showing no signs of slowing. Concerned that this new group was tarnishing the image of the church, a minority of influential members drew a line in the sand. I heard it said aloud, "We are becoming known as the church with that weird group on Sunday evenings." Either I would be fired, or they would withdraw their financial support and their membership.

A central player in leadership threatened my life and things got uglier after that. That person was asked to resign his positions at the church. I had an unnerving anxiety attack and was given a month of paid leave. When I returned, our leadership and I sat around a table and made some difficult decisions. Part of the leadership fought for my position saying, "Our churches are declining and Brian is doing exactly what we asked him to do." The other side countered, "We realize the Quester group is growing, but it isn't the kind of growth we expected." The church was on the verge of splitting, with nearly a quarter of the membership threatening to leave. As long as I was there, they would not be able to resolve it. I was asked to resign and accepted the decision with deep regret.

I had been the initial link and catalyst for the Quester Community, which immediately dissolved, wanting nothing to do with a church that had supported me in organizing it only to fire me when it grew.

Work wasn't easy to find in that rural county. For six months I packed pears in the packing sheds, cleaned streams for the Conservation Corps, and eventually found work as a juvenile probation officer, making two-thirds of my former salary. The financial and emotional hit contributed to a bankruptcy two years later. My shame was doubled. I shuffled around the county in a cloud of disgrace for getting myself fired. I had graduated from both college and seminary with honors and now I couldn't even hold a job in my field.

I was deeply crushed. I was a pastor in a denomination that had witnessed declines of one to three percent every year since 1967. Every church that advertises for a pastor uses virtually the same language: "We want a young pastor with a spouse and children who can take care of the elderly congregation and attract young families." I fitted that bill perfectly: I was only thirty-three when I started, had a spouse and two young children. I provided wonderful pastoral care to the congregation, often being told that my memorial services were the best thing I did. I was successful at reaching younger families in the community through my articles. I led the congregation in creating a program to retain younger people while not threatening the Sunday morning crowd. True, in the beginning I'd made the rookie mistake of attracting people who didn't meld well with the existing congregation, but we had resolved that by creating the Quester Community. In the end, I felt the only thing wrong was that we grew. We grew too big and too fast, and some people got scared. So I was fired—well, technically, I was asked to resign, but it felt the same.

I was devastated and angry, and lost my faith in the Church. How could I ever be a pastor again if churches would rather decline than gracefully negotiate their way through the growing pains of attracting new people? I was royally pissed off and became bitter. In the privacy of my car I threw tantrums: *I am so fucking sorry that we attracted ninety people. Was it twenty you wanted or forty? Did you want me just to lock the door at fifty people, like a theater that's sold out? What the hell do you want from me?*

I wandered through two years, lost and deeply wounded, until Peter and Kathy came to me. "Brian, we had a good thing going with the Quester Community," they'd said. "Some of us miss the gatherings. Is there any chance you would help us start our own church?"

It didn't take me too long to decide. But first I had to work through the ethical issues of starting a church, while still holding my Presbyterian credentials, in the same community where I'd been forced to resign. We started to meet, and eventually decided that the Unitarian Universalist Association of Churches best represented the spiritual values of the group. I then set aside my ordination so that no one could press ecclesiastical charges against me for competing with a local congregation without presbytery approval. For three years we walked together, and eventually chartered as the Unitarian Universalist Community of Lake County. The Quester Community lived on, in a new incarnation and under another name.

Though I enjoyed the open and inclusive approach of Unitarian Universalists, the Presbyterians were my family. They had raised me as much as my own parents had. I wanted to find my place in their fold again, and eventually returned to the Presbyterian Church after moving to Portland.

But it didn't happen easily or quickly. I took a very part-time position as chaplain at an assisted living facility, and then petitioned to have my ordination restored. It took many meetings for me to work through my shame and anger toward the Church. The day my ordination was restored, I stood in the chancel area of a church in front of nearly two hundred ministers and elders. My hands and legs were shaking, but not from the usual nerves. This felt more like PTSD; I was like a woman who decides to give an abusive husband a second chance. I wanted to believe in the church, but I knew I could be hurt again—just like the day in Loveland when I called my mom, wanting to connect, but anxious about opening myself up to more disappointment.

Peter and Kathy had promised me a good dinner out on their patio. As I joined them, I asked, "So how is the church doing? Are you still meeting?"

"Oh yes," Kathy said. "I can hardly keep up with it all. I'm still serving as president of the board."

That was positive news. "Are you still meeting in the Lutheran church?"

"No. We've taken over the old post office," Kathy said. "It's great because it's our space. We don't have to set up and take down every Sunday."

"Is it pretty much the same people as when I left nine years ago?"

"Oh no. We get new people every year. It's at least double the number it was when you left."

That pleased me even more. I'd long carried shame about the events that had unfolded in Kelseyville.

"Look what you started with the Quester Community, Brian," Peter said.

They were just the words I needed to hear. They finally brought me full circle, allowed me to let go of the shame that really belonged to someone else. I needed to forgive Kelseyville Presbyterian Church for not having the courage to persevere through the awkwardness of attempting to grow a church in a time when decline is the norm. I needed to ride out of Lake County with my chin up, proud of what I'd started despite the abuse I took. And I needed to forgive my youthful idealism in assuming that if I attracted people, the church would welcome them.

We sat on the patio under a near-full moon that cast long banners of light across the fields and hillsides. Deer were silhouetted out in the pasture; crickets chirped. The beer was cold, the food elegantly and tastily prepared. But the Giants lost to the Dodgers, making the evening not quite perfect—at least for Peter and Kathy.

Again, I retired to sleep in a foreign bed. But I felt at home; I belonged here. These were my people, after all: we had shared history; we had struggled together and succeeded together; we were bound by more than just place. We had written painful and wonderful chapters of our lives together, and no matter what was written after, we would always have those pages in our book, forever.

I started to weep. Was this reminder of when I was at my best what had prompted the idea for my pilgrimage nearly a year before? Had I ridden 3,400 miles for this moment?

DAY 63
Kelseyville, CA
Rest Day, 15 errand miles

I DIDN'T NEED PHYSICAL REST, since I'd only ridden 170 miles over the last five days, despite the difficult, heat stroke-threatening day surmounting the Hopland Grade. But I looked forward to having a full day to allow feelings to emerge and memories to surface as I casually made my way around the area. The only event scheduled was an evening patio party with a handful of close friends from when I'd lived there.

I tracked down close friends Gary and Pam, who had been part of the original influx of people into the Kelseyville church after I'd written an editorial titled "The Christmas Myth" for the local paper. They introduced me to their friends teasing that I had abandoned them after starting a war with local Christian fundamentalists. They were busy landscaping a large yard on a small farming plot. It was too short a reunion, but they were preparing for their son's wedding later that month, and I had more sights to see.

I rode by the old Presbyterian church and took a couple of pictures, but didn't linger long. I wasn't sure what kind of reception I might get if a church member happened to show up. I cycled around the area for a while, seeing what had changed and what had not. A new marketing campaign had been launched for the town, and six-foot-square replicas of quilting patterns could be seen on the sides of businesses, barns and fences. A new post office had been built—modern and at least three times as big as the former one. Other than that, there hadn't been many changes since we had moved north.

Mostly, I allowed Peter's comment to settle more deeply. I felt my anger about what I considered an unfair dismissal easing. The success of the UUCLC and Peter's gratitude softened all the pain I'd endured in getting there. Plus I began to see the Quester Community in a new light.

In recent years, a whole new movement of experimental Christian communities called emergent churches had blossomed. As I thought about the growing acceptance of these new-style churches, it occurred to me that the Quester Community was really one of the first attempts at an emergent-style church. It didn't completely erase my pain, but it put what had happened in Kelseyville in a new context—first attempts to break through barriers are often not well received. Only after a record of initial successes do people become comfortable with such experimental, risk-taking adventures. I don't know for sure that's what happened, but I could choose to believe it, and it gave me a clue to understanding why a growing program would feel so threatening to so many people.

As the day wore on, I began to feel tired deep in my bones. It had nothing to do with the journey or yesterday's tough ride in the heat. I recognized the feeling from my hospice bereavement work: I was finally letting go the anger and resentment I'd held for so long toward Kelseyville

Presbyterian Church. I didn't realize how much bitterness I had been storing in my body. As I rode slowly and casually through the farms, vineyards and orchards of Lake County, I could feel myself letting it go. I didn't need the anger anymore, it no longer served me. Like extra baggage on my bike, it just slowed me down. I had to unload it and leave it behind.

I enjoyed another near perfect night on Peter and Kathy's patio. We barbecued chicken, drank beer and wine, and watched a bright orange sunset settle over the hills to the west. We reflected on the Quester Community experience in which all of us had participated. We talked about the organizational grief that traditional congregations would experience as they dissolved and made room for new forms of Christian community. We laughed, joked, and in the end, embraced, before saying our goodbyes, not knowing how many years it would be until we saw each other again.

It would be difficult to leave Lake County. Part of me could have stopped right there at Peter and Kathy's, unloaded my bike, pulled my friends together, and said, "I plan to stay. Let's pick up where we left off. What's next?!"

But I knew I needed to move on. My life was in Portland now and, despite the temptation to re-establish myself in Lake County, I looked forward to relishing this newfound feeling of acceptance and forgiveness. When I rode away I would do so feeling much lighter, and with gratitude for the opportunity to finally release the bitterness I'd held onto for so long.

But I wasn't quite done with Lake County yet. Tomorrow was an important day, not just for me, but for all of America. It was the tenth anniversary of 9/11, and the UUCLC would honor the tragic day during their Sunday service. I couldn't wait to worship with them. I felt like a father who has missed seeing his daughter grow up, about to knock on her front door for the first time in years.

DAY 64
Kelseyville to Ukiah, CA
45 miles

I COASTED BY BIKE to the back doors of the old post office—now the Unitarian church—for the service. I wasn't sure what to expect. Would I be remembered? Would people come rushing up to me, saying, "Brian, Brian, it's so good to see you!"? Would there be some hidden resentment that I'd abandoned them, as Pam and Gary had playfully teased?

People filed in. Singles, couples, and a few children strolled past me, showing no sign of recognition. One woman, though, did recognize me. "Brian, what a surprise to see you here."

I knew her face but time had eroded the context. "Hello, remind me who you are."

Her face deflated slightly. "Katie. You married my husband and me."

It came back to me immediately: the large lawn where they had exchanged their vows; an outside reception area for the catered dinner. She'd sought me out because I wasn't the typical minister and she wanted a service more spiritual than religious.

Another couple, whose children were the same age as mine, gave me a warm but quick hug. The hug said it all—this was now a community standing on its own two feet. I wanted to blurt out, "Wow—you guys grew up on me and have a life of your own!" It felt good even as a twinge of grief found its way to the surface. I had provided the initiative and early support. I was no longer needed, but I'd played my part.

The church had beautiful banners hanging in the front, one for each of the seven principles of Unitarian Universalism. The fourth, hanging right behind the lectern, caught my eye. On a banner of purples and blues were the words of the fourth principle: "A free and responsible search for truth and meaning." *That's how this community was born,* I thought. My nakedly honest articles in the paper matched their yearning for an open and honest environment in which to search, grow, learn and love. I knew then why the church sign in Hopland had reminded me of the struggle in Kelseyville. "Don't be such a free thinker that your brains fall out," it had blared. We UU's were free thinkers in a county where free thinking was a threat. I had just underestimated how much of a threat it would be.

I sat toward the back on the left, where I could see everyone and soak in as much of the experience as possible. Attendance had more than doubled from the 20–25 people that we had during the first three years of organization and chartering. Numerous people took roles in the leadership of the service. It was especially rewarding to see that this church was not pastorally dependent, but was run by members of the church itself. It was a grown-up version of what we had attempted to create in the Quester Community fifteen years before. Were the Presbyterians glad that they had severed the cord to this group? Or did they now regret that lost opportunity to be the umbrella organization for this forward-thinking, ahead-of-its-time, communally focused spiritual community?

The service over, we all walked over to the small park adjacent to the old post office. The fifty of us posed for a picture, with me in my cycling clothes kneeling front and center. I had come full circle, being photographed with the child I had left years before. The shame I'd felt at essentially being fired was replaced by pride. These were my people and always would be. Never mind how the Presbyterians felt—I had done well.

As I departed from Kelseyville I knew I was now on the journey home. I'd felt it in different ways in the previous weeks: after reaching my home town of Loveland; successfully propelling myself over Trail Ridge Road; and as I turned north at the Golden Gate Bridge, knowing the rest of the trip would follow the familiar California and Oregon coasts. Lake County, however, was the last stop on my journey of reconnecting with all the people and places that had shaped and nurtured me. I had accomplished what I needed to. Now I could let go and enjoy the remaining miles and days until I reached Portland.

As I left Lake County, I rode by many familiar places. I cycled beside the nineteen-mile- long Clear Lake on roads memorized from past rides. I passed by the ten-acre hillside where permanent structures still stood for the annual Passion Play (a re-enactment of Jesus' arrest, death and resurrection), an event I had played a role in one year. My reactions were mixed, as it reminded me of a time when such things were important to me as a pastor. Now, however, cycling over mountains and through deserts left me feeling much closer to the Sacred than participating in the re-telling of the Good Friday/Easter story. Not that the narrative isn't important; I just feel it's a story for those inside the walls of religion, while I was finding God outside those walls.

I turned onto Highway 20, linking Lake County with Mendocino County and the town of Ukiah. I was especially mindful on this stretch. It's no more dangerous than other stretches I'd been on, but years before I had officiated at the memorial service for a too-young-to-die doctor killed on this road. He was an avid cyclist and was riding his bicycle west during the evening sunset. I had driven along that section many times and sunset is an especially dangerous time along this highway. The angles are such that drivers have to trust their instincts for a few seconds as the road disappears in intense glare. Dr. K was riding in the three-foot shoulder, but a driver blinded by the glare drifted to the right, hit him, and killed him. Strangely enough, the event didn't unnerve me back then. I was too young to be worried about such things.

I absolutely love cycling and nothing short of losing my legs and arms would keep me from the wonderful feeling of cruising down the road under my own power. I love how my body feels when I'm cranking up a mountain, and I love the adrenaline rush when my bike catapults down that mountain at speeds generally reserved for freeway driving. But I know it's risky. I know one day my kids may write about me in the obituary section, "At least he was doing what he loved." Kelseyville had taught me that life is fragile—fired from a position I loved, my life threatened, forced to file for bankruptcy. And here I was, riding on a section of highway where death had visited someone not so different than me. I was grateful to be alive.

Ukiah was to be the last place where I would stay in the homes of Presbyterians. I had contacted the Ukiah church a few days prior and arranged to stay with the associate pastor and her family. She asked if I would be willing to speak to her youth group that night about my experience. I was delighted to do so, even as I yearned to ride back into a place of solitude, much as I had during the first two weeks of the journey. Connecting with the church world had been more overwhelming than I'd expected; I also didn't want any more information in my head. I wanted to spend the last week or so processing the experience of the first nine weeks.

I pedaled to the pastor's house in Ukiah in the mid-afternoon, leaving plenty of time to rest, shower, and prepare to meet the First Presbyterian Church's youth group. I rang the doorbell and waited.

A few seconds later, the door opened. My jaw dropped. "Kelsey, is that you?"

She grinned broadly. "I knew it was you," she said. "After we talked, I started to put it together. Your name's Brian and you're a crazy cyclist. That sounds like my old pastor in Kelseyville, I thought!"

"It's me!" I said. "I can't wait to hear how you ended up here."

Kelsey had been a teenager in the Kelseyville church when the controversy boiled over about the Quester Community. I had no idea how she felt about all that. For all I knew, she might have told me to take a hike and not come anywhere near her, her family, or her youth group.

I was both surprised and grateful that Kelsey was not only gracious toward me, but wanted to engage in the themes and issues at the heart of my pilgrimage. She had been ordained only recently and, as a young mother, was also struggling with the decline of the denomination and increasing absence of youth and young families.

"Kelsey, look," I said. "I don't want to do or say anything to undermine your work and relationship with the youth of this church. If you don't want me to meet them, I'll understand." I was still concerned that, depending how she saw the Kelseyville drama, she might not trust me.

"Absolutely not," she said. "This is a great opportunity for us. You've just ridden—how far? Like three thousand miles? That's the coolest thing in the world to them and they're going to have all kinds of questions. Seriously, we're good."

I took a big breath. "Thanks. That's good to hear."

After dinner, we walked to the church just around the corner from her church-owned home. A handful of youth, aged around fifteen or sixteen, were already anxiously flitting about near the door like moths. They were a high-energy bunch, with the usual manic enthusiasm of that age group. But as the rest of the youth filed in, Kelsey easily redirected their energy. Sitting on old couches, a few cheap church chairs, and the floor, the teens peppered me with a rapid-fire series of questions.

"When did you start this trip?"

"How many flat tires did you have?"

"Did you have to worry about dogs?"

"What kind of bike do you have?"

"How much did it cost?"

After a dessert break, Kelsey brought us back together for the formal part of the evening's activity. She introduced me again, but this time made it more personal: "Brian used to be my minister about fifteen years ago. You know that he's on a long bicycling trip, but I want him to tell you why he's doing it."

I had lots of reasons. But first I wanted to hear what church meant to them. "I'm listening for the shift taking place between religion and spirituality. You're all committed to this youth group and this church. So why are you here, when so many churches have no youth at all?"

They were ready to talk. A dark-haired girl with a roundish figure spoke first. "I think a lot of us are here for each other. We don't actually go to the church. We just like each other."

A thin, tall boy added, "She's right. I don't tell my friends I go to a church youth group. They think it's weird."

"I like being here," a boy with reddish-blond hair said. "We can talk openly here, but I'd never say some of the things in church that I do here. The old folks would flip out!"

Despite Ukiah's fairly healthy youth group, I could still see the national pattern getting ready to play out there. These youngsters would stick with each other through high school, but as they graduated and went off to work or college they would drift away from the church. Their commitment was to each other, not the church. Nothing had changed. Things were no different here.

Back in Kelsey's home, she stepped right into giving her children baths and getting them ready for bed. We talked for a few minutes and reviewed my conversation with the youth. She felt lucky that her church still had youth, but was as concerned as I was. This world was passing away and she wasn't sure what the future held for her. With more than thirty working years ahead of her, she doubted there'd be enough of a church left to sustain a full career in pastoral ministry.

I slept on her couch that night. Given my history in Kelseyville, I wondered whether the day had shown divine justice or divine comedy. Serendipity or synchronicity? Time would tell.

PART EIGHT

Now I Remember!

September 12 – September 21

The *"invisible hands"* of the pilgrimage.

DAY 65
Ukiah to Garberville, CA
91 miles

DETOURING FROM MY USUAL high-fat, high-calorie break-fast, I enjoyed a breakfast sandwich at a little bakery/coffee shop, enticed by a wonderfully aromatic blend of fresh-baked bread and strong coffee. The residents obviously felt the same way: dozens of people flowed through the shop, most taking baked goods with them, while a few of us settled in at tables. I set off for the day's ride happy.

Not too far outside Ukiah I was met with a fairly steep hill I knew was coming, as I'd driven the route many times during the nine years we lived in the area. It forced me to dig deep for a few minutes, but despite its steepness was only a minor obstacle compared to the long days cross-ing the Rocky Mountains and Sierras, where I was often climbing for two, three, or four hours at a time. I was hoping to arrive at day's end in Garberville, 90 miles away. It felt good again not to have hosts expecting me for the evening. That meant I could ride as hard or as easily as I wanted. I could cycle into Garberville anytime, or choose to cut my day short, or I could ride right on through Garberville to the next town— unlikely as that was! I enjoyed the freedom of owning my time.

After successfully climbing the hill and erasing the first quarter of the ride, it was time to stop for refreshments and to let the legs recover. I bought my usual supplies—Gatorade, water, and donuts—and walked out to my bike. Filling up at the gas pumps was a UPS truck. Without a second thought, I propped myself on its back bumper and asked the driver to take a quick picture. I told him it was a family joke. He looked puzzled, but obliged.

The picture was meant to tickle my son's funny bone. In 2002 I had taken Phil, then fourteen, on a coming-of-age vision quest. We cycled 250 miles over four days, crossing the pass of Mount Lassen, one of the Cascades Range volcanic peaks, at 8,500 feet. Because of some poor planning on my part, I ended up carrying the bulk of our gear. On the first day, all the important muscles in my lower body began locking up less than a mile from the top of the day's last serious climb. A UPS truck stopped and offered to shuttle me to the top, an offer I only accepted because I was pretty sure there was still a four-mile climb ahead (there wasn't). Phil had gone ahead, and was waiting for me at the top of the hill, getting somewhat worried. I will never forget Phil doubling over with laughter as the UPS truck pulled up to the top of the hill and let me out. Here I was, on a spiritual vision quest ushering my son from childhood to adulthood, and I hitched a ride in a delivery van.

Just a few miles later, I rode by an "Elk Crossing" sign. Such signs were common on my trip as I traveled through most of the western states, where deer and elk make their home. I hadn't ridden more than 200 yards when, looking to the right, I saw a breathtaking and marvelous sight—sixty elk, shuffling almost in single file along a path heading east into the Mendocino Mountains. It was the largest herd I'd seen in my life.

I left the rolling hills of Northern California, a landscape consisting almost entirely of oak trees scattered over dry, brown, curvaceous hills ripe for wildfires. Next came redwood forests of towering, mammoth trees in a lush, wet, musty environment. I soon came upon a little shop on the side of the road that typefied liberal, creative Northern California. The building resembled a large tie-dyed shirt, a rainbow of colors serving as backdrop to a handful of Hindu sculptures. It was time for a short break and a drink, so I decided to check out this funky place. I walked in and looked at their limited selection of drinks: one small refrigerator offering three choices—water, organic juice, and fermented kombucha.

The man behind the counter jumped to his feet. "Hey, you can't be in here."

What? "I'm just picking up a drink for the road," I said.

"No," he continued, jigging about nervously. "You have to have a card to shop in here."

"What?" I said, aloud this time.

"A medical marijuana card. You can't be in here without a card."

"Oh," I said, surprised and amused at my own naiveté. "Okay, no problem. I just stopped for a drink. Had no idea what I was walking into."

"No problem," he said, relaxing slightly. "Go ahead and get a drink, you aren't doing any harm. But don't linger too long outside. We don't want the cops showing up while you're on the grounds."

I purchased a juice, took a very short stroll around the grounds, and hopped back on my bike, smiling to myself. Just ten years before I'd been a probation officer, yet it still hadn't dawned on me that this shop was anything more than some nature-loving, psychedelic leftover from the sixties now operating as a roadside refreshment stand. My friends at home would shake their heads and roll their eyes when they heard this one.

I spent the next couple of hours stopping at every large redwood tree to take pictures of me and my bike framed against the backdrop of those giants. Most were at least twice as wide as my five-foot bike; one had a single-lane road carved right through the middle of it.

I stopped at a curio shop alongside the road that had redwood burls for sale and thousands of little souvenirs to take home to family and friends. I grabbed a Gatorade and wandered around the shop. A young couple rode up on loaded-down bikes. They were heading south—which, by the way, is the preferred direction, due to the southerly winds. Many cyclists had looked at me and said, "Why are you going north?" I had to explain that I was completing a big circle, and since I would have to ride against the wind someplace, why not up the coast?

The couple told me they were traveling down the Pacific Coast from Portland to San Francisco.

"I just came from San Francisco and I'll be finishing in Portland," I said. "Where in Portland do you live?"

"Southeast Portland," they responded matter-of-factly.

"That's where my grown children live. On Stark Street."

"Really? So do we," they said. "What part?"

"Close to the intersection of 49th and Stark."

"No way! Our house is on that corner."

"Really? My kids live in the apartments on that block," I said, hoping they would know the ones I meant.

They laughed. "That's so funny. Those apartments look down on our house. We know exactly where your kids live."

I rode away feeling I'd gotten a taste of home. I wasn't there yet, but my Portland life was starting to visit me, even on the road. I wanted to start pushing my way home, though I knew that 600 miles still required disciplined pacing.

I landed in granola-loving, dreadlock-wearing Garberville late in the afternoon, found a deli that served a rich and filling lasagna, and bought snacks for the motel room. It was Monday night and the Oakland Raiders would play the Denver Broncos, a rivalry from my long-distant past that's still in my blood. I sat on my bed, opened a bag of caramel corn and a bottle of beer, and allowed myself to become completely engrossed in the game. Just like at home.

DAY 66
Garberville to Eureka, CA
70 miles

THE TRIP HAD BEEN MARKED by numerous shifts in landscapes—from rugged mountains to soft prairies, from isolated deserts
to buzzing cities. I had an option today: I could stay on Highway 101,
with its logging trucks and high-speed traffic, or take a short detour
to the 30-mile stretch called "The Avenue of the Giants." It was one
of those not-to-be-missed opportunities.

Yesterday's giant redwoods had signs drawing tourists to marvel at
those ancient growths, but today's treat was completely different. I was
drawn into a new world that made me feel like Alice entering Wonderland. The sheer scope, size and height of the trees was partly
disorienting and mostly magical. This was an enchanted place. At least
twenty other cyclists were heading south through this same forest. I
might have imagined it, but they seemed to do a double-take at the
sight of one lone cyclist heading north against the wind. Nobody goes
north!

At one fallen tree, I couldn't resist setting up a picture. The exposed
and uprooted trunk was easily 25 feet across and 25 feet high. I added
the photo to my blog with the caption, "Lucky the tree wasn't any
bigger"—insinuating that I'd hit the megaton tree and knocked it over
with my bike. My Heron clan would appreciate the sad attempt at
humor.

I was thankful for the magical quality of the place for I had spent
much of the morning working myself into a state of anxiety. My mind
had turned toward Portland and what I would encounter when I
returned. *What tasks are going to be facing me? How has my cat been?*
What are my kids going to need? What will be the condition of the congre-
gation? I reminded myself that I couldn't take care of those issues now,

and that it was best to enjoy the day before me. I used the magical presence of each tree to keep me focused on the present moment, as my mind kept drifting more than a week and 500 miles ahead. I alternated between growing anxiety and gratitude for the other-worldly gift I was pedaling through.

I exited the redwoods and soon found myself crossing riverbeds that meandered their way to the ocean. The terrain became flatter, less dense, and carried a distinct coastal feel—foggy moisture and wind being common along the Northern California coast. I was nearing the town of Eureka. As I continued to make the transition from the redwoods to the coastal terrain, something began to break loose psychologically. I didn't have words for it, but I felt I was about to shed something and gain a new clarity. The anxiety I'd carried all day melted away; a wave of calm overcame me. It was bigger than just pushing away the anxiety about returning to Portland and all the responsibilities waiting for me. This calm was more about being able to close the chapter—finally—on the struggle that had dogged me and pushed me for 3,500 miles.

As I mused about this growing serenity in my soul, I rode by the sign indicating the city limits of Eureka. The moment made me chuckle. Just as I was exploring this new feeling of acceptance and calm, I entered the town known as "I have found it." Why now and not earlier? The irony was I had ridden through Eureka, Utah, and the only feeling I had was to keep moving before the 100-degree heat bit me for good. I'd slept in Eureka, Nevada, and my only interest was recovering from the day, re-hydrating, eating, sleeping, and psychologically preparing for another day in the barren desert.

I wasn't sure if I was having a real breakthrough or just wishing for a breakthrough, putting too much stock in momentary feelings. Nonetheless, as I entered yet another town named Eureka, I marked the moment in my mind and muttered, "Guess third time is a charm." I smiled at how corny it sounded.

Something felt different inside. Time would tell whether I was just being cleverly playful or whether something real had happened.

DAY 67
Eureka to Klamath, CA
77 miles

I WAS NEARING THE FINISH and the need for daily discipline didn't carry as much weight since I was no longer crossing a mountain range or tackling a desert. I left the motel a good two hours later than usual, after staying up late the night before. I intended to ride a few miles fueled only by a banana and a muffin from the natural food store across from the motel, and the motel's weak courtesy coffee. In McKinleyville, fifteen miles out, I would stop for a farmer-style breakfast that would sustain me for most of the day. Unfortunately, I hit a number of detours due to road construction. The good news was they took me closer to the sea, and I rode through a number of pastures where the cows had an exclusive ocean view. Just a few hundred yards off Highway 101, I felt I was on some Irish isle, wheeling my way across manure-covered roads while cow bells serenaded me as I passed.

But I just couldn't get a rhythm going. It was foggy and cold. I followed the detours, backtracking to my original route so as not to get too far off course, all the time looking for signs to McKinleyville so I didn't ride right past it. But I did! I overshot the town by about two miles, and since it was already noon I had to backtrack to find that breakfast I had bypassed earlier.

An hour later I was on the road again. No more than thirty minutes into it, I hit a large piece of glass, my rear tire let out a loud hiss, and in a few short revolutions I was riding on the wheel rim. Flat tires are annoying, but rear flat tires are especially annoying while touring. All the packs have to come off; then you have to get the chain in the right position, pull back on the derailleur, and wiggle the wheel out of the drop-outs. The process takes three times as long as repairing a front tire. I wasn't really complaining, however—it was only my fourth flat tire over the course of 3,500 miles. I'd expected three times that amount. I was just agitated that it was mid-afternoon and I still hadn't gotten into the kind of rhythm that makes touring enjoyable.

If the late start, detours, backtracking and flat tire weren't enough already, the thick blanket of fog dogged me all day and kept me from feeling comfortable on the bike. I often refer to myself as an "avid fair-weather cyclist." In Portland, most serious cyclists pedal year-round. Me, however—I hang the bike up when the rain starts in October and it doesn't come out again until two or three days of sun get strung together in April. Then I'm on the road nearly every day. This weather reminded me why I don't like to ride in the moist air that permeates western Oregon for most months of the year: by the end of the day, I was coated with a slimy mixture of moisture and sweat that left me cold, uncomfortable and, quite honestly, gross.

I had intended to reach Crescent City, close to the California/Oregon border, but by the time I reached Prairie Creek State Park it was getting dark. The fog had blocked the sun, and I was still riding in groves of tall redwood trees that filter out the light even on a sunny day. The fog was turning to mist and it felt dangerous to be out on the road. All the little misadventures of the day had added up, and I was possibly riding into riskier territory. I kept riding, hoping to find a roadside lodge, since Crescent City was still over twenty miles away. I had sent home my camping gear in the desert: now I was flirting with not having a place to sleep.

At seven in the evening, still fifteen miles short of my original goal, I reached what is listed as the small village of Klamath—although the 780 alleged residents must be hidden in the thick forest in woodstove-heated cabins. I was fortunate to find a couple of motels on the highway, and chose one that had individually quaint cabins with wooden front porches. I settled into my room and made my way back to the Country Market and Diner, due to close at half-past seven. I made it just as they were turning the "Open" sign around to "Sorry, We're Closed."

I was the only person at the tables placed between the kitchen and the shelves of convenience store stock. I ordered with the intention of treating myself well: steak, vegetables, potato, and a good beer. I ate quietly while the cooking crew broke down the kitchen, putting away unused food, scrubbing the counters, and washing dishes.

My first (and only, I thought) beer was just about gone when an attractive, large woman with an easy disposition brought me a second.

"Looks like you could use another one of these."

"Thanks. I hadn't intended to order that," I said, thinking I would need to pay for it.

"This one is on me," she said. She walked back to the kitchen and re-emerged with another mug of cold beer in her hand. "Mind if I join you? My name's Sherry."

I was thrilled. "Please, have a seat. I'd be glad to have the company. I'm Brian."

"I saw you come in on your bike," she said. "You just look like a pretty interesting guy. I was wondering what your story was."

"My story?" I smiled. "That's a big question. I'm not even sure what my story is."

I dove in, trying to find a balance between giving her enough of the story to satisfy her curiosity, but not so much as to bore her. When I got to the part about my divorce and the deaths that followed shortly after, Sherry jumped in.

"I get it," she said. "I didn't take a big trip like you, but I've felt the need to start over. I was divorced three years ago and my world fell apart. I'd dreamed for years of running a retreat center. Last year, I moved away from my life in Southern California, bought this place, and am in the middle of redeveloping it."

"It's a lovely little spot," I said. "My cabin is adorable."

"For now I'm just running it as a motel," she said, "but I'm redeveloping the acreage behind me for groups who are looking more for a retreat center."

I had an impulsive inclination to drop everything, cut my pilgrimage short, and offer to go in with her. "You can redevelop the site," I would say, "and I'll be the marketing and creative director for the retreat center." She might have taken me up on it—but I knew it wasn't right for me. I was enjoying the female attention; I liked the direction her life was taking her. And running a retreat center would be a blast. But Sherry and Klamath were a complete unknown, and my life was still in Portland.

The evening was getting late and I wanted to carve out time to dig into the possible breakthrough I'd had on entering Eureka. I excused myself, and thanked her for the beer and her time. In the tiny, cute cabin I sat down and pulled out a notebook. What was I feeling yesterday? What was the breakthrough that showed up?

I wrote and wrote, searching for words that seemed true. Finally, one sentence emerged: this pilgrimage was less about what was happening in the Church, and more about my *anxiety* about what was happening in the Church. I was grieving over the loss of something for me—an identity, a lifestyle, a place of belonging?

"I feel like I ended up in the wrong place at the wrong time," I wrote. I stuck with the thread that was emerging. I was resentful—resentful to have entered a profession that was dissolving; resentful of the weak resolve of the Church to reverse its increasing irrelevancy; resentful that Kelseyville had too easily discarded me; resentful that the Church had done little to counter the rigid, fundamentalist perceptions of religious leaders in America. In a moment of crystal clarity, I thought, "I don't want to become irrelevant. This is as much about me as it is the Church."

I had gone from anxiety a few days before, to the calm in Eureka, to some deep anger that I allowed to surface. I still hadn't quite put my finger on it, but it was coming. I went to bed with a strange stew of sadness, anger, and mild defiance swirling around in my head and my heart.

DAY 68
Klamath, CA to Gold Beach, OR
75 miles

BEFORE EMBARKING IN THE MORNING, I checked my Adventure Cycling map to assess the number of elevation gains I could expect along the coast. Just a few miles up the road, a short pass separated Klamath from Crescent City, my original destination of the day before. Below the graph was a warning: "Do not attempt to cross this pass in the fog." I strapped my belongings onto my bike on the front porch of the cabin, carried the bike down the steps, and set off confidently. I wanted to make quick work of the pass, cover the fifteen miles in a little over an hour, and then stop in Crescent City for my daily treat—breakfast!

The sun was not out, but the fog was not heavy either; drivers would have no problem seeing me on the road. I hit the base of the climb and the fog still was little more than a light mist. But about a third of the way up I ran into a bank of fog that was thick, scary thick. I stopped. Not only had the map warned me not to attempt this section in the fog, but my gut told me exactly why: there was little to no shoulder on the highway. Where there was a shoulder it was inconsistent, narrowing and widening from two inches to no more than two feet. The road was curvy, as if designed by connecting a series of S-bends. And in addition to normal-sized passenger cars, there was a consistent flow of RV's pulling Jeeps, trailers and boats, with an occasional logging truck blowing by. I stood there paralyzed. I had not been this nervous since the Bozeman experience, when gravel trucks and airport traffic had sped along a no-shoulder frontage road and passed me as if I were a gopher trapped on the road.

I considered my options. I could do as my Adventure Cycling map suggested: coast back down the hill and camp out at the restaurant until the fog lifted. I wasn't pleased at that idea, as the fog had already been socked in for two straight days; I imagined being stuck for one, two, or even three days, waiting for a break in the soupy cloud. I entertained the notion of waiting it out on the side of the road, but I knew it would be only a matter of minutes before I was wetter, colder, and angrier. Finally, I decided to make the attempt and trust I would make it. I attached both my rear red blinker and my front headlamp. They would do little good, but I needed every bit of help I could get. I took a big breath that felt like a prayer and set off, cycling as close to the edge as possible. As the sound of vehicles crept up on me, I assessed whether they were little Toyota hatchbacks that could easily make their way around me, or whether they were timber trucks delivering tons of product and would need all the road plus some of the shoulder to negotiate the constant curves.

I don't know whether I made it over the top due to my focus on riding a straight line, or the extra caution exhibited by drivers in dangerous fog, or dumb luck. I have a feeling that luck played a more significant role than I wanted to admit. But I made it. As I crested the summit and began coasting down the other side toward Crescent City the fog lifted and, amazingly, the sun came out for the first time in three days. My spirits lifted considerably.

I was relieved when a breakfast place presented itself the moment I entered Crescent City. There at the Good Harvest Café I had the best pancakes of the whole trip—evenly cooked all the way through, light and fluffy, a deep, malty taste, and with a crisp, dark-brownish finish. I tipped the cook in addition to the waitress.

"I've been on the road for nine weeks, and these are the best pancakes I've eaten in nearly 4,000 miles," I told the hostess, and beamed at her.

"Well, I guess you're the pancake expert then," she said, smiling back.

I felt good. I'd survived the scare in the fog over the mountain, just eaten the best pancakes of the whole trip—and the sun was out! The glorious sun was out!

Twenty miles later, I crossed another important threshold. Just before the town of Brookings, a six-foot-square sign seemed to stretch its arms toward me, saying "Welcome to Oregon." I stopped, took a picture of it, and immediately texted it to my children and my friend Pam who I had left nine weeks prior in the midst of her grief. I had crossed eight states on this trip; Oregon had the pleasure of seeing me cross it first from west to east, and then south to north. This was the final leg of the journey.

I picked up the pace like a horse that gets barn sour after a long ride. I had scheduled two nights in Bandon, a growing resort town known for its world-famous, exclusive golf courses. My dad and his wife (fourth wife, in case you are confused) were going to make the three-hour drive from Rogue River to meet me there. Coincidentally, my best friend from childhood, Dave (whose parents I had stayed with in Loveland) was vacationing in Bandon with his wife and friends, celebrating his fiftieth birthday. I wanted to get as far as I could today so I'd have a full afternoon and evening next day to relax and enjoy making some long-overdue connections.

The ride—and my mood—improved considerably on this stretch, due mostly to the presence of the sun. I could now see the ocean at the vista points located every few hundred yards along the coast. Wind-surfers were out riding the waves in one cove, with their multi-colored sails and graceful movement. The terrain in this section is pretty much limited to up or down: I climbed short, steep sections to be catapulted down the other side, with just enough momentum to coast up the first hundred yards of the next hill before being forced to dig and grunt my way up again. To my left, rocky cliffs and lush green vegetation fell precipitously to the crashing water below.

I stopped in Gold Beach for the night. I found a motel on the strip that parallels the coastline. The motel was box-like and not very interesting, but it had a comfortable bed. That's all I really needed. I walked a few blocks away to a steakhouse, ignored the prices and refueled in style with a steak and potato dinner, washed down by two beers and followed by coffee and cheesecake. This was living!

I returned to my motel room with a strange buzz from the combination of beer, coffee and sugar. After the effects of the indulgent dinner wore off I sat down to write again. I was still trying to give a name to the shift that I felt as entered Eureka two days before. Yes, I was angry life had placed me in a profession that was disappearing; the defiance I felt was an attempt to battle against being caught in the cross-hairs of life. No, it wasn't resignation I felt, but rather a sad and grateful acceptance. My work was not yet done, but forces were moving inside me that had been stalled for years.

DAY 69
Gold Beach to Bandon, OR
55 miles

I WOKE WITH THAT FEELING of acceptance still caressing me. But I was also physically and psychologically tired. Without intending to, I had ridden four pretty long and difficult days totaling over 300 miles—I was feeling it in more ways than one. Moreover, I'd been dogged by fog through most of Northern California, which had sapped my get-up-and-go. I wandered over to the window, opened the curtains, and let out a shriek. "The sun is out again. Ha-ha!" I felt a surge of energy. I only had a short 55-mile ride to Bandon, on reasonably flat terrain, and I had a rest day planned after I got there. I had no reason to push. This trek really was coming to an end.

I had as uneventful and mindless a ride into Bandon as I could imagine, riding in blissful numbness as if I'd already been given permission to lounge around. I was still turning the pedals, but it felt like the warm-down after a long, punishing ride—except that this warm-down was 55 luxurious miles long.

Just before Bandon, a small, frumpy-looking café was advertising coconut cream pie. It was mid-afternoon; I pulled my bike onto the porch of The Greasy Spoon and ordered a piece of pie and a cup of coffee. I didn't really need either, but I wasn't about to pass up the experience. It was perfect—a buttery, flaky crust with a rich, sweet filling to balance the bitter left-over coffee.

I was a few hours ahead of my dad and his wife when I rolled easily into Bandon. I moved through my normal post-ride routine of checking into the motel, unloading my bike, getting a hot, soapy shower, and putting on my one civilian outfit of green shorts and black t-shirt. I enjoyed a hot, thick and creamy bowl of clam chowder down by the pier and then retreated to my room. My dad was expected in a couple hours, so I thought I would rest my eyes—just for a moment. I woke up over an hour later in one of those "What time is it and where am I?" kind of hazes.

It took a moment of looking around the room to put the pieces together, and slowly come back to my senses. In my half-hazed stupor, the agitating breakthrough that began in Eureka came flooding back.

My mind drifted all the way back to the College of Idaho that I'd visited eight weeks before and attended thirty years prior. I had never intended to be a pastor. I studied religion only because it was my passion, and I couldn't seem to stay away from it. I had a double major because I loved the study of religion, but YMCA programs would be my career, I had thought.

But religion was my soul's real love. I remember gorging myself on Reinhold Niebuhr's *Moral Man and Immoral Society,* followed by his two-volume work *The Nature and Destiny of Man.* Niebuhr, long forgotten by popular culture, was one of the most incisive and powerful voices in the mid-twentieth century, when he offered theological and sociological critiques of Nazism, communism, and the role of democracies in society. He was unique for his time in that he challenged religious conservatives for their narrow view of the Bible, and religious liberals for their naïve idealism about the world. In my mind, he got it just right.

My reading of Niebuhr was followed by a year of honors research on the Protestant response to the Holocaust. I was moved by the faith of the German Protestant pastor, Dietrich Bonhoeffer, who was jailed and hanged for his failed assassination attempt on Hitler. I marveled at his commitment to a faith that challenged tyranny, and inhumane and cruel policies.

In seminary I studied the Rev. Dr. Martin Luther King, Jr.'s speeches and writings, and his brilliant oratory. I was compelled by his ability to apply his religious convictions in calling on America to live more deeply into her own proclaimed values of freedom and liberty. Much later, I was taken by Benjamin Franklin's writing and belief that democracy could only work if the government protected individual rights and churches promoted the common good.

I emerged from my ride-induced stupor and finally remembered—this is why I became a preacher and pastor. I believe in the power of our theological convictions to change, transform and call our society to a higher standard, to more compassionate politics, and a truer reflection of our deepest humanity. I have never felt that honoring the separation of church and state means we must divorce our faith from our politics. How could I ever separate my conviction that America should have universal healthcare from my religious belief that "I am my brother's keeper" and that Jesus' life was about healing the whole person—body, mind and soul? I was both shaped and inspired by the passion, the intellect, and the faith of these and many other figures whose religious convictions shaped our history and our American values.

It was beginning to come into focus. My growing frustration over the years was due to the not-so-subtle pressure that being a pastor was now more about how to save the institution of church. "How are we going to get more young people in the church?" and "Who might be interested in renting our empty space to ease our budget woes?" were now the questions on the mind of many a parishioner and church member. Those were not my questions. I didn't give a flying fuck about keeping a church building open.

I was raised in a time when the Church was the moral pulpit and voice for the community. To be a pastor meant to speak to the broader society and act as America's conscience. That had changed. Now to be a pastor means to speak only to the religious faithful. My obligation was no longer to the theological integrity and voice of ministry; my obligation was now to those who paid my salary, whose greatest concern was how to save the Church, pay the bills, and meet the pastoral needs of those sitting in the pews.

I had finally remembered. I got into this preaching business because I was moved by the faith and commitment of religious leaders who used their theological ideas to serve humanity. Somehow, over the years, the pulpit had turned into a voice-box for the religiously faithful—and somehow I'd got caught in that shift. I believed in the power of the pulpit, but now the pulpit was owned by those more concerned about the survival of the Church than being the conscience of the community.

And so I've been riding. I've ridden hard. I have fought for my life. I've tried to hold on to the one place that used to mirror the best of me and my passions. I've tried to snatch back the pulpit from the hands of those who feel they own it by virtue of their pledges. I never intended to become a pastor, but I was drawn to the pulpit by those who believed in and teased out the powerful dialogue between their faith and their civic identity. My theological heroes were not concerned about serving the religiously faithful; they used their theological ideas to serve humanity.

Finally, I had remembered. A deep breath escaped me. I began to cry softly.

DAY 70
Bandon
Rest Day, 0 miles

MY BED WAS SOFT AND COMFORTABLE with a thick, white, fluffy comforter. I had little on the agenda for the day, so I lay there at least an hour longer than I generally would have. The day ahead was just about nurturing myself, like the day I'd spent in Gardnerville, Nevada, when Gabe took me up in a glider above Lake Tahoe.

My dad and his wife Arlene, in a room across the parking lot in the same motel, also slept in. I was looking forward to reconnecting with my dad; we have not always seen eye to eye on matters of religion and politics, usually arguing without ever coming to any resolution—except to agree that the other was wrong.

We met up and ordered breakfast. Arlene said, "We've loved your blog, Brian. It's the first thing I do in the morning—check to see if you've written and to make sure you're still alive!"

I laughed. "Have you been concerned about me—seriously?"

"Yes. Are you kidding? You were crossing the desert! I prayed for you every day."

My dad nodded in agreement. He isn't as expressive as his new bride, but he raised his eyebrows and said, "You sure had us praying on a few days. I was pretty worried after I read about the car crash in the desert."

"Really, guys, I've been fine," I said. "But I do like knowing that you care."

We drank our coffee while we waited for our breakfast to arrive.

"You know, Brian," my dad said, "I really got what you said about feeling closest to God in the mountains."

"That doesn't surprise me, Dad. The mountains were a big part of our family growing up."

"I do love the church I go to," he said. "I love singing with the people and feel a responsibility to the church. But before I started going there, it was the time I spent fishing, hunting and camping when I felt God the most."

"You know, Dad, we may be closer on our religious views than we think," I said. "I may say that I have a bit of the mystic in me, but that's just the formal name for how you're describing yourself. And I may say I experience the Sacred out there and you say God, but we're really talking about the same thing."

Arlene smiled, saying with no words at all, "I like seeing you two find some common ground. Makes me happy."

It occurred to me that my dad had passed on his values to me. He brought me up in the mountains and by streams. He inculcated in me a love for nature—we shared that. Where we differed was that he hunted and fished, while I cycled and snow-shoed. He hiked and camped, whereas I ran trails and back-packed. But both of us celebrated nature and felt a spiritual presence there. My dad and I had argued for years over religion and politics, but really I was just a chip off the old block.

Dad and Arlene left to drive back to their home in Rogue River. I had nothing scheduled until the evening when I would celebrate Dave's birthday with him. I wandered through town, surveying the shops without getting serious enough to enter them. I walked along the beaches south of Bandon, and meditated on the rhythmic crashing of the waves against large, isolated haystack rocks not far off. I took off my sandals and let the sea tickle my feet with cold, frothy water. For two hours I sat in the cool, sunny air on a Bandon pier, watching seagulls, seals and tourists enjoy themselves and occasionally fight for space. I meandered again through the shops, this time buying fudge and taking more time to appreciate the gift stores and art galleries.

At one gallery I was struck by a piece of art: a five-gallon clay pot simply and elegantly designed in earthy red clay and rusty-brown colors. On the outside, the shapes of several hands had been permanently fired onto the container. The pot seemed to say aloud, "You are safe and held in our hands."

The pot powerfully captured the spirit of my pilgrimage. I'd gone looking for my soul's home after a number of significant losses, and seeing the erosion of the Church and my livelihood as a minister. In the early weeks, I'd felt held by hands that emerged from leaves, trees, lakes and mountains. As I rode away from Mother Church, I felt Mother Earth holding me up. After I had conquered the Rocky Mountains and before I'd put my front tire into the Nevada desert, I was carried by the invisible hands of family, friends and acquaintances, who urged me on when I thought of taking a detour around, through, or over the sobering and terrifying desert.

I loved how the pottery reflected my journey but I left the shop, scared off by the $200 price tag. I hadn't gone very far when I turned right back around. It was the perfect symbol and physical reminder of the pilgrimage: supportive hands on the outside and empty space on the inside. I bought it, had it packed tightly, paid the additional shipping fees, and walked away feeling the joy and the weight of the whole journey, and my gratitude for it surging through my body. I knew this piece of art would forever tell the story of my ten-week pilgrimage.

That evening, Dave called: he and his group had spotted whales far off the coastline and urged me to come early for dinner if I was able. I was treated to the first whale sighting of my life. Far away, too far to see their bodies, little spouts erupted from the surface of the water. Just the physical sign that those massive creatures were swimming out there left me feeling that the day had been a pure gift—connecting with my dad, buying the perfect symbol of the trip, whale-sightings, and then off to celebrate Dave's birthday. "It just doesn't get any better than this," I said to myself.

The five of us enjoyed a delightful meal and good wine (Dave always has good wine!), followed by a birthday dessert with a single candle in it representing his first half-century. We talked about golf, politics, religion, and my pilgrimage. Dave said he'd come across the blog of a person who had ridden from Alaska to the tip of Chile on a tandem, inviting others along the way to ride with him. When he reached the end of his journey, he found himself asking, now what? Dave wondered if I might get to Portland and find myself asking the same question. I wasn't ready to answer that yet, but I intuitively sensed he might be right. I walked back to my motel room with a warm buzz from the good wine, grateful for the full day of rich experiences and relaxed pace.

My mind turned to the remaining miles. I was now close enough to predict that I should be able to ride into the city on Wednesday, September 21. I was excited to be getting back to Portland. I was also sad that this amazing journey was about to end.

DAY 71
Bandon to Florence, OR
77 miles

I LEFT IN THE MORNING with my legs itching to propel me to Portland ASAP—I had only two hundred miles remaining. There was a part of me that wanted to ride straight through the day and into the night, and maybe arrive in Portland before the sun rose the following morning. Of course, it was only a passing thought. I knew how much my body could handle and anything beyond 80 miles would start to punish me. And there was no sense taking the risk of riding on shoulder-less roads in the middle of the night, where a speeding sports car might knock me into a ditch around a tight corner. I dismissed the thought and settled into a pace that would carry me to the town of Florence, where the Siuslaw River reaches the Pacific Ocean.

As I rode, my mind clearly turned toward Portland. I thought about going through ten weeks of mail, picking up my cat, having her get used to me again, and slowly settling back into my pastoral role and community work. I had to work to shut out those thoughts so I could enjoy what was right before me. Once again the terrain allowed for some soft, graceful riding and reflection. There are hills to contend with along the coast of Oregon, but those occasional hills required nothing like the mental preparation needed for the severe ranges of Idaho, Wyoming, Colorado, and Utah.

I rode in a very relaxed state. I had no more taxing physical challenges ahead. With space to reflect, I returned to the themes I'd set out to explore as the pilgrimage began. I had clearly ridden out of Portland with a manipulative and subconscious hope that I could either save Eastminster, or create a whole new role for myself on the back of Eastminster's story. I had thought I already knew the story, and all I had to do was cleverly find a way to broadcast it to the larger community. All the local Portland papers and the national Presbyterian Outlook had interviewed me before I rode my first mile; my blog had over three hundred daily followers.

That's where the pilgrimage started. But by the time I reached Helper, Utah—where I threw a hissy fit at God for the shitty motel—the idealistic veil was peeling away. I wasn't having the impact I'd unconsciously hoped for. The world wasn't suddenly changing just because I was on an over-ambitious pilgrimage. As much grit and determination as I had, it still wasn't enough to hold back the tide of change sweeping through our religious communities.

As this pilgrimage drew to an end, a deeper agenda began to reveal itself. This wasn't really about the Church—it was about me. I was mourning the loss of the Church I knew as a child when its pulpit was actually the community pulpit. I was grieving the loss of a role that seemed to be there while I was in seminary, but disappeared in my early years of ministry—that is, the minister being as responsible for the wellbeing of the community as he or she is for the welfare of the Church as an institution. I was angry that my own religious tradition had no answer to a fundamentalist religious right that had created a toxic environment for debate in the public sphere. I was sad that a role I was once proud to wear on my shirt sleeve I now shared sheepishly, always unsure of public reaction.

I crossed the Siuslaw River and coasted into Florence still feeling reasonably rested after a 77-mile ride. I was riding easily, not pushing, and felt myself decompressing from the long, hard journey. Florence has a small and very attractive four-block waterfront with restaurants, gift shops, and ice cream parlors. The Bridgewater Oyster Bar and Grill was large and roomy, with dark-stained woodwork and red brick walls. I splurged, slurping up a large bowl of seafood cioppino and a pint of pale ale, as had become my custom. I'm not sure whether the meal was actually better than other meals I'd had or whether I was just in the right frame of mind—but I relished every bite as if my taste buds had suddenly come alive.

DAY 72
Florence to Junction City, OR
71 miles

I HAD DECIDED IN BANDON that when I reached Florence I would turn east and head inland. I could have continued up the coast to Waldport, Newport, Lincoln City, Tillamook, and even as far north as Cannon Beach before going east. But I had driven all those sections from Astoria, on the border with Washington, to Florence in past years. Having ridden the complete southern portion, I had now traveled the entire coast. I wanted to see some unfamiliar terrain and, quite honestly, to get away from the cool, moist, windy coast and enjoy the warmer, more temperate inland climate.

The road from Florence to Eugene—Highway 126—can be fairly busy. I looked at my map and found what I believed would be a less-traveled road at the town of Mapleton, just fifteen miles inland. I veered left at the Y-intersection onto Highway 36 and made my way up the two-lane road. What a great decision! I was following the Siuslaw River and the only traffic I saw was an occasional service vehicle. I took time to stop and pick blackberries. I sat on a rock at the edge of the stream, watching the water, and tried not to think of anything.

A woman drove up in a black Jeep. "You wouldn't happen to be Mark, would you?" she asked.

"No, my name's Brian."

"Sorry," she said. "A cyclist on the Cycle Oregon route vanished three days ago not too far from here. You looked a little like him with your grayish beard."

"Oh no, I'm so sorry to hear that," I said. "I rode Cycle Oregon in oh-seven, eight and nine."

She drove away; I hoped Mark would be found alive and well somewhere before too long.

Soon a short, steep climb ushered me onto the edge of the small and inviting Triangle Lake. As I came over the top of the coastal mountains, I began to descend to the Willamette Valley, an area of farming land, sheep and cow pastures, and vineyards linking dozens of small rural Oregon towns, the larger university towns of Eugene and Corvallis, and the state capital of Salem.

I didn't have to wait until I got back to Portland to wrestle with the question Dave had asked: Now what? Just the fact he'd introduced the question got me thinking. I knew I wasn't coming back with some new grand plan for my life. I had not discovered a new calling, nor been asked by some risk-taking investor to create a new kind of church or spiritual community. No woman had swept me off my feet along the way, tempting me to cut my pilgrimage short. But that didn't mean the pilgrimage had been a failure.

I had become clearer about what had prompted the pilgrimage. I was grieving and mourning the impending death of a profession that, at one time, had mirrored my deepest passions and commitments. I had tried to run ahead of the grief and busted my butt to see if I could outwit the losses, but in the end I admitted I would have to let go of an identity that fit me well and that I loved.

I was returning to Eastminster knowing that the members there, too, were wrestling with the reality of trusting and letting go. We didn't know whether we would still be a church in six months or twelve months. I didn't know whether I would still have a job then either. But this was our path. This was our reality. Church and ministry as we knew it was going to pass away, and we could only live through that, trusting and graceful, as a grandfather must live his final months.

I glided down the curved hills from Trinity Lake until I hit the turn for Junction City, just a few miles north of Eugene. I attempted to get a room, but the motel's electricity had gone out. The clerk promised me they would have a room available in an hour or two, so I used the time to haul my gear over to the laundromat for one final wash and dry of my bicycle clothing. I took a picture of myself doing the laundry and included it in my blog, with the Buddhist-inspired caption, "After ecstasy, the laundry." That's exactly how I felt. After ten weeks of being on the road, in my own head, and listening to the wrestling within my heart and soul, I was now returning to committee meetings, writing newsletter articles, feeding my cat, and deciding whether to buy shampoo for normal or oily hair. The ecstasy was ending—a truckload of metaphorical laundry awaited me.

While waiting for my clothes to dry, I checked my emails. A colleague had written: Sharon had read my blog for the first time that morning and recognized the questions I was wrestling with on the pilgrimage. She lived and worked as a pastor in Albany, a town I would travel through next morning on my way to Portland. She was offering lunch in exchange for a conversation about what I'd discovered on the pilgrimage. I accepted.

After leaving the Bay area, I'd decided not to re-enter the church world until I returned to Portland; I was breaking my own rule. But there was energy in Sharon's message. I was willing to make an exception for her.

DAY 73
Junction City to Salem, OR
66 miles

AS I TOOK OFF FROM JUNCTION CITY, my body was still in the valley and on the bike, but my head and heart had already jumped ahead to Portland. I was anxious to see my children again. We had a history of going out for breakfast at least monthly, and getting together to watch Trailblazer games while eating my famous chicken nachos and drinking beer. I had friends who had supported me through the lead-up to the pilgrimage, and I was ready to connect with them and share the experience. I wanted to reconnect with Pam, still feeling bad that I had left her in her time of pain and grief. I was even anxious to return to the church and unravel how this experience had changed them as well as me, and what that meant for our future.

I rode casually through farmland, much of which had been harvested weeks before, timing my ride to arrive in Albany as close to lunch as possible. I crossed the nearly empty parking lot of the church, parked my bike under a mural painted on the wall, and checked in with the secretary. Sharon would be down shortly, the secretary informed me. I waited at the bottom of the steps.

Sharon appeared at the top of the stairs, wearing a flowing colorful skirt. She had large, sparkly brown eyes and exuded an almost manic joy. I recognized her immediately. Years before, I'd been at a presbytery meeting, sitting close to the back of the sanctuary. She was positioned behind the communion table, preparing to lead us through the liturgy for the Lord's Supper. But rather than launching into the usual lengthy Great Prayer of Thanksgiving, Sharon had sung the liturgy in a beautiful and sensual soprano voice. I fell in love with her in the same way a theater-goer falls in love with a star on the screen. I sat in the back thinking, *this is how it's supposed to be. This is how it's supposed to feel.* I knew nothing about her except those thirty minutes we'd shared in worship. I left the meeting and didn't think of her again—until she appeared at the top of the stairs.

"Hi. Are you Sharon?" I asked. Inane question, since I'd recognized her.

"Yes. I'm so glad this worked out. I saw your blog yesterday and then saw you were coming through my area and thought, what the heck, I might as well give it a shot," she said in her energetic, rapid-fire style.

"I saw you at a presbytery meeting years ago. I remember you singing the liturgy."

She giggled. "Yep. That's me. I'm always trying new things and shaking things up."

We walked three blocks to a bustling, pub-style restaurant. She asked for a table somewhat out of the way, which was no surprise: I'd done the same thing dozens of times when I didn't want to be seen by parishioners. This time the strategy didn't work.

Before we'd even arrived at our table, Sharon stopped. "Mom, what a surprise to see you here!"

"Sharon, how marvelous to see you." Her mom's New York accent rang out. "You out for a work lunch today?"

"Yes, this is Brian. I just met him," Sharon said by way of introduction. "He's on this super-human bike trip, writing about the state of the Church. I just happened to catch him while he was riding through."

"Hello, nice to meet you," I said, in the half-hearted way one does to a stranger.

Sharon and I took our leave. Over lunch we talked, the energy of the conversation increasing with each new topic. Sharon had expanded her expertise to include certifications as a yoga teacher and spiritual director, adding to her past degree in music therapy and a masters of divinity (that all us pastor-types have).

"I'm so tired of constantly trying to convince the Church that God can be experienced in different ways, outside our nice buildings," she said.

"I know what you mean. I had great conversations with people outside the Church who don't need any convincing that yoga or cycling or dance or meditation are valid spiritual experiences. But as soon as I walk back into church I feel I have to convince people that those activities are just as valid as praying, singing hymns, and reading scripture."

"I don't want to spend my time convincing—I want to just *do* it," Sharon said, with an emphasis that revealed her frustration with church ministry.

"The irony is that people outside the church are ready for that," I said. "They want to explore their spirituality through dance and movement and nature."

"Yeah, I've decided to call this an embodied spirituality."

The words struck me forcefully. "That's it! A spirituality that is lived out and experienced through our bodies and our senses. That's what I love about cycling. There are times when my body, the rhythm of my legs and my breath, the road, and the surrounding terrain are totally in sync. I don't know any other way to describe it except that I feel in rhythm with God—or as I like to call Her these days, the Sacred."

Sharon smiled at my use of the feminine pronoun, knowing that while I could get away with it in the privacy of the restaurant with her, it's risky business in the Church.

We shared the same frustrations, as well as the same vision for our lives and the Church. I had met a soul companion.

But she had to get back to the office and I still had twenty miles to ride.

Sharon happily posed under the mural at the church as I took a picture to add to my blog and the recorded memories of the trip. We hugged. She returned to her life and I remounted my bike, ready to re-enter mine.

I rode the rest of the afternoon in a playful spirit, deciding to make it a little adventure. I followed smaller country roads, some to the north and others west, until they took me too far off compass. At one point, the road began a sweeping curve, and before I knew it I was heading south again toward Albany. I backtracked, got a little closer to the freeway, and slowly pieced together a series of roads that took me into Salem. Too late, I regretted not planning more of these adventurous side trips into my pilgrimage. I'd packed the trip with a full agenda of long miles, places to visit, and people to see. Sharon had uncorked my spontaneity, if only for a few hours.

That night, the last of my pilgrimage, I splurged on an overpriced downtown hotel room that had a built-in Jacuzzi. I hadn't planned on lavishing so much luxury on myself. The hotel I stopped at had one room available and was willing to give me a 10 percent discount, which still made it three times the price I usually paid. I had the money and I wasn't interested in wheeling around for two hours, looking for the best price. Besides, I wanted to stay close to downtown where I could easily walk to restaurants and be close to the state capitol buildings in the morning as I left town. My bike and grease-stained gear looked incongruous leaning against the wall next to the luxurious mahogany business desk, with the over-sized hot tub in the background. Expensive, yes, but after a muscle-softening soak in the Jacuzzi, I fell into a blissfully deep sleep.

DAY 74
Salem to Portland, OR
71 miles

I HAD UNTIL FOUR O'CLOCK to get into Portland. The church had organized a "Welcome Home, Brian" party, and I had committed to riding up to the church as near that time as possible. If this pilgrimage was my version of a hero's journey, this was as close as I would come to receiving a hero's welcome.

The only stop I had planned for the day was at the state capitol in Salem. As an adolescent, I had dreamt of becoming a U.S. senator; political science was my first declared major in college. Though I chose a different direction, the tug of politics was always there. Remember, my theological heroes were all people who had successfully married their faith with their politics in a way that endowed both with power and integrity. When I look at a church building, I see a symbol of the sacred; when I look at a capitol building, I see a monument to the best that human society can be. Somewhere in the dance between these two partners—the sacred and society—is my life, my calling, and my hope.

My bookshelves are lined with titles that speak to church and state, religion and public life, the sacred and the secular. I was living this out: co-chair to the East Portland Action Plan, an appointed commissioner to the City Charter, a city council-appointed member of the Portland Plan citizen advisory group—not to mention being the alternate to a county commissioner, a seat that would have me serving a district of nearly a quarter million people should the commissioner be unable to fulfill her duties. I was a pastor and a community leader, with a church pulpit and a community pulpit. Couldn't be better for me.

But the pilgrimage was sparked when I saw the foundation I'd built this life on slipping away. Eastminster was on its way toward closure. At a time when churches were forced to double their efforts just to survive, I was unlikely to find another position that would tolerate my heavy public involvement. I could run for political office, but politics itself does not satisfy me. I could find another church, but would probably have to settle for a job description that favored serving the needs of aging members over one that favored the church as the community's conscience and theological center.

I sat on a bench facing the capitol building as government employees scurried between buildings with papers and briefcases under their arms. A little piece of my heart lay in that building. I felt fortunate to be returning to Portland and Eastminster knowing I was just where I needed to be. For now at least, I had a position that honored my love for religious tradition and thought, and my desire to serve the community in a way that was an extension of my theological training and assumed values. I had, for a short stint, a rare position in this age of Church decline.

I also knew it would end. That was sad. But my real sadness was because the days when the church pulpit was also the community pulpit were over. My real sadness was that the discourse between religion and public life had become so warped and toxic that no religious voice was trusted. I want to live in a world where religion and politics are more like first cousins than adversaries. That's the world where I am my best self.

I rode the 70 miles to Portland almost unaware of my surroundings. My head and heart were already miles and hours ahead. I alternated between pushing hard on the pedals, anxious to get home, with easing up, nervous about my re-entry into the world again, like an astronaut breaking through the atmosphere after weeks in space.

It wasn't until I reached the MUP trail in Oregon City that I allowed myself to enjoy the pavement before me and the environment around me. The MUP trail signified that I was back. It was the same section I'd ridden when I took off from Eastminster. It was easy to imagine this was just another daily training ride in the suburbs of Portland.

Getting onto the MUP trail felt familiar, but I wasn't ecstatic. I didn't break down in tears. I was more relieved and just plain tired. As I neared my apartment, I stopped to take a picture of Mount Hood in the distance; it was the first day of fall, yet the mountain still bore snow from the previous winter. It was a familiar sight and one that confirmed I was home.

I stalled as much as I could and tried to stretch out the minutes, as I was over an hour early for the welcome home party. I stopped at my apartment, washed up a little, and then made my way to the church. The sign was lit up with the message, "Welcome Home Pastor Brian!" As I rounded the final corner, church members, family and friends were gathered in the front of the church, clapping, waving and cheering me on through the final pedal strokes. The scene looked eerily similar to the morning ten weeks before, with the same crowd standing in front of the church offering their good wishes and prayers as I pedaled away on an unknown adventure. I said out loud, "I'm home. I'm home. I really am home."

Appetizers were ready in the fellowship hall. I made my way around each small group to share my experiences and express my appreciation for being home. The best moment of the evening came when my lovely, spirited, 22-year-old daughter walked into the reception and blurted, "Oh my God, Dad, you are so ripped!" I hadn't recognized the subtle changes occurring in my body, but my family did. I was ten pounds lighter, significantly leaner and more muscled, and my face had sharper contours than when I left. More than that, however, I returned feeling more grace and more determination. My current world was passing away and I felt more at home with that reality. I wasn't able to save the Church or my position. I wasn't going to restore the Church to the days of glory the faithful yearned for as much as I did.

But I had rediscovered my voice, my passion, and my calling. I would never forget again. I was just where I needed to be—at least for the moment.

POSTSCRIPT

THREE WEEKS AFTER I RETURNED to Portland and my work at Eastminster, one of the members who had had been carrying the weight of the church had a scare. He fell unconscious at church and was taken to the emergency room for tests. That's all it took. The ruling body of the church met and said, "We can't put off the inevitable any longer. Our own health and families are at risk."

Nine months later, on June 30, 2012, Eastminster Church officially closed—but not without leaving a tremendous legacy. The East Portland Family Homeless Shelter was permanently established on the site. A 100-plot community garden had been built and was ready to welcome the largely immigrant community around the church. And, most significantly, another congregation took over the ministry and the mission of the church. The remaining Eastminster members folded into the new congregation and the ministries they had begun continued on, just under a different name—Parkrose Community United Church of Christ. Despite closing, this group that I had served for six years still had a worshiping community in the church building that they had built and known as home.

I lost my job, but not because I had failed. I lost my job in the same way that a hospice chaplain loses a piece of her job each time a hospice patient dies. This would become my story, at least for a while longer. Shortly after the closure, I turned down a position after it became clear that the interview team was looking for a resurrection but wasn't ready to encounter the death that has to accompany new life. I had no interest in becoming their savior. I accepted an interim position in a church that had experienced a ten percent decline in each of the three years prior to my arrival. This church was willing to look in the mirror a little more honestly. This would continue to be my professional reality.

But even during this time my pilgrimage through the West was working on me. My livelihood was in the Church, but my heart and soul were still on the road. An insatiable desire had been sparked in me to discover the new spiritual world that was emerging. My heart was still on the overlook above Lower Yellowstone Falls, where I wanted to lean into the violent power of the water. I was still feeling giddy about the day I was caught in the thunder and lightning storm in Nevada, when it felt as if God and I were in a playful wrestling match. I still had images of Julie, the Mexican restaurant hostess, who was completing her studies in world religions at William and Mary College. I wanted to be in her world, an emerging world of spiritual leadership that likely would have little to do with church as we know it. And I was still haunted by the terrible and wonderful experience of riding through the barren desert. It was there that I felt I came face to face with God. I wanted more of that.

As I neared the end of my interim position, my soul started to organize and plan another pilgrimage that would pick up where I had left off. If this book was largely about coming to terms with the dying of the church, as we know it, and the dissolving away of my profession, the pilgrimage also revealed that my spiritual life was moving more toward religious mysticism—where the experience of the Sacred over-shadows theological beliefs about God.

Another pilgrimage was in the works. In the fall of 2014 I flew to Rome for a pilgrimage that I titled "From Rome to Rumi: A Pilgrimage from the Head of the Church to the Heart of Mysticism." For seven weeks and over 1,500 miles I cycled through Catholic Italy, Greek Orthodox Greece and into Turkey, largely a Muslim nation. I ended in Konya, Turkey, a couple hundred miles above ISIS strongholds, in a town famous for receiving two million pilgrims every year who come to visit the tomb of the Sufi poet and philosopher Rumi. I think another book is in the works!

One final note: Three months after I arrived back in Portland I received a call from my aunt in Minnesota. My mother (my dad's second wife, the one in Loveland, Colorado, who didn't return my call) was being moved from her home to live with my aunt. She was showing signs of advanced Alzheimer's and could no longer care for herself.

I was both sorry and relieved to hear the news. I thought back to those three days when I was in Loveland and waited for her to return my call and possibly visit. It is quite possible that her failure to call wasn't a rejection on her part, but rather a consequence of the Alzheimer's disease. I will never know for sure. But it is what I choose to believe.

The Alzheimer's has, ironically, become a gift. After twenty-three years of estrangement, my mom no longer remembers why she disappeared from my life. She asks me, "Now, who are you?" I get to say, "I am your son, Brian. Remember, you are the one who got me on the bike!"

ACKNOWLEDGMENTS

IT IS SO DIFFICULT TO KNOW EXACTLY who to thank for contributing to the process that resulted in this book. Certainly there are many people without whom this first-time author would have been lost. Specifically, my editor in England, Janet Gelernter, who first coached me with her honest and kind critiques, followed by her sharp editing eye; Bobbi Benson, my business coach and publisher from Wild Ginger Press, who has a keen ability to translate words into images and scattered intentions into a plan; Patty, who supported me in a million different ways as good friends do; Barbara, who believed in me enough to step out financially in support of this project; and the members of Eastminster Church, who took this journey of faith into the unknown with me, supporting me, praying for me, and trusting me as we walked into the belly of the whale together.

I am also thankful for those closest to me, who celebrated my journey and suffered from neglect for the endless hours, days, weeks and months that I dedicated to this project: my delightful children, Phil and Julie, and my lovely daughter-in-law, Tedra; my grandson, Elliot Cooper, with whom I look forward to sharing more life and laughs; Pam, who took the risk to love me at an uncertain and confusing juncture of my life; and Sharon, who gave me a reason to want to finish this labor of love.

Finally I want to say thank you to all the people who played a part in this book and who played a part in shaping me. I have in my life been appreciative and angry, bitter and grateful about some of the experiences and relationships I have had. While I could not have always said this, I am as grateful for the experiences of loss as I am for love. Both your presence and your absence from my life have shaped me in profound ways that continue to generate unexpected gifts and goodness. Know that I will always love each of you for the part you have played in my life. Yes, I have experienced deep loss, but I know now that I am not alone in the world. There are always invisible hands holding me.

Thank you.

ABOUT THE AUTHOR

BRIAN IS A PASTOR, blogger, speaker, overly-ambitious cyclist, community organizer and spiritual pilgrim. He lives between the two worlds of traditional religion and emerging forms of spirituality. His search for the Sacred has taken him into the study of traditional theology, Joseph Campbell's mythology and religious mysticism. His spiritual practice includes regular yoga, cycling pilgrimages, readings from a variety of spiritual literature, exploring the narrative world of movies, and the enjoyment of food, nature, friends and family, and spirited and honest conversation.

He has maintained a lifelong love affair with his bicycle including competitive racing and touring. In addition to this 4,000 mile pilgrimage Brian recently cycled solo from the Vatican in Rome to Konya, Turkey to the pilgrimage destination of Rumi's Tomb, the burial site of the famous Sufi mystic, philosopher and poet.

Brian has an insatiable curiosity to discover the pulse of the world and the rich landscape of the soul. He works with non-profit agencies, businesses and religious organizations which are seeking to rediscover the soul of their organization to better thrive in an uncertain world.

You can follow him at www.pedalpilgrim.com, sign up for his regular blogs, and reach him at brian@pedalpilgrim.com.

CPSIA information can be obtained
at www.ICGtesting.com
Printed in the USA
FSOW04n0846200616
21768FS

9 781943 190058